Destroyer of the Iron Horse

General Joseph E. Johnston, Confederate States Army.

DESTROYER OF THE IRON HORSE

*General Joseph E. Johnston and
Confederate Rail Transport, 1861–1865*

··{Jeffrey N. Lash}··

THE KENT STATE UNIVERSITY PRESS
Kent, Ohio, and London, England

© 1991 by The Kent State University Press, Kent, Ohio 44242
All rights reserved
Library of Congress Catalog Card Number 90–5372
ISBN 0–87338–423–7
Manufactured in the United States of America

Unless otherwise noted, photographs are reproduced through the
courtesy of the National Archives.

Library of Congress Cataloging-in-Publication Data

Lash, Jeffrey N. (Jeffrey Norman), 1949–
    Destroyer of the the iron horse : General Joseph E. Johnston and
confederate rail transport / Jeffrey N. Lash.
        p.   cm.
    Includes bibliographical references and index.
    ISBN 0–87338–423–7 (alk. paper) ∞
    1. Johnston, Joseph E. (Joseph Eggleston), 1807–1891. 2. United
States—History—Civil War, 1861–1865—Transportation.
3. Railroads—Southern States—History—19th century.   I. Title.
E467.1.J74L37   1991
973.7'3013—dc20   90–5372

British Library Cataloging-in-Publication data are available.

Contents

Preface

THE scholarly writing on General Joseph E. Johnston has omitted much concerning his experiences with the Southern railroads during the Civil War. Johnston's use of the Virginia railroads, centering around his evacuations of the Shenandoah Valley in 1861 and northern and central Virginia in 1862, has received extended but still inadequate analytical treatment. His handling of railroad problems in Tennessee and Mississippi in 1862 and 1863, in Georgia in 1864, and in North Carolina in 1865 has attracted only slight attention and critical consideration. The relative neglect of Johnston's and other Confederate commanders' exploitation of the railroads has arisen in part from the preference of Civil War historians for exclusively or principally strategic or tactical studies—or military biographies with this orientation and emphasis—that generally minimize the contribution of the railroads to the solution of logistical and supply problems faced by the Confederate high command. Consequently, the exhaustive study of Johnston's strategy and tactics during the crucial Vicksburg and Atlanta campaigns, however necessary and valuable, has diverted attention from his handling of important logistical and supply operations by using the Tennessee, Mississippi, and Georgia railways. Similarly, writings on his brief delaying campaign in North Carolina have neglected to analyze his approach to railroad problems in the Tarheel State.

This study is offered as a thorough examination of Johnston's use of the Confederate railroads. It is not intended as a biography of Johnston or as a narrative account of his military operations. Rather, it represents a specialized study of one Confederate commander's exploitation of the railroad as a resource of war. Its interpretative focus centers on Johnston's growth in overcoming problems relating to railway logistics. Johnston's professional development should be measured in terms of his ability to understand and use the railroad strategically, logistically, and tactically under the conditions of modern warfare. It should also be assessed with respect to his improvement in relations with Confederate War Department authorities, other prominent Confederate field commanders, and Southern railroad officials—particularly his interpretation and application of the War Department's evolving railway policy. Although his military utilization of the Confederate railroads formed so important a part of his overall generalship, my position is that historians have greatly overrated Johnston as a strategist and logistician. Johnston's continual failure to use effectively the South's railroads seriously damaged his relations with President Jefferson Davis and irreparably harmed the Confederate war effort.

Moreover, the study lends substantial support to the broader and much debated recent thesis that Civil War historians and students of the American military tradition have overestimated the abilities of Confederate generals compared with those of Northern commanders. New studies that concentrate on the use of the Mississippi and Alabama railroads by Rebel commanders are needed, particularly one examining Lieutenant General Leonidas Polk's skillful use of the Southern railroads. Meanwhile, examination of Johnston's handling of Confederate rail transport reveals egregious errors in logistical judgment committed by him and several other high-ranking Rebel generals. Therefore, in further testing the thesis of the overall inferiority of Confederate commanders, historians should more carefully consider the exploitation of the railroad by members of the Confederate high command.

Speaking of Civil War historians, I gladly thank Professors Frank L. Byrne and John T. Hubbell of the Kent State University Department of History for their valuable contributions to this book, which began as a master's thesis in 1974. I am also grateful to numerous reference archivists at the National Archives and the Library of Congress for their assistance in locating the records, maps, and illustrations used in the preparation of this study.

Finally, I wish to dedicate this book to the memory of Captain Robert S. Lash (U.S.M.C. and U.S. Army), a good soldier who loved his country.

Introduction

C IVIL War historians, including those who have recognized the demonstrated superior field command of many Confederate generals, have accurately understood that the Confederate high command never fully exploited the railroad as an important resource of war. Throughout the war Confederate generals, including Joseph E. Johnston, Albert Sidney Johnston, Braxton Bragg, Pierre G. T. Beauregard, John B. Hood, John C. Pemberton, and William J. Hardee (and Federal commanders including Henry W. Halleck, George B. McClellan, and William S. Rosecrans), concentrated mainly on grand strategy and theater tactics. They thus tended to neglect or misunderstand the complex relations between field command, the railroad, and logistics. These West Point–educated officers—excluding Robert E. Lee, the South's most famous graduate of the U.S. Military Academy, and Leonidas Polk, also a West Pointer and easily the Confederacy's ablest railroad general—who in 1861 should have recognized the critical military significance of railway transportation to the Confederate war effort, failed to use the railroad effectively. Many showed ignorance of or indifference to the fundamental mechanical aspects of railroad technology. Avoiding experimentation, they never developed a larger professional concern for the potentially decisive military applications of mechanized transportation—if only to prevent Confederate defeat. Other commanders, equally lacking in ingenuity or adaptability, depended excessively on conventional methods of overland mobility and supply or relegated railroad matters to subordinate engineers or quartermasters.[1] Joseph E. Johnston's erratic wartime record of accomplishment illustrates

1

this serious lack of preparation and imagination despite his extensive background as a topographical engineer.

Born in Virginia in 1807, Johnston graduated from West Point in 1829 and undertook regular army duty as a first lieutenant in the Artillery Corps. He participated in the Black Hawk War of 1832 and served on General Winfield S. Scott's staff during the first Seminole War in 1835.[2] After a short civilian interlude, Johnston rejoined the army in 1837 and won a commission as a first lieutenant in the Corps of Topographical Engineers. During the Mexican War he served gallantly but sustained five separate battle wounds. Scott, in evaluating Johnston's qualifications as an army officer, wryly observed, "Johnston is a great soldier, but he has the unfortunate knack of getting himself shot in nearly every engagement."[3] After the Mexican War, Johnston gained the ranks of captain and then lieutenant colonel in the Corps of Topographical Engineers while directing construction projects in Texas and in the Mississippi Valley. In the Southwest—a section of the country scarcely affected by the railroad-building boom of the 1840s and especially of the 1850s—Johnston expressed a renewed professional interest in railroads. Previously, while serving in the East in 1845, he had devoted himself to mastering the simplest technical aspects of railroad construction. Upon the outbreak of the Mexican War, however, Johnston abruptly abandoned that activity and thereafter neglected it for another six years.

Then, while stationed at San Antonio in December 1851, Johnston agreed to locate a route for and make technical recommendations to a chartered railroad company in his "leisure time" over the winter of 1852. Specifically, the board of directors of the San Antonio & Mexican Gulf Railroad engaged Johnston to make examinations for a proposed hundred-mile line of track between the military post at San Antonio and the busy port of Indianola on the Gulf of Mexico. Daunted by the formidable task, Johnston hastily solicited from the War Department a substantial body of information about the weight and cost of the iron and timber used in railroad building, the precise methods of laying and constructing roadbeds, tracks, and trestles, the price of rolling stock, and the surveying work necessary to ensure construction of a stable and durable railroad line across rugged terrain. His expressed interest in learning how to construct the "best bridge for narrow streams—& for one 100 yds wide" was especially important. A damaged or destroyed bridge resulting from structural weakness or deliberately inflicted harm would disrupt railroad transportation in peace and, even more disastrously, in war. In any event, Johnston deferred to the War Department because, having forgotten much of his experience with railroads in 1845, he sought to renew his knowledge so as not to "make a blunder" and thereby bring discredit on the Topographical Corps.

On receiving Johnston's letter, Colonel John J. Abert, the chief of the Bureau of Topographical Engineers, immediately communicated with Captain William H. Swift, United States Army, of Massachusetts. Swift, a retired military engineer who had acquired "exact knowledge" of modern methods of railroad building, provided the information Abert needed to answer Johnston's questions. Shortly thereafter, Abert strengthened Johnston's preparation as a prospective railroad surveyor by furnishing him with much of Swift's detailed technical information—including a diagram of recommended drainage ditch locations—covering approved European and American methods of designing and constructing railroad cuts, embankments, tracks, and trestles.[4] Abert also explained to Johnston that railroad officials required other facilities to render a railroad operational, including switches, turnouts, sets of double tracks at depots and stations, machine shops, and an assortment of rolling stock. Distinguishing heavy locomotives from lighter engines and freight cars from passenger cars, Abert impressed on Johnston the high financial cost of that equipment ($9,000 for a locomotive and $2,200 for a car) in addition to the expense of transporting rolling stock to Texas. Thus, before the Civil War Johnston had received a thorough grounding in railroad technology, gained an appreciation of the great financial value of railway property, and acquired some experience as a railroad surveyor. Nevertheless, his apparent indifference to and lack of understanding of the technical improvements subsequently introduced in railroad construction and the increasing costs of railroad equipment, his remarkable forgetfulness with advancing years, and his severely limited imagination about the potential military value of the railroad left him largely unprepared to use the railroad as an instrument of war in 1861.

After leaving Texas in 1854, Johnston served as lieutenant colonel in the First United States Cavalry in the trans-Mississippi West, accompanying expeditions sent against Indian warriors and Mormon sectarians. Simultaneously promoted to the rank of brigadier general and appointed quartermaster general of the United States Army on June 28, 1860, Johnston performed administrative duties in Washington until the Confederate bombardment of Fort Sumter in April 1861 and the subsequent secession of Virginia. Having resigned from the United States Army on April 22, Johnston briefly commanded Virginia volunteers around Richmond. He then journeyed to Montgomery, Alabama, to solicit from the recently designated Confederate president—erstwhile U.S. Senator Jefferson Davis from Mississippi—a nomination as brigadier general in the Provisional Confederate States Army. Davis, a West Point graduate and former secretary of war in the Pierce administration, appointed Johnston, and the Confederate Senate confirmed the nomination.[5] Finally, on May 15, 1861, Adjutant General Samuel Cooper ordered Johnston to proceed to Harpers Ferry, Virginia, and assume command of Confederate forces in the Shenandoah Valley.[6]

Johnston's elevation to command in the Confederate army marked the commencement of the last and most distinguished part of his military career. Yet, at fifty-four years of age and with a record of over three decades of active service experience, Johnston seemingly had already reached the height of his powers by May 1861. In physical appearance alone, he struck his contemporaries as a man of impressive military bearing. Although not quite five-feet-nine-inches tall, Johnston kept his slight physique erect. Not considered a particularly handsome man, he nevertheless possessed striking—and indeed extraordinary—features. A high, wrinkled, and somewhat protruding forehead gave the deceptive appearance of larger size to what actually was a small, oval-shaped head. He was bald, and his bushy eyebrows overhung markedly slanted eyes. Several large dark rings were conspicuous beneath his eyes; these skin discolorations created a noticeably weary and haggard expression. A prominent nose suggested an aristocratic background and a nobility of character. Since his Mexican War days, Johnston had maintained a short, well-trimmed beard; initially dark brown, by 1861 it exhibited large patches of gray hair. While it almost completely hid his mouth, the beard failed to conceal, as one especially observant private noted, a decided "peculiarity about his teeth."[7] Neither ostentatious nor flamboyant in habits of dress, Johnston thought nothing of wearing civilian clothing at the beginning of the war; he then donned Confederate gray when the Quartermaster Department furnished him with a general's uniform. A Southern war correspondent near Harp-

President Jefferson Davis, Confederate States of America.

ers Ferry misunderstood Johnston's lack of a formal military uniform, however, and remarked that Johnston on horseback appeared "scarcely distinguishable" from his staff "as he was attired in plain citizens' dress, with a shocking bad stovepipe hat."[8]

Personally, Johnston impressed others as enigmatic and often uncommunicative. Alternately gay and melancholy, he had an unpredictable temperament—marked by alternating fits of irascibility and amiability—that evoked either the unswerving devotion or the implacable antagonism of fellow officers. Friends and acquaintances found him a delightful conversationalist and a man of frequently extreme affability. Simultaneously, he unsettled observers who considered him to be "a sleepy and grim old man" and strangers who felt uncomfortably conscious that he read their "thoughts like an open book."[9] Johnston's self-confessed weakness as a careless writer and his haughty sense of personal honor would present him with serious problems throughout the war when dealing with anyone other than a trusted subordinate, loyal friend, or political supporter. Eventually, he showed a tendency toward insensitivity and even insubordination toward superiors, particularly President Davis and the War Department authorities. Despite these defects in personality and character, Johnston initially inspired the confidence of Davis, who expected him resolutely to defend Harpers Ferry, the site of a Federal military arsenal that Virginia forces captured late in April 1861. There, in the Shenandoah Valley, Johnston would first apply himself to using the railroads of the Southern Confederacy.

·{1}··

Victory and Evacuation in Virginia

T HE Confederate War Department's decision to defend Harpers Ferry, widely known as the "Gibraltar of Virginia," rested on compelling logistical and strategic considerations. At the junction of the Potomac and Shenandoah rivers, Harpers Ferry lay only fifty-five miles northwest of Washington. Therefore, Confederate military leaders in Richmond deemed it essential to maintain railroad transportation links between the fertile food-producing regions of the Shenandoah Valley and their armies in other parts of Virginia and to prevent the envelopment of their positions in northern Virginia through the lower valley passes. Confederate planners also wished to gain secessionist support in Maryland by not invading that state or destroying Baltimore & Ohio Railroad property in Virginia. Specifically, then, Johnston had to hold Harpers Ferry as the strategic key to the Shenandoah Valley, encourage pro-Confederate sentiment in Maryland, and protect his railroad connections running south and east between Harpers Ferry (and Winchester and Strasburg to the rear) and Manassas Junction, a point not far from the encampments of Brigadier General Pierre G. T. Beauregard's army.[1]

Johnston soon confronted these problems of defense when Federal forces from western Virginia and southern Pennsylvania began a concerted movement against Harpers Ferry. In surveying the situation, Major General Robert E. Lee, commander of the Virginia state forces, also recognized the strategic importance of Harpers Ferry. On May 27 he drew Johnston's attention to the Baltimore & Ohio Railroad. Lee urged him to "take measures to maintain it or prevent the use of the road to invaders of the State." Previously, however, Johnston had informed the Virginia military authorities that, as his

7

General Robert E. Lee, commander of the Army of Northern Virginia.

predecessor in command Colonel Thomas J. Jackson of the Virginia militia had instructed the outpost commanders to burn bridges and tear up tracks whenever necessary for their defense, "those instructions were repeated by me." Johnston understated his action. Shortly after arriving at Harpers Ferry, he ordered his engineers to demolish the seventeen railroad bridges from Point of Rocks, a station thirty-six miles east of the town, to Martinsburg, Virginia, an important railroad center eighteen miles north of Harpers Ferry. The destruction of the trestles and the blocking of tracks by huge boulders halted train traffic between the two points, a disruption that complicated the operations of commanders of advancing Federal armies, though ultimately the destruction failed to deter the coordinated Union movement. Still, by wrecking the bridges Johnston gained time to remove to Winchester the arsenal machinery captured at Harpers Ferry. In conducting this operation he recognized the advantage of using the Winchester & Potomac Railroad, although he also exhibited an appalling lack of understanding and an astonishing forgetfulness of the rudiments of railroading that he should have mastered in Texas in 1852.[2]

The Winchester & Potomac Railroad represented a technological anachronism inasmuch as economic constraints forced the firm that owned it to continue using an archaic structure (1841 vintage) on which to operate the company's rolling stock. The track consisted mainly of wood that lacked a solid ballast foundation. Instead of purchasing and laying down the newer and heavier T rails commonly found on other railways throughout the Old Dominion, Winchester & Potomac managers had to use and maintain obsolete strap-iron rails (three-fourths'-inch thickness) fastened to hewn timber stringers and crossties. Because of its weak superstructure, the track could not support locomotives weighing more than twenty-two tons without being crushed or severely damaged. While twenty-two-ton engines passed over all other Virginia railways, the Baltimore & Ohio locomotives of Maryland that steamed across Virginia territory weighed upward of thirty-two tons. These weaknesses of material and construction, coupled with the Winchester & Potomac's limited rolling stock of five locomotives and forty-five cars, reduced the railroad's usefulness for military transportation.[3]

Anxious to evacuate the armory machinery as expeditiously as possible, Johnston supervised the removal operation at Harpers Ferry. Despite the constant employment of their rolling stock, however,

Virginia railways as shown on a war telegram marking map. Courtesy of the Library of Congress.

Winchester & Potomac officials failed to satisfy Johnston's requirements for a more rapid movement of train traffic. Johnston's frustration manifested itself in a rash act. Invoking a doubtful military necessity, he ordered his chief quartermaster to switch several Baltimore & Ohio locomotives and cars (those that Jackson had captured earlier at Harpers Ferry to interrupt railroad communications between Union forces in southern Pennsylvania and western Virginia) onto the Winchester & Potomac track in order to increase the motive power available for the removal operation. Fortunately, a number of Winchester & Potomac engineers intervened and strongly remonstrated against the transfer so as to prevent the company's tracks from collapsing under the weight of the Baltimore & Ohio locomotives. A chagrined and perplexed Johnston quickly countermanded his order. Clearly he had overlooked the technical impracticability of his proposed transfer of rolling stock.

Besides his failure to understand the mechanical problem involved, Johnston suffered a serious lapse of memory that contributed to his action. Almost ten years earlier, in December 1851, he had sought information from the War Department specifically concerning the cost of constructing tracks consisting of T rails as compared to what he described as the "old—including the plate-rail" type. In reply, the Topographical Bureau chief advised him that Northern railroad firms had long since abandoned the strap-iron rail "mode of structure," that type of construction forming an "extravagant kind of road" that proved difficult and expensive to maintain. Moreover, Johnston's attempt to switch rolling stock also displayed a reckless disregard for the safety and integrity of the Winchester & Potomac's equipment and facilities, particularly when he had no assurance that the Confederacy would compensate the company for its costly support of the war effort.[4]

Johnston's error in judgment about the carrying capacity of the Winchester & Potomac tracks proved inconsequential in the end. By the middle of June he had completely evacuated the armory machinery. By then, both Johnston and the War Department had concluded that Harpers Ferry could not be defended from a threatened envelopment by Federal forces. Johnston therefore conducted a strategic withdrawal of his army from Harpers Ferry and consolidated a new defensive position at Winchester, his engineers having demolished a portion of the trestlework supporting the 1,300-foot-long railroad bridge that spanned the Potomac River before they themselves

evacuated the town.[5] Later, the advancing Federal army in mountainous western Virginia encountered stubborn resistance by Confederate troops and guerrillas and experienced repeated delays because
of inadequate field transportation. And when the vacillating Major
General Robert Patterson decided not to cross the Potomac River
northwest of Harpers Ferry, Johnston redirected his attention to the
Baltimore & Ohio Railroad.

Johnston's renewed interest in the Baltimore & Ohio Railroad,
however, occurred in consequence with the arrival at Winchester of
the former Charlotte & South Carolina Railroad superintendent,
Captain Thomas R. Sharp of the Confederate Quartermaster Department. Quartermaster General Abraham C. Myers, a South Carolina native and West Point graduate who had served under Johnston
in the Quartermaster Department before the war, instructed Sharp
to select and then commandeer the finest Baltimore & Ohio locomotives and cars that Colonel Jackson had seized and isolated around
Martinsburg as a part of Jackson's continuing efforts to disrupt communications between Union armies in southern Pennsylvania and
western Virginia. George Wyne, a former civil engineer from Baltimore who later described himself as "an old man" though a "true
southern man," assisted Sharp in executing this order. Sharp (and
the spry Wyne) promptly obtained military protection and teams of
draft animals from Johnston for his work: he had two locomotives
and three thousand tons of railroad iron hauled from Martinsburg
to Strasburg and Leesburg, where he acted as an agent for the Confederate government and sold the engines and iron rails to the
Manassas Gap Railroad Company. By the middle of July, Sharp
succeeded in placing forty-three "first-rate box cars" on the Orange &
Alexandria and Virginia Central railroads, equipment eagerly purchased by those rival firms. Assisted by Johnston, Sharp also subsequently compensated the Winchester & Potomac Railroad for the
damage the company's facilities had sustained at Jackson's and
Johnston's hands in May and June. In February 1862, Winchester &
Potomac president William L. Clark advised Secretary of War Judah
B. Benjamin that "our immense depot building and acres of ground
adjoining *are now* covered with the spoils of that road" taken by
Sharp, who served as that "most energetic and patriotic Agent of the
Confederate States."[6]

Sharp's aggressively executed and virtually unopposed operations,
however, led Johnston to believe that he could destroy Baltimore &

U.S. Military Railroads engine "Commodore" overturned in northern Virginia by Confederate cavalry—a quick method used by both armies to wreck or disable locomotives.

Ohio property without disastrous political and military consequences. This delusion caused him to commit an egregious blunder in the Shenandoah Valley. Toward the end of June, Johnston determined to destroy all the rolling stock around Martinsburg that Sharp had not removed. Fearing that the usually timid and indecisive Patterson might nevertheless soon cross the Potomac and recover the rolling stock at Martinsburg for the Union army's use against Confederate forces in the valley, Johnston sent Sharp, Jackson, and five thousand cavalry troops back to the railroad yards at Martinsburg to accomplish a mission of destruction. At Martinsburg, on June 21, the two Confederate officers supervised the wrecking and burning of 42 locomotives and 386 cars—an equipment loss estimated by company agents to exceed $500,000. While Rebel cavalrymen ignited the "immense quantities" of cordwood and coal that they had stacked around the locomotives and cars, Johnston and a part of his army arrived at Martinsburg and witnessed the devastation. At temporary field headquarters, he then personally judged and released two Baltimore & Ohio managers whom Confederate cavalry officers had arrested and mistakenly accused of attempting to extinguish the fires that had begun engulfing and consuming the rolling stock. The railroaders had desperately fought the flames to save the company's depot and machine shops from the spreading conflagration.[7]

Meanwhile, shocked by Johnston's action, Patterson immediately crossed the Potomac and marched his army against the Confederate forces at Martinsburg. The Union troops opportunely arrived and prevented Johnston's cavalry from completely destroying a "splendid bridge" that spanned a small creek near the railroad yards. In attempting to rescue the Baltimore & Ohio property, Patterson's men "pressed the rebels so hard, that they could not finish the work of demolition to their cruel satisfaction, so they up with the switches and run a large number of cars into the creek, where they upset." Johnston then quickly withdrew his forces south to Winchester. Finally, on June 24, in an exultant mood, Johnston notified Adjutant General Cooper that Jackson had "destroyed all the rolling stock of the road within his reach" below the Potomac River.[8]

Unfortunately for the Confederacy, Johnston's massive destruction of Baltimore & Ohio property raised a groundswell of anger and protest among stockholding and secessionist politicians and simultaneously strengthened the hand of Unionist leaders in the Maryland state legislature. Together with the destruction of the railroad bridges at Harpers Ferry and trestles elsewhere, the wrecking of the rolling stock inflicted a total financial loss of upward of $1 million on the Baltimore & Ohio Railroad. Predictably, editorial denunciation of Johnston's action expressed the shock and outrage of aggrieved proprietary interests in the state. The *Baltimore American & Commercial Advertiser* accused the "Secession troops" and "disciples of Mr. Jefferson Davis" of having committed an "act of wanton vandalism" against Baltimore & Ohio property without the excuse of military necessity. The paper provided graphic descriptions of the scene of the destruction at Martinsburg, reporting in July that "a mass of red hot coals" still filled each of the abandoned coal cars that lay along the extensively uprooted tracks, while the battered locomotives (excepting those engines that the falsely renowned "noble and chivalric" Confederate cavalry had forcibly derailed and plunged headlong into deep ravines nearby) also remained "red and blistered with the heat" of scorching fire. A contributor to the *American* declared that the Rebels had perpetrated a malignant "act of diabolism" at Martinsburg, and a heinous crime "effected by means worthy of the spirits tenanting the nether world."[9]

From a military standpoint the action at Martinsburg demonstrated Johnston's gross underestimation of the value of the rolling stock to the Confederate war effort—despite his self-serving postwar claim that the "orders of the Government required the destruction of all that could not be brought away" to Strasburg.[10] Actually, Johnston had deliberately exceeded or carelessly misinterpreted Cooper's general instructions of June 19. Those orders, like similar messages sent to lesser Confederate officers in northwestern Virginia, urged the military commanders to demolish railroad bridges, tunnels, and tracks as well as to devastate agricultural crops—particularly stocks of food and fodder—that could support enemy infantry and cavalry operations associated with a Federal invasion and occupation of the Shenandoah Valley. The orders had not authorized or demanded an indiscriminate destruction of Baltimore & Ohio equipment.[11] The demolition of railroad bridges at Harpers Ferry and Martinsburg had effectively isolated the rolling stock, and neither the Union army nor Baltimore & Ohio officials could have used that equipment so long as the Confederate army continued to hold that part of the Shenandoah Valley. Moreover, even if Federal forces had seized the rolling stock, Johnston should have recognized the difficulty Patterson's engineer troops or quartermasters would have experienced in using Baltimore & Ohio locomotives and heavy freight cars on the flimsily constructed Winchester & Potomac Railroad. He could have ordered Jackson and Sharp to strip the Baltimore & Ohio engines and cars to supply the Confederacy's machine shops with sorely needed mechanical parts.

The wholesale destruction of the Baltimore & Ohio rolling stock and other railroad property in northwest Virginia appreciably delayed the combined movement of Union armies against Harpers Ferry late in June 1861. However, farther east the Federal army at Washington began making preparations to advance against Beauregard's forces near Manassas Junction. Beauregard responded to the threat by proposing to President Davis an elaborate strategic plan that required Johnston to elude Patterson in the valley and march with reinforcements to Manassas Junction if Beauregard came under attack. Davis accepted Beauregard's plan, albeit in its simplest form. Significantly, however, neither Beauregard nor Davis considered using the Manassas Gap Railroad as a means of transporting Johnston's troops east in the event of battle.[12]

Confident of gaining a crushing victory, Union forces on July 18 attacked the Confederate army along Bull Run. Beauregard immediately advised the War Department of the Federal assault, whereupon President Davis, suddenly perceiving the necessity of using the

General Pierre G. T. Beauregard, commander of the Confederate
Army of the Potomac.

railroad, ordered Johnston to reinforce Beauregard by rail if Johnston
could evade Patterson and mobilize his army. Johnston obeyed
promptly. Easily deceiving Patterson, he led his army away from
Winchester and then pushed his forces through Ashby's Gap in the
Blue Ridge Mountains advancing toward the Manassas Gap Railroad.

Fifty miles short of Manassas Junction, though, Johnston recognized that both he and Davis had neglected to have rolling stock concentrated at a designated point on the railroad. Fearing that he might fail to reinforce Beauregard in time to prevent a Confederate defeat at Manassas, Johnston, in desperation, sent his chief engineer, Major William H. C. Whiting, to Piedmont, the nearest station on the Manassas Gap Railroad. Johnston ordered Whiting to arrange for transportation of the troops as soon as a sufficient quantity of rolling stock could be secured. Fortunately, Whiting found two trains at Piedmont already prepared to ship Johnston's forces the remaining forty miles to Manassas Junction. When the Federal army struck his command along Bull Run, Beauregard urged the railroad officials at Manassas Junction to send all engines and passenger and freight cars (including Baltimore & Ohio rolling stock that Sharp delivered and sold to the Manassas Gap Railroad the previous June) to Piedmont to transport Johnston's troops to the scene of battle.[13]

The mobilizing of Johnston's Army of the Shenandoah initially proceeded smoothly. Brigadier General Jackson and his command boarded cars at Piedmont on July 19 and promptly moved to Manassas Junction. Johnston arrived at the station with another portion of the army on July 20. In his journal, one private praised his commander's handling of the transportation crisis, noting, "troops are being hurried forward by Rail Road to Manassas Junction as fast as possible." Then the entire operation turned into near chaos. Absconding train crewmen, repeated derailments and train collisions on the tracks (injuring a number of troops), and even acts of sabotage by train conductors and engineers interrupted the movement. Johnston furiously demanded that the railroad managers restore regular traffic and enforce discipline, but to no avail.[14] Yet the fiasco sprang primarily from a lack of preparation and coordination of effort; unquestionably, the mishandled Manassas Gap Railroad troop movement resulted from poor planning and faulty execution. Neither Beauregard nor Johnston recognized the complex problems of implementing an almost improvised railway transportation operation, particularly when they assigned the task of handling that operation to civilian railroad officials.

Notwithstanding their late arrival at Manassas Junction, nine thousand troops of the Army of the Shenandoah reached the field in time to help defeat and finally rout the Federal army and win the battle of Bull Run. The *Richmond Examiner*, however, paused amidst the celebration of victory to censure the Manassas Gap Railroad. Declaring that the "laggardness" of the Manassas Gap officials nearly caused a Confederate defeat at Bull Run by delaying Johnston's troop movement to Manassas Junction, the *Examiner* further accused the Virginia railroads (albeit recognizing certain "honourable" exceptions) of having shown a "criminal degree of inefficiency" in transporting Confederate troops in the Old Dominion. The *New Orleans Picayune* agreed, charging that the Manassas Gap Railroad "worked badly" in moving Johnston's forces to Manassas Junction. Two months later, though, the *Richmond Dispatch* preferred to make more optimistic comment, merely noting that two redesignated Alexandria, Loudoun & Hampshire locomotives, the General Johnston and the General Beauregard, had begun operating on the Richmond, Fredericksburg & Potomac and Virginia Central railroads. The renaming of those two "superb engines," the *Dispatch* remarked, ensured that "both the chief heroes of Manassas" would stand high "on the rolls of railroad fame" in the Confederacy.

Indeed, in December 1861 the *Richmond Examiner* still praised Johnston's strategic use of the railroad to achieve a Confederate victory, despite its earlier criticism of the Manassas Gap Railroad. The *Examiner* declared that the "only West Point general that has *mobilized* his army, since the war began, was General Joseph Johnston" in his movements between the evacuation of Harpers Ferry and the "glorious engagement at Manassas." The *Richmond Dispatch*, without specifically referring to the Manassas Gap Railroad, nevertheless also applauded Johnston's "mysterious movements in the Valley, which burst forth like a thunderbolt upon the plains of Manassas." As a more immediate and significant honor than editorial commendation, though, Johnston received promotion to the rank of full general after the battle in July and superseded Beauregard, thereby assuming command of the Confederate Army of the Potomac.[15]

Johnston quickly discovered the necessity of using the railroads of northern and central Virginia for the transportation of supplies to the front in an effort to maintain his army. He also recognized the need to use those railroads to ship sick and wounded troops to the rear, particularly if the Confederate army should ever evacuate its advanced position in northern Virginia. Several railroads met Johnston's requirements for supplies. Besides the Manassas Gap Railroad, which connected Manassas Junction with Strasburg in Shenandoah Valley, the Orange & Alexandria Railroad ran southwest

U.S. Military Railroads engine "Firefly" on the Orange & Alexandria Railroad near Union Mills, Virginia—vintage Civil War rolling stock and trestlework bridge.

from Alexandria, below Washington, past Fairfax Court House to Manassas Junction and thence farther southwest for another sixty-one miles to Gordonsville. The Virginia Central Railroad connected Gordonsville with Staunton in the valley and with Richmond. Thus Orange & Alexandria trains could transport to Manassas Junction the supplies brought from Staunton and Richmond to Gordonsville. Additional stores could be sent north from Richmond to Fredericksburg over the Richmond, Fredericksburg & Potomac Railroad. A privately sponsored legislative proposal to construct a railroad branch line between Fredericksburg and Manassas Junction, though publicly endorsed by Johnston and Beauregard, failed to win approval by the Virginia Senate in February 1862.[16]

Assuming that a sufficient amount of supplies would reach the front by a combination of rail transport and wagon trains, Johnston kept his army at Fairfax Court House, twelve miles north of Manassas

Junction. However, an acute shortage of stores developed by late July, primarily caused by delays in the operation of the supply system adopted by the Commissary Department in Richmond. Insisting on meticulously observing bureaucratic regulations, Colonel Lucius B. Northrop, the Confederate commissary general, instructed his agents to ship all food supplies collected in the valley to Richmond for inspection. Quartermaster agents then reshipped the stores north of Manassas Junction. Johnston and Beauregard argued against the inefficient use of railroad transportation, but Northrop refused to make changes until September, when he completely replaced his previous system of supply. He then sought to accumulate a massive reserve of subsistence stores at Manassas Junction by building an extensive meat-packing plant to the west at Thoroughfare Gap near the Manassas Gap Railroad. The slaughtering and packing operations proved so efficient that, in contrast to the earlier shortage, overaccumulations of butchered beef and pork at Manassas Junction suddenly imposed an equally serious logistical problem on Johnston throughout the fall of 1861 and early winter of 1862.[17]

In addition to oversupply, Johnston faced the difficulty of providing adequate transportation for the removal of sick soldiers from military hospitals in northern Virginia to medical treatment facilities in other parts of the state. After the battle of Bull Run, Acting Surgeon General Samuel P. Moore ordered the medical director of the Army of the Potomac, Surgeon Thomas H. Williams, to establish hospitals at Front Royal and Charlottesville in the Shenandoah Valley, at Manassas Junction, and at Orange Court House north of Gordonsville. Williams obeyed Moore, but the hospitals he established soon proved unable to accommodate increasing numbers of sick troops. He therefore sought authority from Moore to transfer sick soldiers from "Moore Hospital" at Manassas Junction to the hospitals at Orange Court House and Charlottesville. Receiving authorization in October 1861 to ship sick troops south by rail, Williams immediately encountered Johnston's opposition to the use of passenger trains for the transportation of soldiers to the rear. Johnston insisted that special "sick trains" be arranged—consisting of an engine, one passenger car, and one ambulance car—and that Williams should not send the sick on passenger trains, enlarge sick trains by adding more cars, or attach sick trains to passenger trains on the runs south over the Orange & Alexandria and Virginia Central railroads. Johnston hoped to discourage malingering among the troops by forbidding the creation of enlarged sick trains, but, more important, he also sought to prevent any interference with the supply traffic between Manassas Junction and Richmond. His decision, however, arose from a miscalculation of the quantity of available rolling stock, inasmuch as inclement weather and bad roads around Manassas Junction in October, and not a shortage of railroad equipment, contributed to the development of renewed supply problems for his army late in the fall of 1861. Recognizing the abundance of usable rolling stock, Williams requested Johnston's permission to use passenger trains for the transportation of the sick "but was refused."[18] Neither Williams nor Moore could persuade Johnston to reverse his decision.

The combination of railroad transportation problems that Johnston faced in the fall of 1861 led to his decision to create the position of chief quartermaster on his staff. Theretofore he had used Beauregard's chief quartermaster and his own staff officers, such as Brigadier General Whiting, to assist him in handling difficulties with both animal-drawn and railroad transportation. He definitely needed his own chief quartermaster in the steadily worsening crisis of supply. Indeed, despite the earlier overaccumulations of supplies at Manassas Junction, torrential rains in October 1861 complicated the task of transporting those supplies from Manassas Junction overland to Johnston's army at Fairfax Court House. Confronted by a new and more drastic reduction of supplies, Johnston withdrew his army on October 19 to Centreville, a point six miles north of Manassas Junction.

The arrival of severe winter weather and the increasing incidence of disease and sickness among Confederate troops aggravated the supply situation. According to a *Charleston Courier* war correspondent, the "muddiest mud and the ruttiest of rutty roads" connected Manassas Junction and Centreville, while unavoidably the troops had begun "living like pigs—in the mud." Since the roads between Manassas Junction and Centreville had indeed turned into "seas of red mud," Johnston, after weeks of struggling to employ conventional field transportation effectively, contemplated undertaking a railroad construction project to ensure the maintenance of his army. Thereafter, Confederate commanders near Centreville also began urging Johnston to send supplies to the front by rail. As late as January 1862, Major General Edmund Kirby Smith recommended that Johnston use the railroad instead of wagon trains to provision Smith's forces. Smith considered the shipment of stores to Centreville by rail to be both expedient and indispensable because, in view of the impracticable and impassable roads, "this change will be an economy, and in the present condition of the transportation it is a necessity."[19] The success of such an important undertaking, however, largely depended on the ability of Johnston's newly appointed chief quartermaster, Major Alfred M. Barbour, to coordinate the management of men and resources.

Johnston's appointment of Barbour as chief quartermaster of the Army of the Potomac on December 4, 1861—though immediately advantageous and necessary—represented one of the worst decisions that he made in the war. Initially Johnston's selection of Barbour seemed a reasonable and judicious decision, although Barbour ultimately proved detrimental to Confederate logistical operations in Virginia, Tennessee, Alabama, and Mississippi. From Virginia to Georgia, Barbour proved incompetent, inefficient, and extravagantly wasteful of irreplaceable funds and resources.[20]

The descendant of a distinguished Virginia family, Barbour had practiced law and served in the Virginia legislature before the war, representing the district around Charlestown in the Shenandoah Valley. Appointed by President James Buchanan in April 1859 as the military superintendent of the United States Armory at Harpers Ferry, Barbour served in that capacity for two years. Then, in April 1861, he resigned after his participation in the Virginia Convention that passed an ordinance of secession—an ordinance that Virginia voters ratified on May 23, 1861. During his tenure at Harpers Ferry, Barbour had gained a reputation as an efficient administrator and innovative reformer: he capably handled a wide range of ordnance-related activities and construction projects, though none of these included railroads. Temporarily performing special duty at the United States Armory at Springfield, Massachusetts, when the abolitionist John Brown launched a raid against Harpers Ferry in October 1859, Barbour thereafter ardently supported the secessionist movement in Virginia. After his resignation in April 1861, he served as a major and quartermaster in the Provisional Confederate States Army in northern Virginia until Johnston appointed him chief quartermaster in December 1861.[21]

Assisted by Barbour, Johnston continued making preparations early in the winter of 1861 to construct a railroad between Manassas Junction and Centreville. Undoubtedly the building of the "Centreville Railroad," a railroad branch forming a military feeder line, presented

Johnston's former supply line to Manassas Junction, the Orange & Alexandria Railroad, pictured here with U.S. Military Railroads equipment near Union Mills, Virginia.

Johnston with the most difficult railroad problem that he had yet encountered. Recognizing the lack of spare railroad iron as well as his professional limitations as a topographical engineer, Johnston sought to secure both materials and mechanics from the Quartermaster Department and the Orange & Alexandria Railroad. Despite protracted administrative delays, late in December 1861 he obtained War Department authorization to order Major General "Stonewall" Jackson, of Bull Run fame, and the quartermaster agent Sharp (those men having earlier returned to Strasburg in the Shenandoah Valley) to seize several additional tons of Baltimore & Ohio iron and deliver the rails to Manassas Junction. The equipment procured, Johnston then requested Orange & Alexandria officials to lend him tools and skilled laborers for the construction of tracks and a trestle on the proposed line to Centreville. The railroad managers, however, pleaded scarcity of men and resources and denied Johnston any substantial assistance. Johnston then appealed to Quartermaster General Myers for help. Johnston especially needed a technically trained officer who could direct the building of a railroad and bridge on the line to Centreville. Previously, Johnston's chief engineer, Brigadier General Whiting, had reported to Fredericksburg to assume command of Confederate forces in eastern Virginia. Therefore, at Johnston's request, Myers made a wise decision and assigned the seasoned and versatile Sharp to the Centreville Railroad project. Finally, Johnston ordered Barbour to instruct Sharp early in February 1862 to "supervise the construction of the Rail Road between Manassas and Centreville." Johnston promised him "every facility for its speedy completion," including picks, axes, shovels, spikes, and carloads of crossties to be sent north from Richmond.[22]

Sharp executed his orders with remarkable energy. He put three hundred slaves (also furnished by the Quartermaster Department) to work on the railroad. He demonstrated his exceptional technical talents where, despite Johnston's appeals to the War Department for additional technical personnel, there were not enough engineers, mechanics, and carpenters. Guarded by cavalry troops and supervised by Sharp and Johnston's few staff engineers, the black section hands began tracklaying work before the middle of February, and they built the sharply curved segments of the railroad branch "on a beeline from the Junction to Centreville." Sharp's labor gangs tracked the sandy and swampy ground lying between the two points, while army engineers directed the construction of a railroad trestle over Bull Run near Blackburn's Ford; the railroad's terminal lay just beyond Bull Run. Rendered unstable by the use of badly worn Baltimore & Ohio iron rails and unballasted crossties set twice the standard distance apart, the railroad nevertheless became operational late in February. Supply trains constantly ran its length between Manassas Junction and Centreville. Despite the great effort expended to build it, though, the Centreville Railroad ceased operating in March 1862 in the wake of the Army of the Potomac's hasty evacuation of northern Virginia. During the withdrawal, Confederate troops burned the trestle over Bull Run and abandoned the tracks above Manassas Junction, wrecking and overturning four dilapidated Manassas Gap boxcars as they retreated.[23]

Nevertheless, Johnston deserved considerable credit for the completion of the Centreville Railroad project. Though unaided by the Orange & Alexandria Railroad, he showed a willingness and ability

Railroad ruins at Manassas Junction, left in the wake of Johnston's evacuation of northern Virginia in March 1862.

to cooperate with the War Department in using the railroad as a logistical instrument to overcome his supply problems in northern Virginia. Johnston also demonstrated sound judgment in selecting Sharp to assist him in constructing the railroad between Manassas Junction and Centreville. Indeed, without Sharp's crucial contribution, Johnston could not have completed the project without further serious delays. Johnston's other transportation assistant, Major Barbour, managed the project capably, although the railroad construction work constituted a relatively isolated and limited operation. Finally, it should be emphasized that, although President Davis's decision to withdraw the Confederate army late in the winter of 1862 suddenly terminated the railroad's operational usefulness, Johnston's original decision to build the branch line proved justified in view of the continuing transportation crisis in northern Virginia.

The planning and construction of the eventually abandoned Centreville Railroad coincided with the two principal transportation problems that continued to beset Johnston in the fall of 1861: moving sick soldiers to hospitals in the rear and shipping an excessive quantity of supplies to the front. Since October 1861 Johnston had refused to permit the use of passenger trains or to allow the formation of larger sick trains to transport sick or disabled troops to hospitals at Richmond, Orange Court House, Lynchburg, or Charlottesville—a policy that caused much hardship to sick soldiers and prompted sympathetic civilians to send complaints to army headquarters and the War Department. In February 1862, though, Johnston abruptly reversed his decision on sick trains. A combination of circumstances—including the appointment of Barbour as chief quartermaster, the arrival of harsh winter weather, the care of an increasing number of sick troops, and the decreased use of passenger trains—persuaded Johnston to approve the previous recommendation of Medical Director Williams that, besides the regular running of sick trains, additional sick cars should be attached to passenger trains heading south to Orange Court House and other points on the route to Charlottesville. Johnston thus also accepted Williams's recommendation (and the surgeon general's) that all sick troops should thereafter be sent to Charlottesville and none to Richmond; superior medical facilities were available at smaller hospitals located away from the Confederate capital. Nevertheless, two difficulties immediately threatened to disrupt the improved arrangements: the limited power of Orange & Alexandria engines and Major Barbour's dereliction of duty and his arbitrary policy. When advised by a Confederate surgeon on February 3 that the railroad officials refused to cooperate, having concluded that their locomotives could not pull passenger trains to which had been added the weight of a fully loaded sick car, Johnston pressed heavier freight train locomotives into service. The extended passenger trains almost immediately began running to Orange Court House. Moreover, when informed by Williams that Barbour had neglected to make precise arrangements with Orange & Alexandria officials to make up special sick trains regularly, Johnston ordered that "this evil be remedied as speedily as possible" to accelerate the movement of sick troops to Charlottesville. Finally, when Barbour's transportation quartermaster at Manassas Junction, Captain Joseph D. Powell, acting under Barbour's instructions, refused to permit Williams to send sick soldiers home on furlough by rail, allowing only their shipment to Richmond, Johnston overruled Barbour. Disciplined and chagrined, Barbour belatedly ordered Powell to make transportation available for moving the sick to any point in Virginia. Still, Powell defiantly refused to obey orders, whereupon Barbour forced Powell to do his duty.[24] Johnston's preoccupation with the construction of the Centreville Railroad early in February 1862 probably prevented him from effectively controlling railroad transportation of sick troops to the rear, but he was still responsible for ensuring Barbour's efficient supervision of the shipment of those troops southward—a responsibility Johnston neglected to meet.

The other transportation problem that continued to trouble Johnston after the fall of 1861 stemmed from the overaccumulation of supplies at forward depots on the outlying strategic frontier of northern Virginia. Assuming that the Confederate army would conduct a sustained offensive campaign in Maryland or Pennsylvania in the spring of 1862, Commissary General Northrop prepared for an aggressive movement northward by ordering his chief commissary at Thoroughfare Gap, Major Barnard P. Noland, to increase the available reserves of beef and pork (two million pounds' worth) at Thoroughfare Gap and Manassas Junction. Northrop's agents in central Virginia shipped to Manassas Junction an additional three million pounds of stores, prompting Johnston to establish a reserve depot at Culpeper Court House, a point thirty-five miles southwest of Manassas Junction on the Orange & Alexandria Railroad. In January 1862, through his chief commissary of subsistence, Major Archibald H. Cole, Johnston urged Northrop to send all further supplies to Culpeper. Northrop refused. Then, on February 20, President Davis ordered Johnston to prepare to evacuate the Confederate army from northern Virginia. Davis expressed his instructions clearly, but Johnston still badly misinterpreted them, convinced that the president required an immediate and hasty retreat. Fearing heavy losses of supplies attending a precipitate withdrawal, Johnston warned Davis on February 25 that the "accumulation of subsistence stores at Manassas is now a great evil" and that the meat-packing plant at Thoroughfare Gap constituted "a great incumbrance" such that enormous quantities of food and equipment "must be sacrificed in the contemplated movement" to central Virginia. Yet privately Johnston remained confident that he could save all the equipment and commissaries. Returning by special train to Manassas Junction after a conference with Davis in Richmond about the orders to withdraw the army, Johnston conferred with Major Noland. According to a postwar account by Northrop, Noland "spoke of his business and Johnston told him he thought there would be no difficulty of transportation" in removing to the rear within two weeks all the cured meat that Noland had accumulated at Thoroughfare Gap.[25]

Recognizing that the cooperation of Orange & Alexandria officials was of crucial importance to the removal operations, Johnston requested its president, John S. Barbour, Jr., to work the railroad to its "utmost capacity" for the removal to Gordonsville of the stores and equipment from Manassas Junction and Thoroughfare Gap. Barbour, who had long since recognized his railroad as a "very important Military highway," and H. W. Vandegrift, the Orange & Alexandria's chief engineer and general superintendent, promised Johnston an expeditious removal of the supplies, and they received authorization to exercise general supervision over the removal operations. Major Alfred M. Barbour meanwhile instructed his assistants to remove to Manassas Junction the property stockpiled at Centreville. The army quartermasters employed Orange & Alexandria and Manassas Gap rolling stock on the Centreville Railroad and quickly accumulated a huge quantity of stores at Manassas Junction. Simultaneously, in cooperating more promptly and effectively with Medical Director Williams at Manassas Junction, Barbour sent three trains to Bull Run to remove sick soldiers to Manassas Junction, whence they would be moved farther south to Orange Court House and Gordonsville.[26]

At the highest level of command, however, Johnston failed to coordinate closely the efforts of the railroad officials and his own staff quartermasters and thereby created chaos on the railways of northern Virginia. Without first consulting Johnston or Majors Barbour and Cole, the Orange & Alexandria and Manassas Gap superintendents went to Thoroughfare Gap and promised to deliver to Major Noland enough engines and cars to remove two million pounds of packed meat to Orange Court House, the site of one of Williams's hospitals and of a supply depot four miles north of Gordonsville. Subsequently, Johnston's subordinates invoked military necessity, overruled the railroad managers, and seized the rolling stock. Probably reflecting the developing intense rivalry between officers of the Quartermaster and Commissary departments, Johnston's quartermasters refused or neglected to inform the commissary agent Noland of their impressment of the equipment, thus completely disrupting Noland's carefully arranged evacuation plans. For their part, even without such military interference, the railroad officials compounded Johnston's original blunder: he seriously misallocated a great quantity of rolling stock between Thoroughfare Gap, Manassas Junction, and Gordonsville and concentrated most of it at Manassas Junction.

Exploiting the authority of an earlier order of Johnston's that required quartermasters to commandeer an additional thirty-nine Manassas Gap cars and place them upon the Orange & Alexandria and
Virginia Central tracks, that railroad's president, Barbour, urged the
Virginia Central and Manassas Gap presidents to send all remaining
locomotives and cars to Manassas Junction. Complying too hastily,
the railroad executives put the bulk of their combined fleets of rolling stock on the single-track Orange & Alexandria Railroad, over-
loading a line that possessed only four miles of turnout trackage
between Manassas Junction and Gordonsville. Fully 332 engines and
cars had clanked over the sixty-one-mile section of the railroad by
late February. Trains that had regularly completed the run between
Manassas Junction and Gordonsville in six hours now required thirty-
six hours to make the same trip. The delay caused Johnston to complain to President Davis on February 28 about the "wretched
mismanagement of the railroad" below Manassas Junction.[27]

Stunned by the bungling of the railroad officials, Johnston hastily
established a limited form of military control over the northern Virginia carriers then conducting the removal operations by ordering
Captain Sharp to take charge of railroad transportation at Manassas
Junction. Johnston permitted the railroad managers to use their own
employees to operate the trains, but he required Sharp to schedule
and direct all traffic. Therefore, on March 1, Johnston ordered Barbour to instruct Sharp to evacuate systematically the equipment and
supplies from northern Virginia. The instructions required Sharp to
confer with railroad officials and to accumulate enough rolling stock
to remove the army's sick and wounded first, then the ordnance and
hospital stores, and finally the commissary supplies. Also, while reporting regularly and fully to Barbour, Sharp had to keep the Centreville Railroad in "good condition" and continue provisioning the
troops and draft animals at Centreville and Union Mills. Obeying
instructions and acting decisively, Sharp first sent trains west to
Front Royal on the Manassas Gap Railroad to bring to Manassas
Junction the 374 patients in military hospitals in the valley, while
Johnston himself ordered the overland removal to Charlottesville of
the hospital stores and medical supplies at Front Royal. Johnston
sought to move the hospital property safely to Charlottesville on the
Virginia Central Railroad, but he directed Confederate doctors
at Front Royal to "burn all government property" if an invading

Federal cavalry force threatened to capture the equipment.[28] Despite this order, Sharp steadily imposed a closer control over the movement of railroad traffic between Manassas Junction and Gordonsville. Yet even Sharp, for all his resourcefulness, encountered what eventually became insuperable logistical problems created by Johnston and Barbour.

Sharp's most immediate and pressing problem, that of coordinating his orders and operations with those of Brigadier General Isaac R. Trimble, proved especially perplexing and frustrating. Trimble, an "old rail-road man" and a former Baltimore & Ohio civil engineer, received on March 3 Johnston's orders to serve as superintendent of military transportation at Manassas Junction. Unfortunately, Johnston named Trimble to the post without first establishing different operational arrangements among Trimble, the railroad officials, and Sharp. This overlapping of authority and jurisdiction quickly resulted in serious conflict and massive confusion by failing to provide for any unified, centralized direction of the removal operations. On one occasion Sharp countermanded a set of ambulance train orders issued by Trimble, orders that conflicted with Sharp's own. Trimble thereupon complained to Quartermaster General Myers, who in turn sought to learn from Johnston which man exercised superior authority by Johnston's command. Instead of replying, Johnston upheld Sharp's instructions, although he did not remove Trimble as superintendent of military transportation. Besides the conflict with Trimble at Manassas Junction, Sharp could not personally manage the removal operations at Thoroughfare Gap or at Fredericksburg. The limitation proved especially unfortunate for Thoroughfare Gap because Johnston and Orange & Alexandria president, Barbour, had sent most of the Manassas Gap rolling stock to Manassas Junction, thereby depriving Major Noland at Thoroughfare Gap of the equipment he needed to remove the bulk of the cured meat to Gordonsville.[29]

Though Major Barbour had previously sent forty-five cars to Thoroughfare Gap at the prompting of the commissary agent Cole, the shortage of cars continued. Noland thereafter urged Barbour, in vain, to divert more cars from Manassas Junction to Thoroughfare Gap. Nor did Johnston's quartermasters use much of the rolling stock that they did take to Thoroughfare Gap. In anticipating the arrival of the equipment from Manassas Junction, Noland "had the meat placed in piles corresponding to the cars of a train," but

the trains "passed empty and would not take a pound—3 trains." At
Manassas Junction, however, "many trains remained idle standing
there for days" while the meat at Thoroughfare Gap continued to
spoil. Barbour should not have hesitated to send more cars to Noland, particularly in view of the previously expanded facilities for
accommodating additional rolling stock at Thoroughfare Gap. The
War Department had defrayed a part of the Manassas Gap Railroad's
cost in constructing a switch and siding at Thoroughfare Station, a
turnout and tracks that permitted the operation of more rolling stock
near Northrop's meat-packing plant.[30] Obviously, Barbour egregiously failed to do his duty.

As commanding general, Johnston should have demanded an explanation from Barbour and peremptorily ordered an immediate improvement in Barbour's handling of railroad transportation between
Manassas Junction and Thoroughfare Gap. Johnston failed to take
any disciplinary or corrective action, however, merely explaining to
an increasingly impatient President Davis on March 3 that the Thoroughfare Gap operation progressed with "a painful slowness" because "a sufficient number of cars and engines cannot be had." Yet
Johnston clearly was responsible for providing Noland with the required rolling stock, whatever the opposing counsel, delays, and failures of his quartermasters at Manassas Junction. Denied additional
rolling stock before the evacuation of the army on March 9, Noland
reluctantly but dutifully and efficiently destroyed by fire and exposure upward of 300,000 pounds of packed meat. Subsequently, he
angrily censured Johnston's and Barbour's incompetence and negligence in a letter to Commissary General Northrop. Noland's complaints notwithstanding, the heavy losses of supplies in northern
Virginia—largely caused by Johnston's poor handling of railroad
transportation at Manassas Junction—hurt the Confederate war effort and further aggravated a feud that had begun between Davis
and Johnston over other issues in the summer of 1861. Specifically,
the losses at storage depots around Manassas Junction, Centreville,
and Thoroughfare Gap amounted to 1,500,000 pounds of destroyed
or abandoned food and forage, besides the commissaries still loaded
aboard freight cars subsequently damaged or destroyed on the tracks
west and south of Manassas Junction. Johnston also sacrificed enormous quantities of clothing, accoutrements, camp equipment and
baggage, and ammunition, and even fixed heavy ordnance pieces
in his hasty retreat. The loss of meat particularly damaged the

Confederate army in succeeding campaigns in Virginia. As Lieutenant General Jubal A. Early later recalled, the shortages of food "em-
barrassed us for the remainder of the war, as it put us at once on a
running stock."[31]

Meanwhile a third removal operation proceeded, however halt-
ingly, farther south at Fredericksburg on the Rappahannock River.
There, too, Commissary General Northrop had overloaded the supply depots since the fall of 1861. Since Johnston concentrated most
of the rolling stock operating north of Richmond at Manassas Junction, on March 18 Quartermaster General Myers reminded Johnston
of the scarcity of railroad equipment on the Richmond, Fredericksburg & Potomac. Johnston, having relocated his headquarters at
Culpeper Court House, assumed responsibility for the removal of
7,500,000 pounds of supplies from Fredericksburg to Richmond.

To accomplish this formidable task, Myers issued instructions that
Johnston send two heavy engines and eight freight cars to Fredericksburg. Johnston gave the order that the rolling stock be moved to
Fredericksburg but then neglected to enforce it, causing an exasperated Myers peremptorily to direct that Johnston carry out his order.
Virtually reprimanded for his procrastination, Johnston belatedly diverted Manassas Gap cars from Gordonsville to Fredericksburg, an
action that proved to be futile, as Confederate leaders learned later
in March when General Lee and Secretary of War George W. Randolph deemed it necessary to advise Johnston not to send public
property from Gordonsville to Richmond, a city anticipating imminent Federal attack. The threat to Richmond persuaded Johnston
not to move the stores at Fredericksburg to the Confederate capital,
thus removing the diverted railroad cars from active service. The
Manassas Gap Railroad experienced further delay in recovering its
equipment because in May retreating Confederate troops destroyed
seven Richmond, Fredericksburg & Potomac bridges (two of the
structures were six hundred feet long and seventy feet high). This
destruction, coupled with a devastating Federal cavalry attack on another trestle, isolated the Manassas Gap locomotives and cars north
of Richmond. Neither the rolling stock on that line nor the remaining stores at Fredericksburg reached Richmond until late in the fall
of 1862.[32]

As a comprehensive and systematic effort, the removal operations
at Manassas Junction, Centreville, Thoroughfare Gap, and Fredericksburg failed partly because of the War Department's severely

flawed supply methods and its continuing inability to formulate or apply a coherent railway policy. It failed mainly, however, because of Johnston's misallocation of rolling stock and his withholding of direct and timely cooperation from the War Department, the railroad officials, and army quartermasters in northern Virginia. Ironically, Johnston effectively collaborated with the War Department in accomplishing a relatively minor undertaking—the building of the Centreville Railroad—but then adopted a defiant, noncooperative policy toward the Richmond authorities, and so almost willfully failed to use the Virginia railroads to save irreplaceable resources for the Confederacy. Notwithstanding the huge quantities of stores and equipment abandoned or destroyed in northern Virginia caused by these combined failures in administration and command, neither the War Department nor Johnston took effective measures to prevent further heavy losses in central Virginia.

These additional losses of supplies, though, followed Johnston's more immediate and extensive destruction of railroad property in the course of the Confederate retreat from Manassas Junction on March 9. Turning his attention to Thoroughfare Station, Johnston first ordered the burning of "52 freight cars loaded with commissary stores valued at $20,000," but the fire that Confederate cavalry troops "had kindled had failed to consume them." Nevertheless, convinced that by destroying rolling stock and railroad bridges he could prevent or delay a Federal pursuit of his forces, Johnston devastated the Orange & Alexandria Railroad between Manassas Junction and Catlett's Station, north of Culpeper Court House. Johnston ordered the destruction of the railroad depot and a quantity of rolling stock at Manassas Junction, including the Manassas Gap Railroad's highly prized "Locomotive Number 8," which Confederate troops badly damaged before they started marching southward. From Broad Run to Catlett's Station, Johnston continued to destroy railroad property, including demolishing a six-hundred-foot-long bridge over the Rappahannock River. His actions failed to stop a vigorous Union pursuit of the Rebel forces below Broad Run, even though advancing Federal troops struggled to traverse rugged terrain and overcome formidable obstacles posed by "burned bridges, destroyed road-bed, burned and twisted rails, engines and cars partly burned, or otherwise rendered useless" to Union operations.[33]

The destruction of the Orange & Alexandria Railroad below Manassas Junction actually contributed to the further loss of equipment and supplies in central Virginia because it forced the bulk of that railroad's rolling stock to operate on the tracks between Culpeper Court House and Gordonsville. Indeed, the devastation created an excessive concentration of train traffic on that limited portion of the railroad; that congestion in turn hindered the shipment of great quantities of ordnance, quartermaster's, medical, and one million pounds of subsistence stores from Culpeper Court House to Gordonsville. By March 11, having brought his army to Rappahannock Station on the Rappahannock River, Johnston prepared to remove the stores. He instructed Major Barbour to remove the ordnance stores first, making such arrangements with the "R.R. Agent as will most speedily accomplish this object." The railroad managers struggled to reduce the volume of traffic on the tracks, but they could not break the bottleneck between Culpeper Court House and Gordonsville. Johnston, however, erroneously concluded that incompetent handling of transportation by the railroad officials accounted for the continuation of an extremely heavy concentration of Orange & Alexandria and Virginia Central locomotives and cars operating upon those lines. He complained to President Davis on March 13 that "the management of this railroad is so wretched that it is impossible to guess when the removal of those stores will be completed" at Culpeper Court House. Managerial incompetence was scarcely the problem; rather, poor generalship as manifested by his misallocation of rolling stock and needless destruction of railroad tracks and trestles created the condition in which train traffic on the twenty-six-mile Gordonsville and Culpeper Court House segment of the Orange & Alexandria line came to an almost complete halt. On March 17, Johnston again querulously explained to President Davis that the shipment of troops and commissaries farther south to the line of the Rapidan River remained "greatly delayed by the condition of the country and by the railroads." His patience exhausted, Johnston led the advance elements of his army to Rapidan Station on March 18. His quartermasters then abandoned large reserves of spoiling meat, although they salvaged and completed the removal of other supplies to Gordonsville—a costly and wasteful operation that dragged on into late May.[34]

Though he had created the problem of an excessive amount of railroad traffic below Culpeper Court House, creditably Johnston also employed numerous engines and cars to transport troops to Richmond and Charlottesville— an action that eventually eliminated much of the congestion of railroad equipment on the Orange & Alexandria and Virginia Central railroads. The substantial completion of the removal operation in central Virginia afforded Johnston the opportunity to concentrate on exploiting the railroads of the Old Dominion for strategic purposes. Although Johnston's decision to use rolling stock to transport troops south and, simultaneously, to reduce the quantity of railroad equipment on the central Virginia railroads sprang from both necessity and expediency, his action also caused further hardship to the sick soldiers whom he had earlier removed to Orange Court House from Front Royal, Centreville, and Manassas Junction.

After the evacuation of the Confederate army from northern Virginia early in March, Johnston ordered the closing of the military hospital at Orange Court House. Then, during the army's retreat toward the Rappahannock, he decided to reopen the facility. Although the arrival of additional numbers of sick soldiers thereafter quickly overcrowded the hospital, Johnston decided not to remove the patients farther south (only four miles) to Gordonsville, where they would have received better treatment and from which point they could have been forwarded to other hospitals at Lynchburg or Charlottesville. At this juncture, Medical Director Williams, who stood deprived of railroad transportation because Johnston already designated all available trains for use by those quartermasters then engaged in transporting troops to Richmond, described to Johnston the extreme "discomfort" that the sick soldiers would endure if Johnston did not remove the patients to Gordonsville. As Williams later explained to Surgeon General Moore, however, Johnston had "replied that it could not be avoided, as the transportation of the troops was of the first importance."[35] Johnston failed to advise Williams of his intention to use all available rolling stock to reinforce Richmond with additional troops; this lack of communication and coordination of effort reflected his earlier and similar withholding of information and assistance from Williams, Noland, and the railroad officials in northern Virginia. As a result, the sick troops at Orange Court House suffered unnecessary delay in being sent to well-equipped hospitals in the rear. Ironically, Johnston took measures to transport sick soldiers from Front Royal and Manassas Junction to Orange Court House and then refused to send them the four miles to Gordonsville.

Johnston's assignment of priority on the shipment of troops to Richmond in mid-March 1862 sprang from reasonable and even urgent considerations, although he should have allocated spare rolling

stock for Williams. Indeed, even earlier in March, he had considered
using the railroad as a means of moving troops quickly to threatened
points. At that time, while commanding at Rappahannock Station,
Johnston learned that thirty-five thousand seaborne troops of the
Federal Army of the Potomac, supported by the Union navy, stood
prepared to invade the Peninsula and threatened to attack Major
General John B. Magruder's twelve-thousand-man command at Yorktown. Despite the peril to Richmond, Jefferson Davis dismissed
Johnston's proposed plan to reinforce the capital massively in the
event of a Federal landing upon the Peninsula. On March 13
Johnston expressed the view that by a "proper management of the
railroad" around Gordonsville, "20,000 or even 30,000 men might
be thrown into Richmond in a single day." He also urged the president to permit him to impose an absolute and extraordinary "military control" over the Virginia Central Railroad to avoid a repetition
of the civilian-related management problems that had hindered
his efforts in using the Manassas Gap and Orange & Alexandria
railroads. Johnson further recommended that Davis remove the
Northern-born Virginia Central general superintendent, Henry D.
Whitcomb, and replace him with Colonel Robert L. Owen, the military superintendent of the East Tennessee & Virginia Railroad who,
in the fall of 1861, had fiercely battled with bands of bridge-burning
Unionist saboteurs in East Tennessee.[36]

Militarily, Johnston's intelligent and imaginative plan reflected his
growing perception of the practical use of the railroad to achieve a
strategic concentration of force. Yet he conspicuously failed to appreciate the necessity of maintaining an effective working relationship
between the Confederate War Department and the Virginia Central
Railroad, whatever his unfounded suspicion of Whitcomb. Then,
too, Johnston framed his proposal in ambiguous and sweeping terms.
He should have clarified his recommendation about the proposed
appointment of Colonel Owen, specifically indicating that Owen
should temporarily assist Whitcomb in the execution of a critical
strategic operation. Johnston implied that Owen should permanently
supersede Whitcomb, which probably misrepresented his true intention. Moreover, the selection and use of the quartermaster agent
Sharp in that crisis should have struck Johnston as giving him a
course of action superior to the choice of Owen. In view of such
considerations, Davis prudently rejected Johnston's proposal for an
arbitrary assumption of military control over the Virginia Central.

Undeterred, Johnston continued to perceive the railroad as a strategic instrument of war. His opportunity to reinforce the Confederate capital by rail came when he answered Lee's instructions on March 27 to send ten thousand troops to Richmond with the message that he had "ordered about 7500 men" from Gordonsville "by railroad to move tomorrow and 2500 to be transported" by troop trains from Fredericksburg. Satisfied with Johnston's performance, Lee then requested him to send a large number of cars from Gordonsville to Charlottesville for transporting Virginia recruits to Staunton in the Shenandoah Valley.[37] In both situations, Johnston cooperated with quartermasters and with officials of the Virginia Central and Richmond, Fredericksburg & Potomac railroads to execute the operations successfully. He thereby demonstrated his ability to make effective strategic use of the Virginia railways by coordinating troop train movements upon widely separated railroad lines.

Following his reinforcement of Richmond and the diversion of rolling stock to Charlottesville, Johnston ordered Sharp to supervise the extending of sidings on the Virginia Central Railroad. He might have remembered that Quartermaster General Myers, late in July 1861, had suggested that he use some of the Union prisoners—those taken at Bull Run—to repair the damaged section of the Orange & Alexandria between Manassas Junction and Fairfax Court House because, Myers explained, the slave "labor requisite cannot I understand be procured in the vicinity of the Road." Although Johnston decided not to rebuild that segment of the railroad at that moment in the summer of 1861, subsequently the pressing need to expedite the transportation of troops from Gordonsville to Richmond persuaded him to use not Federal prisoners of war but rather black prison inmates and other slave laborers for railroad work. Therefore, on April 1, Johnston ordered Sharp to procure from Major Barbour a gang of black "Penitentiary Convicts" from Richmond and, from a quartermaster agent at Fredericksburg, enough "negroes to make 200 with Rations" for the purpose of "lengthening the turnouts on the Central R Road between Gordonsville & Richmond" so as to facilitate the passing of troop trains upon the tracks.[38] Although by completing this work Johnston again demonstrated an improved appreciation of the strategic value of the railroad, he earlier failed to build or extend sidings on the Orange & Alexandria north of Gordonsville to accelerate the movement of supply trains. He thus clearly revealed his persistent misunderstanding of the potential uses of the railroad in solving logistical problems relating to overland mobility and supply.

Having improved the Virginia Central tracks below Gordonsville, Johnston thereafter steadily reinforced Magruder's command at Yorktown until he himself proceeded to Richmond in mid-April to assume command of all Confederate forces on the Peninsula. Though Richmond constituted the hub of Virginia's railway network, Johnston proved unable to protect the railroads that radiated north from the Confederate capital, despite the stationing of troops at Gordonsville, Fredericksburg, and Hanover Junction. By late May 1862, the relentless Federal movement against Richmond forced Johnston to abandon the railways completely, resulting in their devastation by retreating Rebel troops and raiding Federal cavalry. Nor could he indefinitely protect the Richmond & York River Railroad, which crossed the Pamunkey River east of Richmond before it extended to the Union army base at West Point. Fearing that Union gunboats would soon attempt to bombard the railroad bridge spanning the York River, the Richmond & York River president, Alexander Dudley, sought the intervention of General Lee who, as military adviser to President Davis, referred him to Johnston. Further, in a separate communication, Lee recommended that Johnston cooperate with the railroad officials in obstructing the Pamunkey River to hinder its navigation by Federal warships. He also urged Johnston to help Dudley "hold the bridges" until the railroad could be safely abandoned by the Confederate army that prepared to retreat slowly west toward Richmond.[39] Presumably Johnston aided Dudley, although eventually an extended portion of the Richmond & York River line fell under Federal control.

Thwarted in his efforts to use with full effectiveness the railroads north or east of Richmond in defeating the Federal army on the Peninsula, Johnston turned with greater confidence to the Richmond & Petersburg Railroad, which ran south from the capital to connect the Old Dominion with the states of the Confederacy's Atlantic seaboard. At this juncture Johnston proposed a second plan to President Davis regarding a coordinated strategic concentration of force at Richmond by rail. In view of the worsened military crisis, the operation he now anticipated would be conducted on a grand scale. Thus, late in April 1862, Johnston boldly recommended that Davis strip the garrisons of Wilmington, Charleston, Savannah, and other Southern seaports and ship the troops to Richmond where, with other Confederate forces, they would inflict a crushing blow upon the Federal army. Davis and Lee criticized this elaborately devised but unfeasible scheme, principally for its lack of clear recognition of the formidable management and technical problems involved in implementing such a massive troop movement to Virginia, as well as the danger of rendering the Confederacy's vital seaports vulnerable to amphibious assaults.

The rejection of Johnston's second proposal for a massive strategic concentration of troops at Richmond limited his use of the railroad to theater tactics. Consequently, late in May Johnston shipped from Petersburg to Richmond three brigades of infantry commanded by Major General Benjamin Huger. In sharp contrast to his lack of foresight in the Manassas Gap Railroad troop movement fiasco of 1861, Johnston made advance arrangements with Richmond & Petersburg officials to allocate and concentrate enough rolling stock at Petersburg for the transportation of Huger's command to Richmond, an operation executed with celerity and precision. Fittingly, Johnston's skillfully handled movement of Huger's brigades to Richmond concluded his use of the Virginia railroads. On May 31, 1862, at Seven Pines, Johnston sustained two disabling wounds, and Robert E. Lee then assumed command of what became the legendary Army of Northern Virginia.[40]

Throughout his command in the Old Dominion, Johnston showed an inconsistency in his handling of railroad transportation. From Harpers Ferry to Richmond, his fundamentally sound perception of the potential of the railroad to increase the mobility of his army evolved steadily, and he grew appreciably in his ability to exploit the Virginia railways to achieve limited strategic objectives. Otherwise, apart from his building of the Centreville Railroad, Johnston seriously failed to make effective use of the railroad to solve his supply problems. Johnston's striking inconsistency—marked by wide divergence between his conceptual views and practical uses of the railroad—also revealed itself in his contradictory policy of either plundering or destroying Baltimore & Ohio rolling stock and in his erratic relations with the War Department and railroad officials. Significantly, Johnston exhibited a reckless disregard for the preservation of rolling stock and other railroad property belonging to the Virginia carriers. His repeated abuse and destruction of that equipment sprang from his radically mistaken opinion that Union commanders depended heavily upon rail transport in undertaking and sustaining overland invasions of Virginia. Johnston believed that, short of crushing Union forces in battle, he could cripple or delay Federal military movements by destroying rolling stock, railroad tracks, and trestles in the enemy's front or rear—a self-serving delusion to which he clung obstinately throughout the war. Finally, Johnston's extensive and productive employment of Captain Sharp further reflected his uneven approach to the railroad. The detailing of Sharp was an inadequate arrangement, though it frequently relieved him of excessive dependence on technically incompetent quartermasters such as Major Barbour and Captain Powell. Johnston failed to consider the superior advantage of recommending and procuring Sharp's early appointment as military superintendent of transportation for the Confederate Army of the Potomac. Unfortunately, Johnston's inconsistent handling of the Virginia railways anticipated his disastrous misuse of the Southern railroads in the strategically critical Confederate West.

·{2}·

Paralysis and Conflict in the West

J OHNSTON'S handling of the railroads in the Confederate West should be viewed against the larger strategic background of decisive military operations occurring in both the East and the Mississippi Valley. General Braxton Bragg's invasion of Kentucky in September 1862 produced excitement throughout the South and raised high hopes in Richmond for the achievement of Confederate independence. Concurrent with Bragg's Kentucky campaign, Robert E. Lee led his Army of Northern Virginia into Maryland and threatened to invade Pennsylvania. The Confederate government confidently expected a series of strategically decisive victories that would simultaneously defeat two Union armies and ensure European intervention and Federal recognition of the Confederacy's de jure independence. The first stunning setback to the Richmond government's hopes for independence was Lee's withdrawal from Maryland following the bloody Battle of Antietam. The final blow came four weeks later when Bragg notified the Confederate authorities that the Army of Tennessee had returned to Chattanooga after sustaining heavy losses at Perryville, Kentucky. Bragg's unsuccessful Kentucky campaign only emphasized the steadily deteriorating Confederate military situation in the trans-Appalachian West. After the battle of Perryville, Major General William S. Rosecrans's Army of the Cumberland advanced south into Tennessee and encamped around Nashville. Major General Ulysses S. Grant distributed the forces of his Army of the Mississippi across northern Mississippi. Together, the two Federal armies threatened vital Confederate interests. Rosecrans's army lay only 120 miles northwest of Chattanooga, and a Federal capture and occupation of Chattanooga would expose

General Braxton Bragg, commander of the Army of Tennessee, 1862–
1863. From *Battles and Leaders of the Civil War,* ed. Robert Underwood
Johnson and Clarence Clough Buel (New York, 1880), 3:601.

northwestern Georgia to invasion and break one of the three railway
axes that connected the Atlantic coastal and Mississippi Valley regions of the Confederacy. Farther west, Grant's army could concentrate and move east along the Memphis & Charleston Railroad
toward Chattanooga or resume its advance down the Mississippi Valley against the stronghold of Vicksburg.[1]

Lieutenant General John C. Pemberton, commander of the Department of Mississippi and East Louisiana.

In response to the more immediate Federal threat to Vicksburg, President Davis appointed Northern-born Lieutenant General John C. Pemberton to the command of the newly created Department of Mississippi and East Louisiana. Davis's appointment of another department commander to strengthen the Confederacy's Western defensive system failed to satisfy Bragg, who perceived a need for a supreme commander in the West. Bragg sent Lieutenant General Leonidas Polk to Richmond to request Johnston's appointment to that position. In conveying Bragg's request for Johnston, Polk also advised Davis that he and his fellow officers had lost confidence in Bragg's ability to guide Confederate affairs in Tennessee. Davis, who considered Bragg an especially competent commander, refused to dismiss him and hesitated to grant Johnston another independent command. The president particularly feared a repetition in the West of Johnston's costly and unnecessary destruction of supplies and equipment in the evacuation of northern Virginia. Despite presidential inaction, demands for Johnston's immediate appointment poured into the Confederate capital from all quarters of the West. Yielding to the pressure, Davis devised an ingenious solution to his dilemma. He retained Bragg as commander of the Army of Tennessee and designated Johnston supreme commander of all Confederate troops in the West. Davis recognized that Johnston could not directly command any field army from headquarters at Chattanooga, but he still charged him with the coordination of military effort between the two widely separated Confederate armies east of the Mississippi River. In effect, Davis appointed Johnston his chief of staff between the War Department and the two army commanders within Johnston's jurisdiction.[2]

On November 13, 1862, Johnston reported to the War Department and learned of Davis's action. He expected eventually to resume command of the Confederate army in Virginia, despite his slow recovery from wounds sustained on the Peninsula. In August 1862, he assured Quartermaster General Myers that, although he wished to return to the front in northern Virginia, he preferred not to take command of Lee's army near Richmond to "wait [Major General George B.] McClellan's leisure" on the Peninsula. Johnston expressed bitter disappointment over his new assignment to duty. He not only hesitated to assume and exercise authority over such a vast geographical region, but he also believed that his transfer to the West represented Davis's and the War Department authorities' ingratitude for his service in Virginia. As Johnston prepared to depart from Richmond for Chattanooga, Mary Boykin Chesnut, the perceptive diarist, overheard the general grumbling that "they may give Lee the army Joe Johnston trained." Johnston and his adjutant general, the West Point–educated Colonel Benjamin S. Ewell of North Carolina, and his chief quartermaster, Major Barbour, traveled over several railroads to Tennessee and, although delayed by three separate derailments on their journey south, safely reached Chattanooga on December 4.[3]

Johnston's frustration and perplexity about his appointment to the Western command sprang from logical considerations as well as from personal feelings of resentment. His jurisdiction embraced much of the territory of the seceded states of Tennessee, Alabama, and Mississippi. Bragg's army around Murfreesboro, Tennessee, and Pemberton's forces in Mississippi lay beyond the range of any rapid concentration of force. Johnston's objective assessment of the possible military uses of the railway system in those states scarcely encouraged him about the practicability of joint army operations. Collectively, the railroads of the three states formed a disjointed system of transportation. The careless arrangement of the railroads grew out of the essentially commercial purpose for which the states had helped finance railroad construction in the 1850s. The several state legislatures, largely dominated by slaveholding interests, promoted intrastate railway building in order to facilitate the shipment of King Cotton to ports on the Gulf of Mexico or the Mississippi River. The railroad companies eagerly built their lines to monopolize as much of the intrastate cotton traffic as possible. As a result, the developing interstate railway pattern across the Deep South assumed an increasingly disorganized form.

Moreover, compared to the Confederacy's Atlantic coastal railway system, the Western railway network contained a paucity of trackage—a condition perpetuated by a scarcity of good-quality iron. The many broad rivers running across the territory of the trans-Appalachian seceded states compounded the severe shortage of track. The railroad companies of those states therefore carefully maintained their bridges and trestles because the destruction or disrepair of a single bridge could break railway connection between river banks indefinitely. Still, the near uniformity of track gauges among individual railroads partially offset the flaws of the Western railway system. Identical gauges permitted the transfer of one

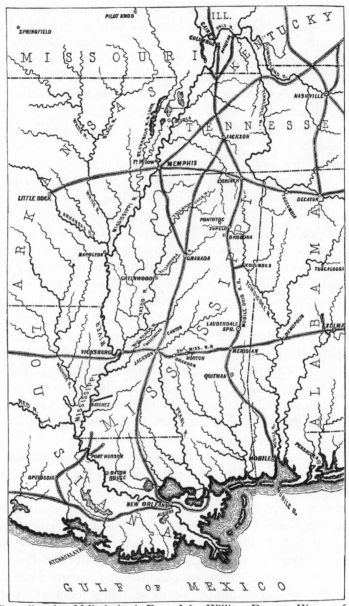

The railroads of Mississippi. From John William Draper, *History of the American Civil War* (New York, 1870), 3:206.

company's rolling stock onto the line of almost any other. In addition, most of the railroads of the Gulf States had comparatively longer trunk lines than the Atlantic coastal railroads. These conditions eliminated the numerous gauge changeovers that slowed troop train movements in the East.

Despite its structural and technical defects, the railway system of Tennessee, Alabama, and Mississippi strove to support Confederate military operations from the outbreak of the war. The system offered Confederate commanders roughly three main lateral axes. From its Memphis terminal on the Mississippi River, the Memphis & Charleston Railroad extended east along the Mississippi and Tennessee border and across northern Alabama to Chattanooga, Tennessee. A series of railway links in Georgia connected the Memphis & Charleston's Chattanooga terminal with the Atlantic seaports of Savannah and Charleston. While Johnston may not have perceived any threat to his railway connections southeast of Chattanooga, Grant's Army of the Mississippi occupied a series of strategic points along the Memphis & Charleston Railroad from Memphis to Burnsville near the Mississippi and Alabama border. The second major lateral line of railroad transportation of any strategic significance consisted of a series of links that Southerners informally termed the Savannah & Vicksburg Railroad. This line connected the Atlantic seaports with the stronghold of Vicksburg on the Mississippi River; it also joined the seceded states east of the river with Lieutenant General Edmund Kirby Smith's Trans-Mississippi Department over the Vicksburg, Shreveport & Texas Railroad. The barge transportation that linked the railheads on the two river banks, however, could not be protected from interruption or destruction in the event that Federal military or naval forces descended or ascended on Vicksburg from Memphis or New Orleans and possibly rendered useless the railroad west of the Mississippi.

The third railroad connecting Charleston and Vicksburg and other points on the Mississippi formed only a partially completed line between Montgomery, Alabama, and Meridian, Mississippi. The combination of a four-mile trackless gap and the unbridged Tombigbee River—a gap between Demopolis and McDowell's Landing, Alabama, on either side of the Tombigbee—separated the Alabama & Mississippi Rivers Railroad into two segments. Completion of a railroad connection and bridge between Demopolis and McDowell's Landing would, however, more directly link Charleston and

Vicksburg via Montgomery, Selma, and Meridian. The Southern Railroad connected Meridian and Vicksburg via Jackson, the Mississippi state capital.

Consideration of the system's north-and-south-running railroads could not have offered Johnston increased confidence that the Western railroads could effectively support the military operations of his department commanders. In eastern Tennessee, the Nashville & Chattanooga Railroad connected Bragg's army around Murfreesboro with the Atlantic coastal states. As long as Bragg maintained his position near the railroad, Nashville & Chattanooga freight trains could haul an adequate amount of beef and subsistence stores from Chattanooga to Murfreesboro to meet the Army of Tennessee's supply requirements. In central Tennessee three railroads, collectively forming what railroad executives called the Nashville & Decatur Railroad Line, connected Nashville on the Nashville & Chattanooga with Decatur, Alabama, on the Memphis & Charleston below the Tennessee River. The Tennessee & Alabama Railroad extended from Nashville to Columbia, Tennessee; the Central Southern Railroad ran from Columbia to Athens, Alabama; and the Tennessee & Alabama Central Railroad linked Athens and Decatur. Neither Johnston nor Bragg had yet discovered that the Nashville & Decatur was in extensive disrepair. All of western Tennessee's railway lines had fallen under Federal control.

Farther south, Alabama's railways offered Johnston few logistically useful lines. The Alabama & Tennessee Rivers Railroad extended northeast from Selma to its terminal at Blue Mountain. There, a fifty-nine-mile trackless gap broke railway connection between Blue Mountain and a Western & Atlantic Railroad spur line at Rome, Georgia. Johnston would thus have to use a number of railroads to transport troops over a circuitous route from Tennessee to the Gulf States. Bragg's forces would have to travel from Murfreesboro to Chattanooga in Nashville & Chattanooga cars. At Chattanooga, the troops would take Georgia's Western & Atlantic trains and continue to Atlanta. Four other railway companies would have to supply the rolling stock needed to forward the troops from Atlanta to Mobile on the Gulf of Mexico. Alternately, he could send troops over a number of railroads between Chattanooga and Demopolis. After a four-mile march from Demopolis to McDowell's Landing and after crossing the Tombigbee River by steamboat or barge, Confederate forces could proceed by rail farther west to Meridian or Jackson.

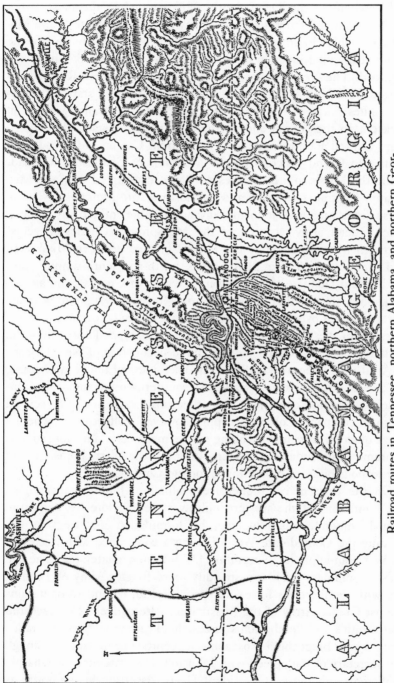

Railroad routes in Tennessee, northern Alabama, and northern Georgia. From John William Draper, *History of the American Civil War* (New York, 1870), 3:59.

Elsewhere in the Deep South, Mississippi had the most elaborately developed railway system of any of the Gulf States. The Mobile & Ohio Railroad left Mobile and extended north to the strategically vital junction of Corinth on the Memphis & Charleston Railroad. The New Orleans, Jackson & Great Northern Railroad departed from New Orleans to run north to Canton, a station twenty-five miles north of Mississippi's state capital and railway nexus at Jackson. In the central and northern parts of the state, the Mississippi Central Railroad extended north from Canton to Grenada and thence to Grand Junction on the Memphis & Charleston Railroad, while the Mississippi & Tennessee Railroad diverged from the Mississippi Central at Grenada and ran northwest to Memphis. None of these lines promised Johnston any appreciable military usefulness. The Federal army's control of the Memphis & Charleston across northern Mississippi broke the railway linkage between Mississippi and Tennessee. While Mississippi's north-and-south-running railroads could facilitate the southward advance of Grant's army against Vicksburg, they could offer Pemberton's forces only a group of transportation lines over which to receive supplies brought from the trans-Mississippi West through Vicksburg or stores shipped north from the Gulf Coast. The Federal reduction and occupation of New Orleans in April 1862 effectively nullified the usefulness of the New Orleans, Jackson & Great Northern Railroad's southernmost segment for Confederate logistical operations in southeastern Louisiana.[4] The several railroad companies of Mississippi, however, collectively owned a great quantity of valuable rolling stock, machinery, and iron; and as supreme commander of the Department of the West, Johnston bore the responsibility of protecting it for the Confederacy.

On the basis of comprehensive evaluation, Johnston recognized the limitations of the western railway system before his departure from Richmond, thus influencing his formulation of strategy for defending the Confederate West. During a conference with Secretary of War Randolph on November 13, Johnston contended that the Western railroads could not speedily unite Bragg's Army of Tennessee with Pemberton's forces in Mississippi for combined operations against Grant's Army of the Mississippi. Alternatively, he suggested that Smith's and Pemberton's forces should unite and crush Grant's army while Bragg held Rosecrans in central Tennessee. Although the secretary of war agreed with Johnston, his strategic views sharply conflicted with those of President Davis. Asserting his authority as commander in chief, Davis insisted that the three Confederate armies remain separated and that Bragg's troops reinforce Pemberton only when militarily necessary. Randolph found his position untenable and produced a "profound sensation" in the South by submitting his resignation to the president on November 15.[5]

Johnston departed from Richmond for Chattanooga still hoping that President Davis would accept Randolph's strategic plans. Davis disappointed him. The chief executive left Richmond on December 7 and went to Johnston's headquarters at Chattanooga. After inspecting the Army of Tennessee at Murfreesboro, he directed Johnston to send two infantry divisions to Jackson, Mississippi, for the temporary reinforcement of Pemberton's troops around Vicksburg. Johnston obeyed and designated Major General Carter L. Stevenson's nine thousand troops for transportation from Murfreesboro on December 18. Exploiting his experience with the Virginia railroads in conducting large-scale logistical operations that involved urgent and extraordinary military intervention in railroad company affairs, Johnston also recognized the necessity of imposing a similar form of limited military control over railroad firms in the Deep South to accomplish an extensive strategic transportation of troops in the West. Therefore, on December 23 he ordered Major Charles F. Moore, his assistant chief quartermaster, to proceed to Atlanta and thence to points farther south and west to accelerate the railway movement of Stevenson's divisions to Mississippi. Johnston granted Moore "authority to impress cars" and to "dispatch & detain trains when necessary to secure prompt transportation" for Stevenson's troops.[6] Notwithstanding Moore's efforts, the operation proved ineffective and indecisive because of long delays in the movement of troop trains across the Deep South. Two of Stevenson's brigades reached Jackson by December 28, enabling those units to support other Confederate troops in the repulse of Major General William T. Sherman's attack on Vicksburg near Chickasaw Bayou. The other four brigades required ten more days to complete their railway journey to Mississippi.

The prolonged delays in the movement of Stevenson's troops to Mississippi confirmed Johnston's doubts about Davis's strategic judgment. The three railroad derailments that impeded his journey to Chattanooga earlier in December alerted him to the badly deteriorated condition of the eastern Tennessee railways. In view of Moore's inability to expedite train traffic despite his establishing a

limited military control over the Southern carriers, Johnston refrained from criticizing the eight railroad companies that furnished
transportation for Stevenson's divisions, retrospectively observing
that the "management of the railroad trains was at least as good as
usual in such cases." Rather, he concluded that the dilapidated condition of the Western railroads largely accounted for the delays in
Stevenson's troop movement to Mississippi, informing President
Davis four months later that "the [Tennessee, Alabama, and Missis-
sippi] railroads are in worse condition now than they were then."[7]
Though Johnston was correct in his narrow technical assessment,
neither he nor the War Department authorities yet perceived the
need for comprehensive joint planning and improved cooperation
among the railroad managers, Confederate field commanders, and
the War Department in mobilizing the Southern railroads for coordinated strategic and logistical operations in the West.

However slow their progress westward, the movement of Stevenson's divisions from Tennessee to Mississippi coincided with Federal
General Rosecrans's preparations to attack the Army of Tennessee at
Murfreesboro. Bragg, acting without Johnston's authority, responded
to the threat by issuing orders that prohibited "Railroad transportation except for ordnance and commissary stores" on the Nashville
& Chattanooga and Memphis & Charleston lines between Chattanooga and Murfreesboro. Having received a complaint on December 14 from the chief quartermaster of Lieutenant General Smith's
Department of the Trans-Mississippi that Bragg's action stopped
the shipment of badly needed shoes and clothing west on the Memphis & Charleston line between Chattanooga, Tennessee, and Stevenson, Alabama (where the Nashville & Chattanooga then ran north
to Murfreesboro), Major Barbour urged Johnston to address the
problem.[8] Johnston, however, neither upheld Bragg's orders nor ordered the resumption of the transportation of clothing to Smith's
command. Davis's order that Confederate troops be sent from Tennessee to Mississippi by way of Chattanooga and Atlanta required
Johnston to suspend further ordnance and commissary shipments to
Bragg until Johnston had completed the transportation of Rebel
forces from Murfreesboro to Chattanooga. By the time Stevenson's
divisions had evacuated Tennessee and entered Georgia, Bragg, apparently with Johnston's concurrence, again prepared to repel a
Federal attack by drawing more ammunition and food over the railroads from Chattanooga. Bragg's action further delayed renewed

shoe and clothing shipments to Smith's tattered troops west of the Mississippi River.

Rosecrans struck Bragg late in December 1862 at Stones River. After three days of bloody battle, Bragg withdrew his army along the Nashville & Chattanooga Railroad but sent large numbers of captured Federal soldiers to Atlanta. Partly to protect his railroad communications, he left one infantry corps at Shelbyville above Duck River and another corps at Tullahoma, twelve miles farther south on the railroad. Later, Johnston ordered Major Moore to remove the Federal prisoners that Bragg had captured at Murfreesboro from Atlanta by rail to Richmond at the rate of a thousand a day. Referring to the East Tennessee & Virginia Railroad, Johnston required Moore to march the prisoners "over that part of the Rail Road between the two Bridges recently burned" by Unionist saboteurs near Knoxville. Meanwhile, farther west, Grant hastily withdrew from his forward position along the Tallahatchie River in northern Mississippi. The destruction by Rebel cavalry of his supply base at Holly Springs on the Mississippi Central Railroad forced him to abandon his attempted rear investment of Vicksburg. Shortly thereafter, Confederate troops (including part of Stevenson's command) repulsed Sherman's attack on Vicksburg near Chickasaw Bayou.[9]

The break in Federal military operations against Confederate forces in Mississippi at the close of 1862 coincided with the eruption of controversy and acrimony within the Rebel high command in the west. Since the outbreak of the war, Confederate quartermasters in northern Louisiana continuously shipped a heavy volume of corn and meat to points on the Vicksburg, Shreveport & Texas Railroad. The railway company's trains carried the stores to DeSoto on the west bank of the Mississippi River, and barges then transported the goods across the river to Vicksburg. Southern Railroad trains took the stores on to Jackson, where New Orleans, Jackson & Great Northern and Mississippi Central trains hauled some of the supplies to Grenada for the subsistence of Confederate troops encamped above the Yalobusha River. Other Southern Railroad trains carried the bulk of the stores from Jackson to Meridian, the company's eastern terminal. Then, Mobile & Ohio trains shipped the stores from Meridian to Mobile for distribution among private merchants who had earlier contracted with the two railroad companies for the interstate transportation of the supplies. This pattern of trade and traffic abruptly disintegrated late in November, however, when Lieutenant General

Pemberton decided to accumulate a greater quantity of corn and bacon in his army's supply depots at Grenada. When informed of the Southern and the Mobile & Ohio companies' activity in the Mobile supply traffic, he endeavored to divert all the corn and meat entering Mississippi to his army around Grenada and to other Confederate troops in that state. Thereafter Pemberton commandeered Southern Railroad, New Orleans, Jackson & Great Northern, and Mississippi Central rolling stock to accomplish that purpose. He also ordered the seizure of Mobile & Ohio rolling stock below Meridian, although his quartermasters seldom employed that equipment. Finally, Pemberton placed the transportation and distribution of the supplies under the supervision of quartermasters in his department. Owing to his preoccupation with Grant's movements early in December, Pemberton neglected to control closely the carrying trade of the Mississippi railroad companies. But this laxity ended on December 12, when he promulgated his notorious "corn order," forbidding the Mobile & Ohio to ship to retailers or merchants "in Mobile and elsewhere out of the department" any of the corn and bacon brought into Mississippi through Vicksburg. His quartermasters accordingly imposed extralegal controls over railroad traffic and positively prohibited the Mobile & Ohio and Southern railroads from making further shipments to civilians.[10]

The vigorous enforcement of Pemberton's corn order over the winter of 1862 and 1863, despite countermanding orders from Richmond, provoked massive protest throughout Mississippi and southern Alabama. Manifesting the outcry in highly condemnatory terms, the *Mobile Advertiser and Register* called the continuation of Pemberton's flagrantly illegal action "simply preposterous and a public outrage," calling for Johnston's and the War Department's intervention. Subsequently, a number of prominent railroad officials, civil authorities, and relief association members sent Johnston formal complaints about Pemberton's action. In particular, the secretary of the Mobile Supply Association advised Johnston that railroad transportation for that organization and other relief groups stood "so much interfered with by military orders" that Mobile remained "almost entirely cut off" from its primary source of corn supply along the Mobile & Ohio Railroad in Mississippi. The association's secretary therefore requested Johnston to authorize private shipments of corn over that railroad in an effort to feed the forty thousand hungry inhabitants of

Mobile. Johnston refused to revoke peremptorily Pemberton's order, but he referred the complaints to Pemberton with the ill-founded expectation that his subordinate would lift what effectively constituted a domestic economic embargo imposed by the military on private merchants. Pemberton, resentful of Johnston's supposed interference, refused to "alter the spirit" of his order. Robert H. Slough, the mayor of Mobile, nevertheless urged Johnston to order an immediate change in Pemberton's railroad policy. In responding to Slough's appeal early in February, Johnston instead suggested that southern Alabama could furnish Mobile with an "abundance of corn." Trying to avoid a direct confrontation with Pemberton, he also refused to grant the wishes of Alabama governor James G. Shorter, informing him on February 8 that he could not "meddle with General Pemberton's mode of supplying his troops" because of his distance from Mississippi. Rather, Johnston requested that Shorter suggest to Slough "how Mobile may be supplied." Not unexpectedly, Shorter failed to appease Slough or alleviate the food shortage in Mobile.[11]

Johnston's misunderstanding of the corn supply situation in Mississippi and Alabama continued until February 16, when newly designated Secretary of War James A. Seddon accurately described the problem for him. He drew Johnston's attention to the vociferous complaints raised by Mississippi railroad officials and emphasized that Pemberton's corn edict flagrantly violated War Department orders against the assumption of unauthorized military control over any railway company's property or carrying trade. Seddon declared that the complaints about Pemberton's quartermasters "have been incessant" and that "imputations upon their integrity have come again and again to the Department." The secretary of war pointed out that Pemberton's "control over the railroad system of the State" of Mississippi imposed an "embargo on the domestic trade of an entire people." Acknowledging that Pemberton still refused to obey War Department orders to lift or modify the railroad ban, Seddon granted Johnston discretionary authority to uphold or revoke Pemberton's edict but, short of that, urged Johnston to take "such measures to reconcile the apparently conflicting interests of the two communities and military departments as may be proper." Failing to balance the demands of Pemberton and the needs of Mobile merchants and citizens, however, Johnston concluded that satisfying Pemberton's immediate supply requirements constituted a more pressing consideration than relieving Mobile's critical and chronic food shortage. He permitted the corn order to remain in force for the rest of the winter of 1863.[12]

Johnson thus displayed serious errors of judgment. He failed to appreciate the vital necessity of maintaining a cooperative relationship between Pemberton and the Gulf States' political authorities and railroad officials. Thus he possessed clear War Department authorization to rescind Pemberton's edict, his unwillingness to exercise that authority strained the relationship between the Confederate military and public authorities—besides depressing public morale—in Alabama and Mississippi. Initially, Johnston erroneously concluded that the corn order reflected Pemberton's immediate and expedient decision to utilize the Mississippi railroads for assistance in the maintenance of the Confederate army around Grenada. Thereafter he failed to recognize that Pemberton's action amounted to an arbitrary assumption of continuing military control over the railway firms' rolling stock and an illegal monopolization of their carrying trade.

Moreover, Johnston's obstinate refusal to comply with Mayor Slough's request for intervention on the ground that southern Alabama offered the Gulf port an alternate source of corn displayed a disregard of two other considerations. Confederate quartermasters in southern Alabama constantly sought to procure corn in that section of the state. They then shipped the corn to Confederate armies in Tennessee and Virginia, not to competing Alabama merchants. Slough's request for the resumption of corn shipments to Mobile should have suggested to Johnston that southern Alabama's corn supply failed to provide an adequate amount of food for the city's starving population. Nor could Johnston have reasonably expected Governor Shorter to resolve the crisis without military assistance and cooperation; yet Johnston abruptly withdrew his support of Pemberton's corn order a few weeks after he received Seddon's letter, when, in the middle of March, it appeared that Pemberton's mismanagement of the Mississippi railways threatened to aggravate an especially acute shortage of sugar and molasses for Confederate troops in Tennessee. Johnston disciplined his troublesome subordinate by repealing Pemberton's ban in Mississippi.[13] In retrospect, it should be emphasized that the whole episode once again conspicuously revealed Johnston's severe limitations as a logistician in using the Confederate railroads to overcome problems of supply, and the affair further demonstrated his continued lack of professional growth in this sphere of generalship since his initial command in Virginia.

Despite his failure to curb Pemberton's abuse of authority, Johnston correctly recognized that the Army of Tennessee suffered more severe food shortages than Pemberton's troops endured in northern Mississippi. Nashville & Chattanooga trains struggled early in the winter of 1863 to carry a sufficient quantity of corn and beef to Bragg's troops, but the shipments fell far short of their needs. The increasingly critical supply situation around Tullahoma prompted Johnston to send his assistant adjutant general, Major Arthur D. Banks, in search of additional sources of food. Fortunately, Banks found unexploited reserves in northern and central Alabama. From Mobile, on January 13, he reported to headquarters that he had located "a good supply of provisions on hand between Columbus and Decatur." Although primarily a cotton-growing zone, the belt between Columbus, Georgia, and Decatur, Alabama, promised an abundant supply of corn and meat for the Confederate army. A shortage of field transportation, however, coupled with the long journey of animal-drawn wagon trains from northern Alabama to central Tennessee over a rugged terrain, necessitated the immediate use of the Central Southern and Tennessee & Alabama Central railroads. By March, Banks's quartermasters had secured so little field transportation in northern Alabama and southern Tennessee that they could not even "collect the supplies at depots on the [Tennessee & Alabama Central] railroad, the country having been stripped completely of every description of wagons and carts." Therefore, the operation of railroad trains on those lines could ensure a faster shipment of northern Alabama and central Tennessee provisions to Bragg's veterans around Tullahoma. Freight trains could carry supplies from Decatur north to Pulaski, Tennessee, or from Columbia, Tennessee, south to Pulaski. At that midway station, quartermasters could transfer the provisions to wagon trains. The wagon trains could then transport the supplies to Fayetteville, the railhead of a Nashville & Chattanooga spur track that ran only twenty-five miles east to join the main line at Decherd.[14]

Probably remembering his successful building of the Centreville Railroad in northern Virginia the previous winter under similar circumstances of supply shortages and inefficient field transportation, Johnston considered the three railroads that formed the Nashville &

Decatur Railroad Line as a means of increasing the flow of supplies to the Army of Tennessee. Unfortunately, the two railroads that constituted the seventy-mile Columbia and Decatur section of the railway offered neither Bragg nor Rosecrans any practical logistical use in January 1863. In the late winter of 1862, after the fall of Nashville, retreating Confederate troops acting under higher military authority tore up thirty-four miles of the segment's track and burned numerous bridges and trestles. The destruction proved so widespread and costly that three railroad presidents—those managers whose lines connected Nashville and Decatur—complained and appealed to General Albert Sidney Johnston in an effort to secure indemnification for commandeered, displaced, and damaged locomotives and rolling stock as well as for burned bridges and substantial losses of commerce and revenue.

In any event, the rugged territory over which the railroad ran presented formidable obstacles to a rapid reconstruction of the tracks and trestles below Columbia. Ulysses S. Grant (victor of the battle of Chattanooga in November 1863) remembered the railway as passing "over a broken country, cut up with innumerable streams, many of them of considerable width, and with valleys far below the roadbed." Obviously, Johnston could not have immediately repaired or used the temporarily Union-controlled Tennessee & Alabama Railroad between Nashville and Columbia, but he expressed interest in putting the Central Southern and Tennessee & Alabama Central railroads between Columbia and Decatur in working order. Late in January he approached Bragg to determine the feasibility of a repair project between Columbia and Decatur. Johnston deliberately delegated authority and responsibility for railroad repairs, deciding by late January to give Bragg not only the power to rebuild the Central Southern and Tennessee & Alabama Central lines but also to transfer to him the "line of Rail Road from Chattanooga to West Point, Georgia" to serve Bragg's "military purposes" in eastern Tennessee and northern Georgia.[15]

Cognizant of his extensive jurisdiction over railroad transportation in Tennessee and Georgia, Bragg informed Johnston that he had already initiated a reconstruction project, having sent his chief engineer to examine the damaged sections of the Central Southern and Tennessee & Alabama Central railroads. The engineer estimated that the reconstruction of the trestles alone would require at least two months' work. Bragg assured Johnston, who remained at headquarters at Chattanooga, that the repair project would receive his close attention and that he had "ordered timber to be prepared" for rebuilding the bridges. Johnston therefore assumed that Bragg would immediately begin the work, particularly since the completion of the project offered the Army of Tennessee substantial relief from food shortages. Irresponsibly, however, Johnston neglected to follow Bragg's progress; not until March did he learn that Bragg had failed to begin the reconstruction project. Bragg's delay in January and February stemmed partly from his indifference to what he understood to represent the principles and special provisions that constituted Confederate railroad policy. The policy, as indefinitely formulated and erratically applied by the War Department's Railroad Bureau after December 1862, forbade direct military interference with the private affairs of Southern railroad companies—particularly the managerial allocation of their capital resources—but it encouraged railroad officials to apply for and employ army troops in situations where neither railroad workers could be used nor slave laborers hired or impressed. Moreover, the War Department offered subsidies to railway firms or private contractors for railroad repairs when militarily necessary or when the companies lacked funds or materials with which to repair their own facilities.[16]

Bragg's first important opportunity to apply Confederate railway policy occurred in the spring of 1862. After the death of Albert Sidney Johnston at the battle of Shiloh in April, Bragg prepared to assume command of the Army of Mississippi, a forerunner of the Army of Tennessee. Obeying War Department orders, Bragg exercised supervision over the construction of a line of railroad between Selma, Alabama, and Meridian, Mississippi. Previously, in December 1861, President Davis recommended that the Confederate Congress appropriate $150,000 for the completion of the Alabama & Mississippi Rivers Railroad (commonly designated the Selma & Meridian Railroad); in approving Davis's request, the Congress voted to furnish the railroad officials with the required funds. Therefore, late in April 1862, Bragg sent Major John W. Goodwin—his superintendent of military transportation and a former general superintendent of the East Tennessee & Virginia Railroad—to Meridian to survey the proposed route to close the gap between Selma and Meridian. Goodwin had particular orders to examine that portion of the line designed to cover the four-mile stretch of territory between Demopolis and McDowell's Landing, Alabama—those points divided by the unbridged Tombigbee River and rendered more difficult for railroad or wagon transportation by swampy outlying ground near the river. Having received Goodwin's favorable report on the proposed construction work, however, Bragg, later in April, recalled Goodwin and then accepted the services of Colonel Samuel Tate, who also served as general superintendent of the Memphis & Charleston Railroad. Early in July, Bragg sent Tate to Demopolis to superintend the railroad construction project in western Alabama, instructing him to assist the railroad officials by granting them full authority and military support to expend the appropriated congressional funds to purchase or impress materials and to hire or impress slave laborers to complete the vital railroad connection at Demopolis. Bragg also ordered Tate to send him regular progress reports covering the work accomplished under Tate's direction.[17] Significantly, however, Bragg subsequently recalled Tate to Tennessee, where Tate continued to serve Bragg by maintaining and repairing the Memphis & Charleston Railroad from Chattanooga, Tennessee, to Corinth, Mississippi.

In view of his previous experience with the Alabama & Mississippi Rivers Railroad project, Bragg understood the broad provisions of the War Department's railway policy as they applied to the reconstruction of damaged or destroyed railroad tracks and trestles in Tennessee. More important, however, from the standpoint of Johnston's contribution to Bragg's delay in repairing the railroads between Columbia and Decatur, it should be stressed that in Virginia Johnston frequently used slave laborers, Quartermaster Department resources, Confederate engineer officers, and the former railroad superintendent Thomas R. Sharp to build or repair railroad facilities in the Old Dominion, particularly for the Centreville Railroad. Yet in Tennessee he failed to remind Bragg of such methods of restoring railroad communications. Consequently, despite his earlier supervision of Goodwin and Tate on the yet uncompleted Selma & Meridian Railroad construction project, Bragg remained inexcusably indifferent—if not irresponsibly oblivious—to the reasonable presumption that the War Department stood prepared to offer a generous subsidy to Central Southern and Tennessee & Alabama Central officials for a repair project.

The principal cause of Bragg's delay, however, was his great concern about the maintenance and repair of the Nashville & Chattanooga Railroad—the main line of communication between Chattanooga and his army at Tullahoma. In the wake of Albert Sidney

Running Water Bridge on the Nashville & Chattanooga Railroad, under reconstruction by Union troops—a typical trestlework bridge in the Confederate West.

Johnston's evacuation of Nashville in February 1862, the Nashville & Chattanooga, besides the Tennessee & Alabama, had suffered a succession of devastating property losses from contesting Union and Confederate armies in Tennessee. Bragg, who had assumed command of the Army of the West in June 1862 (redesignated the Army of Tennessee the following November), inflicted heavy damage on the Nashville & Chattanooga in consequence of his hasty retreats from both Chattanooga and Murfreesboro, ordering the destruction of "several of its Locomotives and about Two Hundred, out of Three Hundred cars" to prevent that equipment from being captured by Federal cavalry. Then, too, between Bragg's burning of the railroad bridge over the Tennessee River at Chattanooga and the wrecking of tracks by retreating Rebel troops and raiding Union cavalry, long portions of the Nashville & Chattanooga had been destroyed; by February 1863 the railroad ran one hundred miles north of Chattanooga to Wartrace, or for a distance extending only two-thirds of its total operational length. Though Bragg had repeatedly devastated the Nashville & Chattanooga in 1862, in January 1863 he cooperated with the Nashville & Chattanooga superintendent, Colonel Edmund W. Cole, in assigning details of troops requested by Cole to work on the railroad between Chattanooga and Tullahoma, because Bragg himself considered the work a "case of urgent necessity." Bragg therefore ordered subordinates to assign troops to Major Goodwin, his superintendent of military transportation at Tullahoma, for work on the Nashville & Chattanooga to ensure the steady supplying of the Confederate army in eastern Tennessee. However, he neglected simultaneously to allocate men or materials to repair the equally important Central Southern and Tennessee & Alabama Central railroads farther west. He continued to send men to Cole and Goodwin, forwarding troops in February and April.[18]

Meanwhile, in Richmond both the Confederate Congress and the War Department expressed interest in a proposed reconstruction of the Central Southern and Tennessee & Alabama Central railroads. On January 29, Representative Thomas J. Foster of Alabama introduced a resolution in the House of Representatives requesting that the Committee on the Quartermaster's and Commissary's departments consider the "expediency of repairing the Nashville & Decatur Rail Road from Columbia Ten to Decatur Ala." The House adopted Foster's resolution, but this failed to expedite railroad repairs in Tennessee. As late as April 21, 1863, the committee still neglected to report favorably on Foster's resolution, although it referred the question to the Special Committee on Military Transportation for further consideration.[19]

While members of the Confederate House of Representatives procrastinated on the issue of railroad repairs, Commissary Department officials in Richmond and at posts in the Deep South grew increasingly impatient over the continuing delay in starting the railroad reconstruction project in central Tennessee. Early in February, the commissary agent O. C. Boone, then at Huntsville, Alabama, informed Commissary General Northrop that the trestlework over the flood-swollen Elk River below Pulaski, Tennessee, remained in disrepair—a condition that prevented the railway shipment to Pulaski of the supplies that abounded in the fertile region between Columbia and Decatur. Northrup immediately referred the matter of a bridge-rebuilding project to the Engineer Bureau, making a "warm personal appeal" on Boone's behalf. The commissary general's proposal received prompt approval. On February 4, Major Alfred L. Rives, the acting Engineer Bureau chief, prepared a letter for Johnston informing him of Secretary of War Seddon's granting to Johnston full extraordinary authority and discretionary power to undertake railroad repairs in Tennessee. Significantly, Seddon did not order Johnston to rebuild railroad tracks and trestles but nevertheless urged him to assign an engineer to estimate the cost of repairs and, if Boone's $10,000 estimate proved correct, then Johnston should act on his considered military judgment.

Unfortunately, Rives's letter of February 4 miscarried. Meanwhile, Boone, not apprised of the failure of communication, sent a message to Northrop from Alabama on February 16 complaining of the army's failure to repair the railroad in the effort to save "large quantities of corn." At this juncture Northrop again referred the matter to the Engineer Bureau. Having returned to Richmond from duty elsewhere in the Confederacy, Colonel Jeremy F. Gilmer, chief of the Engineer Bureau, sent to Johnston on February 19 a copy of Rives's letter, reminding Johnston that Seddon deemed it important to commence a repair project, and again advising Johnston of the availability of a government subsidy for the railroad officials if they would repair their railroad facilities with military assistance. Gilmer then assured Northrop that he had, by authority of Seddon, urged Johnston to provide the railroad officials with the military protection from Federal cavalry and Unionist saboteurs without which the railroad managers refused to undertake repairs of the Central Southern and Tennessee & Alabama Central railroads even if the War Department defrayed their costs of procuring labor and materials. Belatedly, Johnston received Gilmer's letter on March 16. The message shocked him. Before replying to Gilmer, he communicated with Bragg, questioning him about the total cost of repairing the line of railroad between Columbia and Decatur. Confused and indecisive, he asked Bragg if the work should not be begun and informed him that the "Engineer's Department offers $10,000 toward defraying expenses." Johnston then regretfully notified Gilmer that the bridges would require two months' work for completion. Bragg, who had displayed as much negligence as Johnston, delayed even longer before ordering Major Goodwin to suspend work on the Nashville & Chattanooga, to hire the necessary contractors and laborers, and to purchase repair materials at Chattanooga with which Central Southern

Colonel Jeremy F. Gilmer, chief of the Confederate Engineer Bureau.

and Tennessee & Alabama Central officials could undertake the reconstruction project.[20]

The reconstruction of the Tennessee & Alabama Central and
Central Southern railroads, beginning at Decatur, started late in
March. While the railroad officials and slave labor gangs struggled

with relaying tracks between Decatur and Pulaski, farther south Goodwin and army engineers prepared to raise trestles over the Tennessee and Elk rivers and intervening streams. The reconstruction of the tracks progressed rapidly, but the rebuilding of bridges proceeded slowly because of rivers and streams swollen by the incessantly heavy spring rains and posed a more formidable undertaking. Encouraged, however, by what appeared to be the prompt and energetic prosecution of the reconstruction project, on March 28 a *Mobile Advertiser and Register* war correspondent reported that the bridge over Sulphur Branch, north of Decatur, and a "trestle work 72 feet high, is now being completed." He further reported that, under Goodwin's able supervision, "preparations are also being made to build a bridge 600 feet long over Elk river, the State line of Tennessee, and over Richland Creek, near Pulaski." Confidently, he explained that Confederate military leaders planned to put the three lines of railroad "in good running order to Columbia and Nashville" because "this road at the present time is of the highest importance to us." Appreciating the need for more expeditious repairs, on April 1 Johnston ordered Major M. B. McMicken, the acting chief quartermaster of the Army of Tennessee at Tullahoma, to determine from Goodwin—who had since proceeded from Decatur to Athens, Alabama—how much more time would be required to make repairs to the railroad lines between Columbia and Decatur. McMicken sent a message to Goodwin asking if "anything further [can] be done to hasten completion of Road?"[21]

Besides having the formidable task of bridging flooded rivers and streams, Goodwin proved unable to expedite railroad repairs because he depended on a private contracting firm's agents, George P. Gates and W. S. Higgins of Macon, Georgia, to procure timber for the reconstruction of the Elk River and Widows Creek bridges in southern Tennessee.[22] Consequently, the railroad bridge and supporting trestlework over the Tennessee River north of Decatur (which Federal cavalry had destroyed in April 1862) and two other trestles below Pulaski remained uncompleted until the middle of June. A Southern war correspondent at Huntsville, Alabama, reported on June 19 that the Central Southern Railroad "has been put in operation by the Government from Decatur to Pulaski," and the line would "soon be completed to Columbia. Through its aid large supplies are brought from the interior of Tennessee." By then, however, Johnston had assumed command of Confederate forces in Mississippi, while the

Army of Tennessee's worst winter food shortages had long since ended. Meanwhile, the Engineer Bureau compensated the Central Southern and Tennessee & Alabama Central railroad companies for the resources the firms had expended in the reconstruction project, reimbursing the firms with $60,000 worth of Confederate Treasury Department bonds bearing 8 percent interest, or six times the War Department's estimate of repairs.[23]

Because he had originally undertaken the repair project on his own initiative and encouraged Johnston to believe that he would successfully complete it, Bragg bore heavy responsibility for the failure to repair promptly the Central Southern and Tennessee & Alabama Central railroads over the winter and spring of 1863. Bragg used his chief engineer and Major Goodwin, his military superintendent of railroads (but not Major John S. Bransford, the Army of Tennessee's chief transportation officer at Chattanooga), to complete railroad repairs. Yet he neglected to employ Memphis & Charleston superintendent Tate on the reconstruction project in April, despite Tate's able direction of the Alabama & Mississippi Rivers Railroad project at Demopolis in the summer of 1862. Tate, a man of "great intelligence, indomitable energy and excellent judgement," had in January been favorably considered by Pemberton in Mississippi to be the military superintendent of railroads west of the Alabama River. Thereafter Tate, passed over by Pemberton, had obeyed Bragg's orders in Tennessee, although Bragg failed to use him for the Central Southern and Tennessee & Alabama Central project. Bragg did, however, order him to rebuild damaged sections of the Memphis & Charleston Railroad between Chattanooga, Tennessee, and Tuscumbia, Alabama, over the winter of 1863. As a result of his "indefatigable exertions," Tate completed that work by early April.[24] Bragg should then have ordered Tate to assist Goodwin on the Central Southern and Tennessee & Alabama Central railroads, but neither Bragg nor Johnston recognized the necessity of employing him there.

Nor did Bragg or Johnston recommend or urge the personal involvement of Anthony L. Maxwell Jr., the head of the foundry firm of A. L. Maxwell and Co. of Knoxville, Tennessee. Maxwell, a New York native who had built bridges in Massachusetts in 1850, had settled in Nashville, Tennessee, by 1860. Indeed, late in January 1863, when both Johnston and Bragg first confronted the Columbia and Decatur railroad problem, Tate recommended to Pemberton the services of Maxwell, whom Tate considered "an excellent and energetic Bridge Builder," having "one hundred efficient hands with all the necessary tools" prepared to undertake railroad reconstruction projects in northern Mississippi. Not Pemberton, though, but Bragg made immediate use of Maxwell, whom the *Knoxville Register* also considered "that most prompt and skillful of architects" and that "prince of bridge-builders." In January and February Maxwell, working under a contract with the Engineer Bureau, assisted Bragg by rebuilding burned bridges over the Wautauga and Holston rivers on the line of the East Tennessee & Virginia Railroad northeast of Knoxville. Maxwell had completed the reconstruction by March, whereupon Bragg sent him to Chattanooga. By importing timber from Georgia and by employing skilled workmen and black laborers, Maxwell had finished rebuilding the Lookout Creek bridge on the Memphis & Charleston Railroad southwest of Chattanooga by early April.[25] Though Goodwin hired Maxwell's agents, neither Bragg nor Johnston engaged Maxwell for work north of Decatur, thus aggravating their failure to assign Tate to the Central Southern and Tennessee & Alabama Central repair project later in April. And though Maxwell stationed a mobile railroad reconstruction crew at Chattanooga and stockpiled building materials for the framing of trestlework bridges, Bragg overlooked those superior advantages and instead ordered Goodwin to oversee the procurement of black laborers and timber for use principally by the railroad officials—an inefficient method of operation in view of the severe supply crisis in Tennessee.

For his part, Johnston's recollection of the difficulties attending the building of the Centreville Railroad in northern Virginia in the winter of 1862 should have suggested to him the more challenging problems that Bragg confronted in retracking stripped Central Southern and Tennessee & Alabama Central roadbeds and rebuilding bridges on those railroads. Johnston was not ignorant, though apparently forgetful, of the methods of building trestles and constructing railroad tracks. As a topographical engineer at San Antonio, Texas, in 1850, Johnston had proposed to the War Department his own plan for constructing a suspension-type wagon train bridge over the Pecos River, while in 1852 he had sought and received detailed technical information from Colonel John J. Abert, the chief of topographical engineers, about building railroad tracks and trestles before attempting to survey a route for the San Antonio & Mexican Gulf

Railroad in Texas.[26] Therefore, Johnston could not have pleaded inadequate professional preparation to excuse his failure to direct Bragg in the railroad reconstruction project in middle Tennessee. Moreover, as supreme commander of Confederate forces in the West, Johnston should have carefully observed and evaluated Bragg's progress and intervened when Bragg began to hesitate and procrastinate. The weak and belated suggestion to Bragg on March 6 about the advisability of a repair project also reflected Johnston's almost cavalier disregard of Secretary of War Seddon's urgent desire for prompt repair of the Central Southern and Tennessee & Alabama Central railroads. Yet Seddon might have procured an order from President Davis peremptorily directing Johnston to rebuild the railroads: the secretary of war's scrupulous observance of punctilious Confederate railroad policy proved inadvisable in view of the urgent military need for reconstruction.

Ultimately, neither Davis nor Seddon reprimanded Johnston for his failure to rebuild quickly the Central Southern and Tennessee & Alabama Central railroads over the winter and spring of 1863. Commissary General Northrop, however, censured Johnston, reporting to President Davis on February 1, 1864, that "no effective solution was taken by General Johnston in a matter so vitally important after the battle of Murfreesborough." Ironically, although Johnston neglected to hasten the repair of the Central Southern and Tennessee & Alabama Central railroads, he apparently approved of Major Barbour's complaint to Quartermaster General Myers in April 1863 about the dilapidated condition of the Western railroads and the consequent difficulty in supplying forage to the Army of Tennessee. Scarcely suppressing his exasperation, Myers denied responsibility, however, and explained that the "Government has always refused to exercise any authority over the Roads." He advised Barbour that Colonel William M. Wadley, a former Southern railroad superintendent and the head of the War Department's Railroad Bureau (established December 22, 1863), had the "duty of making all contracts, and arrangements of a general character with Rail Road companies." Compounding his inconsistency, in previously replying to a complaint from Pemberton about the poor condition of the Southern Railroad in Mississippi, Johnston had referred Pemberton to Wadley. Yet he thereafter failed to use the Railroad Bureau chief to solve his own rail transport problems in middle Tennessee. Moreover, Johnston revealed a lack of imagination and willingness to improve the situation in Tennessee and Alabama by making specific recommendations to the War Department about how Confederate railway policy could be more effectively formulated and systematically applied in the West. Further reflecting his indifference to the outcome of the Central Southern and Tennessee & Alabama Central repair project, Johnston left Chattanooga on March 12 and went to Mobile to conduct an inspection of the Gulf port's defenses.[27]

Johnston arrived at Mobile on March 14 and discovered an acute shortage of sugar in army depots and warehouses. In stark contrast to the deprivation of the civilian population, the garrison troops at the Gulf port enjoyed an abundance of corn, although they lacked sugar. Johnston understood that a scarcity of beef afflicted Confederate troops throughout the South and that nothing could accelerate production of new cattle herds in Texas or in the Atlantic coastal states. The marked deficiency of sugar and molasses around Mobile, however, struck him as an unnecessary hardship. Since the fall of 1862, the troops around Mobile, in Tennessee and Virginia, and in other parts of the Confederacy depended on those supplies as nutritional substitutes for a regular beef ration. Confederate commissaries purchased sugar and molasses from private producers in northern Louisiana. They then transported the stores to points on the Vicksburg, Shreveport & Texas Railroad for shipment to DeSoto. After barges carried the supplies across the river to Vicksburg, Pemberton's quartermasters forwarded the stores by rail to Alabama for distribution among the troops around Mobile. Supply trains moved the rest of the sugar and molasses to Rebel forces in Tennessee, Virginia, the Carolinas, and Georgia.

Initially, Johnston mistakenly assumed that the sugar and molasses shortage at Mobile resulted from Pemberton's almost exclusive use of rolling stock for the shipment of corn from Vicksburg to Grenada, Meridian, and Mobile. Thus on March 12 he instructed Pemberton to ship balanced proportions of corn and sugar to Mobile. To that end, he directed Pemberton's attention to the employment of Vicksburg, Shreveport & Texas rolling stock to achieve a heavier volume of sugar shipments from Monroe to DeSoto. He reminded Pemberton that "the returning trains from Vicksburg [DeSoto] can bring valuable quantities [of sugar and molasses from Monroe] without delaying the transportation of subsistence stores" from Vicksburg to Mobile. In pointed retaliation for Pemberton's rebuke of the previous January, Johnston sarcastically informed him that "other

departments have greater difficulty in obtaining food than yours."
Johnston's analysis of the sugar and molasses shortage reflected a
partially inaccurate understanding of the situation, because Pemberton's use of the railroads to ship corn had not created the supply
deficiency in early 1863. Rather, the problem had arisen the previous
January in consequence of the military and civilian allocation of
available rolling stock to transport sugar and molasses, as opposed to
the military monopolization of other railroad equipment to ship corn
to Confederate forces in Mississippi.

Johnston's chief quartermaster, Major Barbour, who remained stationed at Jackson, Mississippi, after January 1863, explained the situation to Johnston the following March. Barbour advised Johnston
that previously Major General John B. Floyd, commander of the Virginia state forces, had complained of sugar and molasses shortages
among his troops. Floyd had served as secretary of war in the Buchanan administration and had directed Barbour in the latter's prewar capacity as military superintendent of the United States Armory
at Harpers Ferry. In this situation, however, Floyd urged Barbour to
increase the quantity of rolling stock devoted to the shipment of
sugar to Virginia. Consequently, Barbour appealed to Pemberton to
address the problem, but Pemberton offered no assistance. Barbour
further informed Johnston that besides Pemberton's use of rolling
stock for corn shipments, "much private freights" of sugar passing
over the railroads accounted for the sugar shortages elsewhere in the
Confederacy. He recommended that Johnston reallocate rolling
stock, assigning preference to "freights for Virginia troops over private freights." Johnston hesitated to adopt Barbour's proposed solution. He feared to exacerbate further the continuing corn order
controversy surrounding Pemberton's monopolization of rolling stock
in Mississippi and Alabama and therefore avoided pressing more private railroad property into government service. Rather, adopting a
more reasonable and realistic solution, Johnston resorted to using for
Confederate supply whatever spare rolling stock he could locate in
the Deep South. Fortunately, he found availaɔie equipment at Mobile and sent Pemberton revised instructions on March 15. Refrain-
ing from approaching the railroad officials or from impressing their
equipment, Johnston suggested that Pemberton make arrangements
to have that equipment placed on the Southern Railroad to increase
the sugar shipments from Vicksburg to the Gulf Port. In a more tem-
perate tone than that he had taken on March 12, Johnston asked

Pemberton if "an occasional train load" of sugar "could be sent over in the mean time?" Further, he recommended that Army of Tennessee commissary officers sell sugar for the beef "which is to be obtained in no other way," while more tactfully reminding Pemberton that "you are aware that it [beef] is very scarce in all our armies" east of the Mississippi River.[28]

Johnston's earlier criticism of Pemberton's management of the Louisiana and Mississippi railroads lacked validity or justification. He could not have expected Pemberton to possess a thorough knowledge of the supply requirements of Confederate troops in Alabama, Tennessee, and Virginia. Early in February, he refused to interfere in Pemberton's "mode of supply" because he himself lacked knowledge of the particular supply needs of Confederate troops in Mississippi. He also overlooked the difficulties that Pemberton's commissaries and quartermasters faced in collecting sugar and molasses in northern Louisiana and the railroad transportation of those supplies to DeSoto. Although Pemberton possessed general authority over commissaries and quartermasters in east Louisiana, he could scarcely have exercised direct supervision over their activities beyond the Mississippi River. Certainly he could not have regulated the Vicksburg, Shreveport & Texas Railroad's carrying trade as stringently as he could use the military control he imposed on the freight trade of the Mississippi firms. Johnston not only failed to grasp these facts but also remained uninformed about the critical event that largely accounted for the scarcity of beef and the paucity of sugar and molasses reaching the Deep South by March 1863. Fully six weeks before Johnston ordered Pemberton to make sugar shipments to Mobile, Federal General Sherman proudly assured his brother, United States Senator John Sherman, that "since I broke the railroad leading west [of DeSoto] most of the necessary supplies to Vicksburg have come from Red River, and we now stop this."[29]

Sherman's action reduced the amount of beef, and the corn and sugar that reached Natchez by way of the Red River required either steamboat transportation up the Mississippi River to Vicksburg (frequently hindered during February and March by Federal gunboats) or wagon shipment to a point on the New Orleans, Jackson & Great Northern Railroad for transportation to the state capital.[30] Pemberton, despite his centrally located headquarters at Jackson, thus could not have forwarded sugar shipments from DeSoto or have swelled the volume of corn and sugar sent over the railroads from Jackson to

Mobile or other points farther east. Johnston's ignorance of the Federal railroad wrecking operations opposite Vicksburg stemmed from his and Pemberton's inability or unwillingness to cooperate or communicate fully. Obviously, he did not bear responsibility for the sudden and drastic curtailment of sugar shipments from Monroe, and his instructions for a balanced proportion of stores to be sent from Vicksburg to Mobile, as well as his approach to achieving a more effective use of rolling stock for supply shipments to Virginia, displayed sound logistical sense. Doubtless, too, both Pemberton and Barbour failed to apprise Johnston of the railroad break west of De-Soto because they seriously underestimated the devastating effect of that development on the Confederate supply situation east of the Mississippi.

Johnston's use of the railroads of the trans-Appalachian West reflected a continuation of the patterns of inconsistency and contradiction that marked his use of railroad transportation in Virginia. Though he showed considerable improvement in planning and coordinating extensive troop movements by rail— as in the shipment of Stevenson's divisions across the Deep South—he nevertheless continued to underestimate the value of the railroad as a critical logistical resource and instrument of mechanized war. His failure to rebuild promptly the Central Southern and Tennessee & Alabama Central railroads demonstrated his fundamental lack of sound strategic and logistical judgment. Concerning Confederate railway policy, Johnston remained almost willfully ignorant of the practical collaborative relationships existing between the War Department's Engineer and Railroad bureaus and the Dixie railroad companies. Moreover, he communicated less directly and cooperated less effectively with Tennessee and other Western railroad managers than he had with officials of Virginia railway firms. His self-imposed isolation and withholding of cooperation complicated the War Department's task of achieving substantially increased coordination of effort between the Confederate military and the Southern carriers to overcome the successive railroad transportation crises that threatened to destroy vital Confederate interests in the West. Johnston's inability to mobilize the Southern railroads in support of Confederate logistical operations in the West and his irresponsible indifference to the value of rolling stock and other railway property would shortly result in a stupendous transportation failure in Mississippi.

·{3}·

The Grenada Disaster

ALTHOUGH largely preoccupied with supply problems in Alabama, Johnston's awareness of events in Mississippi caused him to make decisions of greater military importance than those concerning the feeding and clothing of troops at Mobile. On March 19 he left Mobile and returned to Tennessee, where he closely followed the progress of Grant in Mississippi in the latter's determined attempts to take Vicksburg. Then, early in May, he learned that Grant's whole army had crossed the Mississippi River at Bruinsburg, below Vicksburg, and had started marching on Pemberton's stronghold. The military situation deteriorated so rapidly as Pemberton maneuvered unskillfully against Grant that Secretary of War Seddon ordered Johnston to leave Tennessee and hurry to Jackson to take command of all Confederate forces in Mississippi. Johnston boarded a special train and left Tullahoma on May 10. The trains that followed him carried 3,000 Army of Tennessee troops, while 5,500 soldiers and cavalrymen boarded cars at Charleston, South Carolina, for the railway journey to Mississippi.[1]

Stevenson's troop movement from Tennessee to Mississippi showed Johnston the considerable logistical difficulty involved in the transportation to Jackson of a force of nearly equal size. He and his staff moved quickly, though, traveling to Mobile by way of Atlanta and Montgomery. Johnston and his aides then took cars at Mobile and speedily proceeded over the Mobile & Ohio to Meridian. With the rearward troops in mind, Johnston, as soon as he arrived at Meridian on May 13, questioned Southern Railroad officials about the quantity of rolling stock available for the transportation of the 8,500 troops soon expected to reach Meridian in successive contingents from Mobile and Selma. The railroad managers confirmed Johnston's previous knowledge: they lacked a sufficient quantity of operational rolling stock with which to forward the reinforcements on to Jackson as rapidly as the troops arrived at Meridian. Indeed, early in February 1863 both Lieutenant General Pemberton and Southern Railroad vice president Morris Emanuel had advised Johnston of the deteriorating condition of the company's engines and cars caused by the scarcity of iron needed to repair the rolling stock. Pemberton and Emanuel had urged Johnston to issue an order transferring iron from the government-operated Shelby Iron Works in Alabama to Vicksburg for the purpose of repairing the machinery, but Johnston had either refused or neglected to order the procurement of the iron for the railroad firm.[2]

Disregarding the fact that he had contributed to the immediate shortage of railroad equipment on the Southern Railroad, Johnston in desperation sent a message to Milton Brown, president of the Mobile & Ohio Railroad, then stationed at Mobile. He appealed to Brown "as a patriot to lend the Southern Railroad as many engines and cars" as that company required for the shipment of the troops to Jackson, and he urged the measure on Brown as of the "utmost importance to the country." He then advised the Mobile & Ohio superintendent and Colonel Lawrence J. Fleming that "public necessity" required the use of "rolling stock from your road" and requested that Fleming furnish the equipment without hesitation or delay, an appeal to which Fleming favorably and expeditiously responded. Johnston's appeals to Brown and Fleming, although motivated by his sense of urgency, displayed an unusual deference to Southern railroad managers. In Virginia and Tennessee, he generally treated such officials with detachment and distrust. Johnston also showed his first realistic recognition of the intense commercial rivalry between Southern railroad firms. Indeed, his respect for the Mobile and Ohio and Southern Railroad companies' track rights sharply contrasted with his attempted switching of Baltimore & Ohio locomotives onto the Winchester & Potomac tracks at Harpers Ferry, Virginia, in 1861.[3]

Having received assistance from Brown, Johnston left Meridian for Jackson and assumed command of Confederate forces there amidst an alarming military crisis. Grant's army marched rapidly on Jackson in implementation of his plan to attack Vicksburg from the east. Johnston could not reinforce Pemberton and retreated to Canton, the

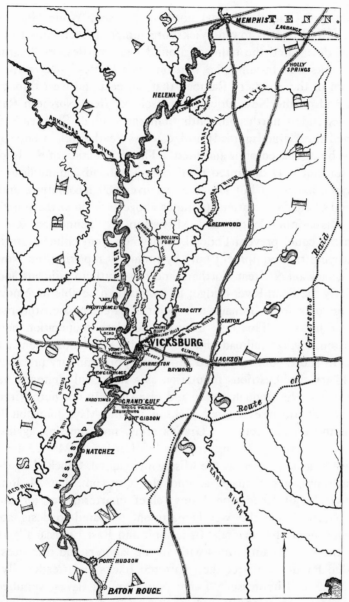

Railroad approaches to Vicksburg. From John William Draper, *History of the American Civil War* (New York, 1870), 3:26.

Mississippi Central terminal north of Jackson. While Grant drove Pemberton's troops toward Vicksburg, units of Sherman's Fifteenth Corps devastated the railroads around Jackson. Besides "tearing up the tracks and burning the iron on piles of ties" over a five-mile section of the Southern Railroad that ran east and west through the city, and on the New Orleans, Jackson & Great Northern Railroad that extended north and south from the capital, Sherman's forces burned the "large [railroad] bridge across Pearl River, twenty barrels of tar being placed on it and fired." The destruction of the bridge at Jackson not only disrupted Confederate railroad communications in central Mississippi but also isolated over 680 locomotives and cars around Grenada, a station 105 miles above Jackson at the junction of the Mississippi Central and Mississippi & Tennessee Railroads. Johnston could prevent Federal cavalrymen from either capturing or destroying that equipment only by promptly repairing the New Orleans, Jackson & Great Northern and the Southern railroads and particularly the Pearl River bridge; he would then be able to remove the rolling stock from Grenada to a point of safety beyond the river by way of Jackson. This task necessitated close cooperation between Johnston, civilian railroad officials, and the War Department authorities. In short, Johnston faced in Mississippi a military problem that would try the illustrious reputation as a masterful strategist he had won in the Shenandoah Valley and elsewhere in northern Virginia.[4]

After Sherman evacuated Jackson in mid-May, Johnston began preparing for an attack on Grant's army, now pressing against the gates of Vicksburg. To this end, he left Canton on May 23 and reestablished headquarters at the Mississippi capital. Shocked by the extensive property damage around the city, on May 24 Johnston ordered Major Livingston Mims (chief quartermaster for the enlarged jurisdiction the War Department prepared to designate the "Department of Alabama, Mississippi, and East Louisiana") to provide the railroad authorities with all the laborers and resources they needed for the repair of their battered tracks and trestles. By May 31, Mims had impressed "Large Numbers" of slaves, supplied the railroaders with materials and mechanics, and commenced immediately the reconstruction project.[5] His work gangs finished tracklaying and bridge building around Jackson early in June, but the construction of another trestle over Pearl River presented him with a more formidable and arduous undertaking. Although Mims's mechanics used the still smoldering structure's stone piers to help build the new bridge, the construction work dragged into mid-June. By the time Johnston marched his army toward Vicksburg two weeks later, Mims had succeeded in assembling and raising only half the trestlework.[6]

While Mims's work crews struggled to raise the new structure over the Pearl, Johnston acted quickly to protect his railroad communications to Meridian and Mobile. A sudden wave of Federal cavalry attacks against the Southern Railroad and a threatened Union movement against Confederate positions near Corinth, Mississippi, prompted Johnston on June 9 to order a cavalry force at Corinth to "destroy as much of the [Memphis & Charleston] railroad as possible." He then ordered the commanding officer at Meridian to send a detail to Chunkey's Creek bridge, a few miles west of Meridian on the Southern Railroad, to protect the trestle from a "Marauding force of federal cavalry" and further sought to "cut off the enemy" raiders approaching the Southern Railroad station at Brandon, east of Jackson. Perplexed and frustrated by the serious railroad problems that suddenly confronted him and complicated his efforts to raise the siege of Vicksburg, Johnston called on the Memphis & Charleston superintendent, Colonel Tate, for assistance. On June 25 Johnston sent a message to Tate, then at Huntsville, Alabama, inquiring, "Can you come to Jackson? I want to confer with you about RRd matters."[7] The proposed conference never occurred, however, because the fall of Vicksburg on July 4 resulted in Johnston's evacuation of Jackson and his suspension of railroad repair work in central Mississippi. Despite this, Johnston showed much willingness to seek the assistance of an experienced railroad man in solving his military transportation problems—a more cooperative attitude than that he had exhibited in Virginia and Tennessee.

The Confederate military crisis in Mississippi, however, quickly turned to disaster. The Union army's investment of Vicksburg finally compelled the capitulation of that strategic bastion to Grant. When Johnston learned of Pemberton's surrender of Vicksburg on July 4, he retired toward Jackson. Acting on the assumption that Grant would pursue his command and besiege the capital, Johnston decided to suspend the work being performed on the Pearl River bridge. On Johnston's orders, his assistant adjutant general at Jackson, Lieutenant Colonel Thompson B. Lamar, directed Major Mims to "take immediate steps to preserve the bridges now being erected over pearl river from injury, and to save as much of the materials

Major General Ulysses S. Grant, Union conqueror of Vicksburg.

from destruction as possible." Although Mims promptly halted the bridge-building work, his efforts proved unavailing: the timbers that he had stacked on the left bank of the Pearl remained there when Sherman's army confronted Johnston's forces west of the stream.

Considering his position untenable in view of Sherman's partial encirclement of the city, Johnston instructed his engineers to throw pontoon bridges across Pearl River against the evacuation of Jackson. Then on July 14, fearing that Federal cavalrymen would raid Grenada and seize the rolling stock concentrated there, Johnston ordered Brigadier General James R. Chalmers, whose cavalry command protected the three railroads above Jackson, to hold his troops in readiness to move east and to burn "railroad bridges and rolling stock" as he fell back to the Mobile & Ohio Railroad in eastern Mississippi.[8] Significantly, he ordered indiscriminate destruction of the railway equipment, although he knew that railroad officials had removed a large number of locomotives and cars to Grenada for security before Grant occupied Jackson in May.

Unquestionably, Johnston ordered the destruction of the rolling stock with the same indifference and recklessness that marked his destruction of Baltimore & Ohio and Orange & Alexandria railway property in Virginia in 1861 and 1862. In Mississippi, however, he could not have pleaded ignorance of its value to the railroad officials or to the Confederate war effort. In February 1863, a special committee appointed by the board of directors of the New Orleans, Jackson & Great Northern Railroad had sent Johnston a resolution that called for the redeployment of Confederate forces near the southern terminus of the railroad near New Orleans, troops that Pemberton had withdrawn from southern Louisiana. The committee members unsuccessfully urged Johnston to restore Confederate cavalry to the duty of protecting their rolling stock from further Federal attacks because the company had earlier "sustained severe losses in cars, rolling stock, and particularly of machinery which cannot now be replaced." Therefore, Johnston should have recognized the great financial and commercial value the railroad officials still attached to their property, especially because they had removed their remaining rolling stock north to Canton and Grenada for safety in May 1863.[9] Despite knowing the railroad officials' anxiety about their imperiled property, Johnston allowed his railroad order to stand. He then withdrew his army east to Brandon, committing the capital to Sherman's occupying army.

Southern newspapers lamented Johnston's evacuation of Jackson and, in their commentary on his withdrawal, hotly debated the extent to which his retreat had harmed the Confederate transportation system. Soon after the fall of the capital, the *Memphis Appeal*, then publishing from Atlanta, informed its readers that Grant had isolated all the rolling stock around Grenada. The *Montgomery Mail* disputed the *Appeal* 's story, however, declaring on July 21 that "one of the general superintendents of the Government" had replied that "the loss of the rolling stock is not so great as represented by *The Appeal*." The *Mail* regretted the sacrifice of eighteen first-class locomotives but declared that "the balance of the engines and cars were brought away, and are being distributed wherever they are most required in all portions of the country." The *Richmond Whig*, however, credited the *Appeal* 's account and reported on July 23 that the evacuation of Jackson had resulted in the loss of the rolling stock of three Mississippi carriers and that "the motive power alone consisted of over forty engines." The Richmond paper further maintained that "to have saved this invaluable property required only the construction of a temporary bridge across Pearl River" and pointed out that "six weeks of time were allowed for this work, which might have been done in six days." The *Whig* then censured Johnston's military judgment by angrily inquiring, "what were the railroad and military authorities thinking about" in June and July, when the bridge-building work had progressed so slowly. Further, unknown to Johnston, a much disturbed President Davis saw the *Whig*'s story about the Mississippi rolling stock that Johnston abandoned around Grenada and advised General Robert E. Lee on July 28 that "heavy losses are said to have been sustained, in the Southwest, of locomotives and machinery, which cannot soon, if during the war, be replaced."[10]

Johnston's withdrawal from Jackson led to another devastation of the city's railway facilities and those of Canton farther north, at the junction of the Mississippi Central and New Orleans, Jackson & Great Northern railroads. At Canton Sherman's forces—besides uprooting railroad tracks—destroyed five locomotives, thirty cars, two turntables, and thirteen railroad buildings. Farther south, at Jackson, from July 17 to July 23 units of Sherman's pioneer corps ripped up iron bars on the New Orleans, Jackson & Great Northern and the Southern railroads. Sherman also ordered the demolition of the uncompleted Pearl River bridge. A battery of Union artillery quickly formed along the river's west bank, the Federal soldiers unlimbering the field guns and planting them in a position to deliver a raking, converging fire upon the structure. Then, with devastating accuracy, the cannoneers began "knocking down the stone piers to the Rail-

road bridge" by "firing solid shot into them." As soon as his wrecking crews and gunners had finished their work, Sherman returned to
Vicksburg.[11]

In the interim, and in spite of Johnston's instructions to retire toward the Alabama border, Chalmers hesitated to evacuate his position at Panola on the Mississippi & Tennessee Railroad. He balked
at Johnston's order to destroy the rolling stock around Grenada without making any attempt either to remove or to safeguard the 75 locomotives and 610 cars at Water Valley, Grenada, and other points on
the Mississippi Central in the direction of Canton. Recognizing the
enormous financial and military value of that equipment, Chalmers,
on July 17, requested the Mississippi Central's president, Walter A.
Goodman, then at Okolona on the Mobile & Ohio Railroad, to suggest other methods by which he could discourage a Federal seizure
of the rolling stock. The request shocked Goodman. He immediately prepared a hasty, albeit well-reasoned, reply in which he urged
Chalmers as a last resort to strip the engines and cars of their price-
less mechanical parts instead of burning the rolling stock wholesale. Subscribing to Goodman's ideas, Chalmers forcefully reminded
Johnston that the railway property, if preserved, could continue to
support the Confederate war effort. Then on July 19, in a dispatch
to his intimate friend Jefferson Davis (whose brother, Joseph Davis,
then served as a director of the Mississippi Central), Goodman protested the "Military orders" that had called for "the destruction by
fire of railroad equipments to the value of $5,000,000" and he in-
sisted that the "order should be countermanded if not a necessity."[12]

Notwithstanding Chalmers's exertions to save the locomotives and
cars in northern Mississippi, Johnston refused to revoke his railroad
order. Expecting Chalmers to execute it in his absence, he left Brandon and repaired to Mobile for an inspection of the Gulf port's fortifications. Goodman, who had hurried to Grenada for a conference
with Chalmers and the railroad authorities there, again apprised
President Davis of Johnston's determination to burn millions of dollars' worth of irreplaceable rolling stock. Opportunely, however,
Davis had already instructed Secretary of War Seddon to counter-
mand Johnston's railroad order. On July 22, he assured Goodman
that Confederate commanders would spare the railway property "unless it is clearly necessary to prevent its capture by enemy. With
energy and good management, the greater part of it could be sent
down to Meridian." Carrying out Davis's instructions, on July 24

Seddon sent a laconic message in which he informed Johnston, "The President directs that efforts be made to bring away the equipments, which should be taken down the road for removal as far as may be necessary."[13]

While a train carried the secretary's letter to Mississippi, Chalmers received important news from another quarter. Still believing that he could persuade Johnston to order the removal of the rolling stock from Grenada, Chalmers questioned Colonel Edward D. Frost, the Mississippi Central's general superintendent, about the condition of the railroads between Grenada and Jackson. In the absence of detailed knowledge, Frost expressed his opinion that the railways sustained lighter damage in July than they had in May. After further inquiry, on July 25, Chalmers advised Johnston's adjutant general at Brandon, Colonel Ewell, that "it is confidently thought by the railroad authorities here that with the aid of the Government" toward the procurement of enough slave laborers, "the road between this place and Jackson can be put in working order within two weeks." On reflection, however, Chalmers wisely decided to verify the railroad officials' views. On July 26, he instructed Frost and the New Orleans, Jackson & Great Northern's general superintendent, Thomas S. Williams, to conduct a close inspection of the railroads and bridges between Grenada and Brandon, reporting their findings directly to both Johnston and himself. As Chalmers had apparently feared they would, on July 29 Superintendents Frost and Williams prepared a drastically revised estimate of the amount of time needed to complete railroad repairs north of Jackson. While Frost took the original report north to Chalmers at Grenada, Williams delivered a copy to Assistant Adjutant General Ewell at Johnston's headquarters at Brandon. The railroaders disregarded the slight damage done to the Mississippi Central Railroad above Canton, although they pointed out that "about 800 feet bridging is destroyed." A closer inspection of the destruction that Federal troops had inflicted on the New Orleans, Jackson & Great Northern and Southern railroads north and east of Jackson, however, dashed their ill-founded hopes for an expeditious removal of their rolling stock to Alabama. So Frost and Williams informed Colonel Ewell that "13 miles of [the New Orleans, Jackson & Great Northern] track are torn up, the ties burned, the iron bent. Fourteen bridges burned." Having beheld the charred ruins of the Pearl River bridge, both men regretfully advised Ewell that "all the heavy bridging over Pearl River and in the bottom is burned." They pointed out that "not more than 3 miles of the [Southern Railroad] track have been torn up," but they necessarily concluded that "we are of the opinion it will require 800 hands one month to put these roads in repair so as to run our rolling stock to the Alabama River."[14]

Johnston left Mobile late in July and arrived at army headquarters at Morton, Mississippi, on July 31. After studying the railroad superintendents' damage reports, he took the initial step toward mounting another reconstruction project at Jackson. Without mentioning the rolling stock around Grenada, Assistant Adjutant General Lamar informed Chalmers on August 1 that Johnston "authorized" Frost and Williams "to impress a sufficient number of negroes to repair the Railroads of which they respectively have charge" and that Chalmers should "afford them all needful assistance."[15] Despite Chalmers's earlier request for the "aid of the Government" by which he, Chalmers, could direct the hiring or impressment of black tracklayers, Johnston failed to order Major Mims to furnish Chalmers with funds and resources toward the mobilization of another slave labor force. His indecision, or refusal, proved particularly injudicious, and Chalmers, who had gone to Canton to aid the railroad officials, later reported to Johnston that he had also encountered "a great unwillingness on the part of citizens to hire hands lest the work should bring the enemy back" to Jackson and Canton. However, convinced that he had dealt decisively with the problem of railroad repairs around the capital, Johnson replied on August 2 to the secretary of war's letter of July 24. After explaining that the "order concerning rolling stock of Mississippi railroads was to destroy rather than permit it to fall into the enemy's hands," he assured Seddon that, as Sherman had returned to Vicksburg, "the superintendents of roads have been promised protection if they repair."[16]

Johnston's intention to repair the Jackson railway facilities received special notice in the *Atlanta Appeal*, the paper's Mississippi war correspondent having reported on August 8 that Johnston had finally "determined upon" a plan to remove the "rolling stock of the Mississippi Central, which are of so much importance to us at this crisis of our affairs." The reporter warned, however, that only a prompt repair of the tracks and trestles around Jackson could save "the valuable trains of cars, locomotives, etc., that were sent up the Mississippi Central Railroad for safety." Declaring that "nothing is wanting but the proper energy and a sufficient [slave labor] force to begin and complete the work," he stressed that Johnston had "the power and right to bring them out" and that "the military should see to it at once." Further, the immediate construction of "a temporary trestle bridge" across Pearl River would meet "the emergency," while a sturdier structure could be "built hereafter, did the policy of the country demand it." A considerably chagrined correspondent advised his editor on August 16, however, that the reconstruction work had still not begun, although he hoped that the recently arrived Mississippi governor, John J. Pettus, would "urge before General Johnston the necessity of repairing" the railway facilities around Jackson, "the country being very anxious about the rolling stock up in North Mississippi."[17]

Inasmuch as Johnston received on August 2 a direct War Department order to remove the Mississippi rolling stock from Grenada to a safe point east of Pearl River, his dilatory approach to the problem of railroad repairs manifested willful insubordination. Although he recognized that he had not promptly obeyed his superiors, he seized on two reasons to justify his procrastination. First, his views regarding a removal of the railway property to Mobile or Selma gave him cause for postponing the reconstruction work. On July 14, he ordered the destruction of the rolling stock without knowing exactly how many engines and cars the railroad officials had removed to Grenada in May. On August 2, after learning the financial value of that equipment from the secretary of war, Johnston rightly inferred that the railroad officials had placed scores of locomotives and hundreds of cars on the tracks above the Yalobusha River. Yet he believed that Alabama's disjointed railway network and a developing Federal threat to Mobile would render a removal of that property to Georgia both technically impracticable and militarily inadvisable. He remembered having seen scores of inactive cars in the Mobile yards late in July and also recognized the continued existence of trackless gaps "in each of the two railroad routes through Alabama, as difficult to pass as that I am censured for not having closed." Johnston's recollection of the idled rolling stock at Mobile and his opinion that the Mississippi locomotives and cars could not easily move beyond Selma or the Gulf port "for use in the East" persuaded him to leave the equipment around Grenada. In anticipating a Federal attack on Mobile from Pensacola early in August, he also thought that "it would not have been judicious to collect all the spare engines and cars of the department at one point." Distracted by that worry,

Johnston also feared that Grant, in planning his next move after Vicksburg, contemplated operating simultaneously against Mobile. Preparing for such a contingency, he reasoned that Grant would forgo seizing the rolling stock near Grenada and march through Jackson to Mobile or advance on the Gulf port by way of Memphis and Corinth or via New Orleans.[18] Consequently, he allowed the Mississippi railway property to remain around Grenada and awaited Grant's movement as a confirmation of his strategic judgment and as an excuse for his prolonged inaction in not hastening the completion of railroad repair projects around Jackson.

Johnston's unwillingness to employ his engineers or troops for railroad repair work served as his second reason for deferring the reconstruction projects. After President Davis rescinded Johnston's rolling stock order, Secretary of War Seddon referred the matter of railroad reconstruction in Mississippi to Colonel Gilmer, the head of the Engineer Bureau and an officer whom Davis promoted directly to the rank of major general on August 25, 1863. Gilmer sent a dispatch to Johnston on August 6 and urged him to direct his chief engineer to "rebuild temporarily and promptly" the Pearl River bridge. Not receiving an acknowledgment of his message, on August 8 he sent a letter to Johnston again attempting to spur the Confederate commander into action; another "earnest appeal" followed on August 14. Gilmer assured Johnston that the War Department sanctioned his use of army engineers for the rapid repair of the Pearl River bridge and that if Johnston could not procure enough black laborers for tracklaying work, then Johnston should employ troop details to accomplish that task.[19] Gilmer's proposal should not have struck Johnston as a radical or unprecedented practice: Johnston had used black penitentiary convicts to extend railroad sidings in Virginia and, in critical situations, granted the quartermaster agent Sharp almost blanket authority over railroad transportation in that state. Moreover, shortly after the fall of Vicksburg in July, Johnston issued orders to repair promptly wagon train plank roads running from Jackson to Brandon. Fearing that Sherman's forces would intercept his retreat from Jackson and capture the Confederate army's ordnance and supply trains foundering in narrow, muddy, and deeply rutted roads east of Pearl River, Johnston instructed subordinates to employ army teamsters and to impress slave laborers to rebuild corduroy roads. Emphatically, Johnston explained that work on the main route "must be attended to immediately. Make details from drivers &

impress hands. Get the labor by all means as the repairs of the road" required expeditious action.[20] Johnston employed Confederate troops and impressed black laborers for wagon train road repair work to hasten his retreat from Jackson in the face of Sherman's pursuit, but he refused to adopt such measures to reconstruct railroad tracks and trestles to save irreplaceable rolling stock and railroad iron after Sherman's evacuation of Jackson and his withdrawal to Vicksburg.

Indeed, in July, Johnston categorically rejected Gilmer's proposal for an extraordinary employment of Confederate troops on the Mississippi railways. Concerned that by putting his engineers and soldiers to work on the railroads he would further demoralize his command, infringe on the jealously guarded property rights and commercial interests of the New Orleans, Jackson & Great Northern and Southern Railroad companies, and violate the War Department's hands-off railway policy, Johnston insisted that the railroad authorities should repair tracks and trestles without direct military intervention.[21] Yet, earlier in July, he had defiantly ignored the Mississippi firms' property rights and the Confederate government's scrupulously observed laissez-faire railroad policy by ordering the destruction of the railroad bridges and rolling stock around Grenada without authorization from Richmond.

Ultimately, Johnston's refusal to employ his troops on the railroads, his failure to order an immediate impressment of slave laborers, and his reluctance to grapple with the problem of railroad reconstruction around Jackson sprang from his increasingly unreasoning preoccupation with Confederate military affairs in Alabama. Since its withdrawal to Vicksburg on July 23, the Federal army had not seriously acted against Confederate forces at Morton or Mobile. Reports of an unexpected wave of Federal cavalry forays into northern Alabama and of an impending Union movement on Mobile from Pensacola, however, persuaded Johnston to delay railroad repairs around the capital. Instead of rebuilding the Pearl River bridge, he sent three infantry brigades to Meridian and Enterprise in order to "protect Selma and Demopolis in case of raids" and to "join the garrison of Mobile should that place be threatened" by an overland attack from Florida. Johnston decided toward mid-August that another reconstruction task around Jackson would waste government resources and further deplete his attenuated command. Fearing that a removal of the Mississippi railway equipment to Mobile or Selma would expose that property to Federal invaders, he decided that the rolling stock around Grenada occupied a safer position than any point east of the Pearl River and therefore "no change [of location] was made."[22]

Johnston reversed his decision on August 15 when he recognized an imminent peril to the rolling stock in northern Mississippi. The startling news that Grant and Sherman had launched 2,500 Federal cavalrymen from Yazoo City, Mississippi, and Grand Junction, Tennessee, on a converging attack against Grenada stung him into action. He hurriedly sent a force of 2,700 cavalry to Grenada from Canton and Okolona to support Chalmers's 1,100 troopers, the latter already heavily outnumbered by Union cavalry above the Yalobusha. Despite Johnston's action, the Federal brigades captured Grenada on August 17 and started a conflagration that destroyed a quarter of the town. They razed the junction's railroad depots and machine shops and burned the closely packed engines and cars that sat unguarded in the Grenada yards. The Federals found a portion of the rolling stock that railroad managers had previously removed to Grenada from Water Valley conveniently "covered with fence rails, ready to be set on fire." Johnston's reinforcements encountered the routed detachments of Chalmers's command below Grenada, and the Confederate troops then retreated along the Mississippi Central tracks toward Canton, firing more of Walter Goodman's rolling stock.[23]

Reports of the destruction of the railway equipment in northern Mississippi streamed into Johnston's headquarters at Morton over the succeeding days. On August 21, after having assured himself that the Federal raiders had evacuated previously Confederate-controlled portions of northern Mississippi, Johnston advised Adjutant General Cooper that the Yankee cavalrymen had "destroyed much of the rolling stock" around Grenada. Later that day, in a desperate attempt to rescue the engines and cars that had escaped destruction by fire on the railroads above Jackson, he finally decided to furnish Superintendents Frost and Williams with the slave laborers that they needed for another reconstruction project around the capital. He ordered his cavalry chief at Canton, Major General Stephen D. Lee, to ascertain "if Mr. Frost will repair the road" and to "promise him protection and impressment of negro labor."[24] Johnston's belated offer of direct military assistance for the repair of the central Mississippi railroads struck Williams as a piece of egregiously inept generalship. He complained to the editor of the *Meridian Clarion* late in August that he "was very much disgusted with the whole [Grenada] affair" and that he could not understand why Johnston had kept Chalmers's and Lee's commands "idle in the pine woods where there is nothing to guard, while a point at which there were millions of invaluable property should be left unprotected."[25] Despite his anger with Johnston, Superintendent Frost favored Johnston's suggestion for reconstructing the companies' tracks and trestles. Johnston thereupon instructed Major Mims to procure "as many laborers, wagons, and teams, as the engineers of the railroad companies required" for the repair or the railroads around the capital as well as for the "rebuilding of the railroad-bridge at Jackson."[26] Despite Johnston's action, the loss of rolling stock in Mississippi shocked and infuriated the Richmond authorities, particularly Secretary of War Seddon, who had conveyed President Davis's instructions requiring Johnston to remove the railroad equipment quickly to safety. Bluntly, Seddon demanded "prompt and complete information" from Johnston's chief engineer, Lieutenant Colonel Samuel H. Lockett, concerning the full extent of the "destruction of rolling-stock beyond the Pearl River Bridge."[27]

Meanwhile, accounts of the railroad destruction in Mississippi quickly spread across the Northern states, where newspaper editors exulted over the Confederate disaster. The Southern press, naturally, deplored that calamity. On August 22, the *Mobile Advertiser and Register* charged that neither Johnston nor his subordinates had made any serious effort to save the rolling stock and that "the vain hope seems to have been indulged in that the enemy were unaware of its existence or situation, or careless of its importance to our interests." The *Advertiser* concluded its condemnation of Johnston and his field officers by declaring bluntly that "it is difficult to conceive how such a great oversight could have blinded the Confederate military authorities." The *Atlanta Appeal* agreed, pointing out that Confederate commanders had allowed seven weeks to pass "without replacing the bridge over the Pearl at Jackson, (which could easily have been done)" toward a removal of the rolling stock beyond the river. The editor of the *Jackson Mississippian*, then at Selma, Alabama, bitterly complained that "this time was frittered away by those whose duty it was to use dispatch in securing this rolling stock, and that vast amount of property is consequently destroyed." Without accusing Johnston of precipitating the Grenada catastrophe, he nonetheless commented: "We have never been able to learn whose duty it was to employ and direct this labor, nor why the matter was so shamefully neglected." Reflecting on the Confederate failure to replace the Pearl River bridge, the *Daily Chattanooga Rebel* declared that Knoxville bridge contractor Anthony L. Maxwell "would have built two like it while Grant was besieging Vicksburg." The *Rebel* further asserted that the Grenada debacle demonstrated that, when either army destroyed a Southern railroad "with all our negro labor at hand, the Yankees re-build it in half the time we consume in a like undertaking." But the *Meridian Clarion*, eager to preserve Southern morale, saw "no use grumbling" about the loss of the locomotives and cars, although it admonished supporters of the Confederate cause to "save all we can, and agree 'never to do so any more,' if we are let off this time."[28]

Whatever the Southern editorial comments on the Grenada affair, Johnston's failure to remove the Mississippi rolling stock to Alabama in the summer of 1863 constituted a monumental blunder. In August, raiding Union cavalry and retreating Confederate troops together badly injured or totally destroyed upward of 600 engines and cars—equipment belonging to three railroad companies—around Grenada and other points farther south on the Mississippi Central Railroad. Jefferson Davis, in adding to that figure the nearly 190 other railroad vehicles that Federal cavalrymen in July burned on the tracks above and below Jackson, all because of Johnston's failure to rebuild promptly the Pearl River bridge in June, accurately estimated in 1865 that the loss of equipment aggregated "a very large number of locomotives, said to be about ninety, and several hundred cars were lost." Johnston weakly asserted nine years later that, despite the heavy toll of engines and cars taken, "enough for the business of the [Mississippi Central] road escaped" and that the destruction of that property "was not a military loss, however, and was not felt by the transportation department." In truth, the sacrifice of the Mississippi Central equipment ruined the carrying trade of that company and that of two other firms until long after the war.[29] The total financial loss amounted to some $10 million, or twenty times the value of the Baltimore & Ohio property he had destroyed in Virginia. Worse still, the destruction of the rolling stock dealt the Confederate transportation system a stunning blow. From this flows one indisputable truth about Johnston as a strategist and logistician: he never recognized the crucial importance of railroads and rolling stock to the Confederate war effort. Notwithstanding this, it should be emphasized that in his July 22 message to Walter

Goodman, even President Davis expressed a willingness to permit the destruction of the Mississippi Central rolling stock at Grenada to prevent its capture by Federal cavalry. Davis did, however, in his July 24 message to Johnston, order Johnston to make efforts to rescue and remove the endangered rolling stock. Since Johnston should have interpreted those instructions to include a reconstruction of the Pearl River bridge, his failure to rebuild the bridge constituted flagrant insubordination. Acting to the full extent of their authority, Seddon conveyed Davis's orders to Johnston, and Gilmer urged Johnston to execute them, but Johnston still refused. Consequently, the public condemnation of Johnston in all quarters of the Confederacy sprang from a correct assessment of his disobedience, an expression of willful misconduct that resulted in the disaster at Grenada.[30]

The Grenada affair scarcely ended with the destruction of the rolling stock and Johnston's belated offer of military assistance to the railroad officials for another reconstruction project around Jackson. Johnston, with his egregiously poor judgment, doubted the military necessity or expediency of making the proposed repairs to the railroads and to the Pearl River bridge. The fundamental cause of Johnston's renewed procrastination, though, was not a specific strategic objection but rather a reflection of his opinion of the lack of practical usefulness and of the technical difficulty of a serious effort to recover the remaining rolling stock and railroad property around Grenada, including the stacks of iron rails still isolated north of Jackson. Although he had already ordered Major Mims to assist the railroad officials in rebuilding their tracks and trestles around Jackson and Canton, Johnston decided to obtain another damage assessment report on the Pearl River bridge and the railroads around Jackson. Consequently, on September 3 he instructed Lieutenant John W. Glenn, a Mobile-based Engineer Corps officer whom the War Department had assigned to temporary duty at Jackson on July 18, to inspect the destruction of tracks and trestles from Brandon to Jackson and from Jackson to Canton and Grenada.[31]

Glenn submitted his inspection report to Johnston on September 10, stating that "the entire tressel work through Perl [sic] River bottom is destroyed—about 500 yards in all. The bridge across Perl River is gone & the masonry piers partially destroyed." Glenn advised Johnston that the railroad officials would require five weeks' time and two hundred black laborers to repair the Brandon and Jackson section of the Southern Railroad and to construct a temporary bridge across the Pearl. He then described the more extensive damage done to the twenty-four-mile Jackson and Canton segment of the New Orleans, Jackson & Great Northern Railroad. The Engineer Corps officer reported that Federal cavalry had thoroughly devastated half of that portion of the railroad and had inflicted more damage on the line farther north, leaving the "ties all burned & nine tenths of the iron badly bent." Glenn estimated that a separate force of four hundred black hands would need five weeks to restore that stretch of track to a "passable condition." Though the railroad officials and their work crews had already repaired the Mississippi Central tracks between Canton and Grenada, they required an additional hundred slave laborers for two weeks to reconstruct the entirely destroyed "tresselwork & bridge crossing the Yalobusha" River north of Grenada. The Yalobusha trestle needed rebuilding since much of the stranded rolling stock lay above the river. The railroad officials, furnished with War Department funds, would have to hire seven hundred slave laborers and expend $80,000 to complete all reconstruction work, Glenn reported. In short, Glenn's findings agreed in all important particulars with the conclusions drawn by railroad officials Frost and Williams the previous July. Yet Johnston failed to act promptly on the first report, and his neglect resulted in the destruction of most of the rolling stock around Grenada.

Nevertheless, in the most important part of his damage assessment report, Glenn strongly recommended the recovery of undamaged railroad vehicles and the salvaging (for use by government machine shops) of the wheels and other unharmed mechanical parts of burned engines and cars as well as the "immense quantities of scrap iron" still isolated around Grenada. Appraising the remaining railroad property to be worth about $10 million, Glenn proposed that, should the "commanding Genl decide to recover the above stock, the work necessary should be commenced immediately," and that Johnston should order the removal of all the equipment from Grenada to Canton, where Confederate cavalry could protect it from renewed enemy raids. Glenn recommended that Johnston then order the rolling stock removed from Canton to Jackson and across Pearl River "as the track progressed" and "convoyed by a sufficient force to prevent any successful raid against it." Should Johnston supply

the railroad officials with laborers promptly, Glenn confidently concluded, the railroad men could complete the reconstruction work
earlier than the five weeks he otherwise anticipated.[32]

Ignoring Glenn's work and his ability to repair damaged tracks and
trestles, on September 11 Johnston sent him back to Mobile where
he resumed work on the fortifications at Fort Gaines under the direction of Brigadier General Danville Leadbetter, the chief Engineer
Corps officer at Mobile, and under Major General Dabney H.
Maury, commander of the Department of the Gulf. Simultaneously,
Johnston himself proceeded to Montgomery, Alabama, leaving Lieutenant General William J. Hardee in temporary command of Confederate forces in Mississippi. At this juncture, D. H. Kenney, the
general railroad iron commissioner under the Engineer Bureau, expressed his intention to reconstruct the Pearl River bridge. Hardee,
however, either obeying Johnston's orders or acting on his own authority, advised Kenney, "Protection cannot be given to rebuild the
Pearl River bridge, nor is it practicable."[33] Not until February 1864
did the Confederate military provide protection for Kenney's work
crews at Jackson.

Notwithstanding Glenn's reasonable and intelligent plan and Kenney's intention to rebuild the Pearl River bridge, Johnston continued
to vacillate. He refrained from more direct and effective military intervention in an effort to expedite railroad repairs in central and
northern Mississippi. As a partial concession to the War Department, however, he reluctantly forwarded to Quartermaster General
Alexander R. Lawton a copy of a contract proposed by the Mississippi & Tennessee Railroad company, an agreement that would
have obligated the Confederate government to insure the Mississippi
& Tennessee ($6,000 a month) to enable the firm to reopen that
railroad north of Grenada with what little rolling stock the company
still possessed. The renewed operation of the railroad, as both the
railroad managers and army commissaries agreed, would have facilitated moving food supplies from northwest Mississippi to the
east. Though Johnston refrained from specifically endorsing the proposed contract, War Department officials eagerly supported the
agreement.[34] In failing to execute Glenn's plan or to support the
Mississippi & Tennessee contract, Johnston again demonstrated contempt for railroad officials, underestimating their financial interest
in railway property, and showing his disparagement of the value of
rolling stock to the Confederate war effort. He also manifested his

continuing insubordination and recalcitrance toward the War Department authorities concerning the Pearl River bridge.

Johnston especially resisted stubbornly and defiantly control by the War Department authorities early in October. Secretary of War Seddon, who since late August had recognized the importance of saving Mississippi rolling stock between Jackson, Meridian, and Mobile and of salvaging the remaining rolling stock and railroad iron at Grenada, urged Johnston to protect railway equipment and to furnish protection and material resources to Engineer Corps officers assigned to his staff toward the rebuilding of the Pearl River bridge and the recovery of the machinery and iron. In reply, Johnston assured Seddon that "military officers have instructions to prevent injudicious exposure of rolling stock to capture & to protect it when possible & not to permit it to fall into enemy's hands." As for rebuilding the Pearl River bridge and recovering machinery and railroad iron from Grenada, Johnston explained to Seddon that "for the object you mention, relaying 9 or 10 miles of R. R. will also be necessary. I will give all assistance & protection in my power, but my force is very small."[35] Johnston's responses proved that he had learned little about making judicious military applications of railroads, even in the wake of his disastrous Grenada blunder. He still insisted on destroying rolling stock to prevent its use by Federal forces. To avoid direct military intervention, he also demanded that railroad officials and slave laborers, assisted by army engineers and protected by cavalry troops, rebuild railroad tracks and trestles without the use of troop details.

Then, instead of obeying Seddon and reconstructing the trestle over the Pearl, Johnston directed his attention to repairing a less strategically critical railroad bridge near Pelahatchie Station west of Morton on the Southern Railroad. The structure formed only one of the many trestles on the railroad connecting Meridian and Jackson, including the Chunkey's Creek bridge that Johnston had protected from Federal cavalry in June. Previously, on July 20, before Johnston had decided to rebuild the Pearl River bridge after the second Federal occupation of Jackson, Major Barbour, then at Morton, advised Johnston of his efforts to procure the repair of the Pelahatchie Creek bridge, which had sustained severe damage at the hands of retreating Confederate forces after the second fall of Jackson. Barbour nevertheless assured Johnston that he would restore quickly the broken communications between Morton and Jackson; it posed a task

"which the railroad men say can be done" by "hiring twenty men."
Barbour thereupon requested the railroad officials to proceed with
the repair work in return for eventual government compensation.
Sadly, Johnston had refused to take similar prompt action on the
Pearl River bridge later in July—precipitating the Grenada disaster.

Subsequently, in October 1863, Assistant Chief Quartermaster
Moore, then stationed at Meridian, notified Johnston that the Pelahatchie Creek bridge had again suffered heavy damage, apparently
on this occasion from high floodwaters. Significantly, Moore requested "authority to have men detailed from the troops at Brandon" to reconstruct the trestle. Moore's message stunned Johnston.
By the middle of October he had nearly completed preparations to
receive President Davis, who had already left Richmond to conduct
an inspection of Confederate forces in Tennessee, Alabama, and
Mississippi. Fearing that any neglect in repairing the Pelahatchie
Creek bridge would prevent Davis from reaching Brandon by rail,
Johnston ordered Barbour to advise Ewell: "Genl Johnston desires
the bridge made immediately—It can be done in a few days." Moore
succeeded in repairing the trestle over Pelahatchie Creek before
Davis reached Meridian, but his accomplishment failed to prevent
additional difficulty with the Southern Railroad. The special train
that carried both Davis and Johnston toward Brandon "ran over a
cow & was thrown from the track" on the night of October 22 near
Pelahatchie Station. Neither Davis nor Johnston sustained serious injury, though, and the two men boarded another train sent from Meridian to take them to Brandon and then to bring Davis back to
Meridian.[36] In short, by using Confederate troops, Johnston quickly
rebuilt a smaller bridge to avoid a presidential reprimand. Yet he
continued to refuse to employ those same troops and still procrastinated in the matter of repairing the railroads and the Pearl River
bridge for the recovery of irreplaceable Confederate rolling stock.

Finally, yielding to pressure, Johnston decided to provide military
commanders and railroad officials with slave laborers and the services
of Engineer Corps officers to reconstruct the railroad facilities around
Jackson, where previously he had required the railroad managers
to use black laborers and to repair damaged tracks and trestles
with only indirect and limited military assistance. Johnston understood, however belatedly, that he needed to secure slave laborers to
complete the work. Therefore, on November 8, he sent a message
to Major General William W. Loring, then at Canton, instructing

Loring that "if you cannot otherwise obtain it, impress labor to work on the roads." Loring obeyed and began mobilizing a slave labor force to make repairs to the railroads between Canton and Brandon. Then, early in December, Loring advised Johnston that the "well organized pioneer corps" under his command could swiftly build another Pearl River bridge if Johnston desired it. Johnston could entrust the raising of another trestle to the head of Loring's pioneer corps because he had proved himself "a thorough mechanic & [he] can construct any kind you may wish." Loring pointed out, however, that his previously assembled black "Rail Road party is moving very slowly" between Canton and Brandon. Further encouraged by Major General Lee at Canton, on December 9 Johnston advised Lee that he had ordered his chief engineer, Lieutenant Colonel Lockett, to assign two engineer officers to the work of superintending the rebuilding of "bridges on the Big Black and Pearl rivers," and that they should report to Lee for further orders. Encouraged by these developments, the *Brandon Republican* reported that the Confederate engineers expected railroad repairs between Brandon and Jackson to be completed by January 1, 1864, "provided the river don't rise so as to prevent them from building the bridge across Pearl river."[37] Reconstruction of the Pearl River bridge finally began by the middle of December, but a combination of circumstances prevented its completion. The arrival of stormy winter weather, a shortage of carpenter's tools, and Johnston's departure from Mississippi for Georgia later in December 1863 contributed to the protracted delay.

Nevertheless, as late as February 1864, Secretary of War Seddon kept making efforts to recover the rolling stock from Grenada. He instructed Johnston's successor in command, Lieutenant General Polk—who proved himself to be the Confederacy's most effective railroad general—to remove the railroad equipment as soon as Polk could rebuild the Pearl River bridge.[38] Polk's vigorous efforts, however, proved fruitless; early in February Sherman launched a devastating raid against the Confederate railroad center at Meridian, destroying railroad tracks around Jackson and the trestlework of the Pearl River bridge for a third time. Determined to succeed where Johnston had failed, however, the energetic and enterprising Polk planned to build another railroad bridge across the Pearl River early in May. By then, however, President Davis had ordered him to reinforce and join Johnston's Army of Tennessee north of Atlanta to repel an imminent Federal invasion of northwest Georgia.[39] Although the Confederates later succeeded in restoring railroad communications through Jackson by replacing the bridge, the rolling stock at Grenada never reached the East. Between Federal attacks, Johnston's inaction, and Polk's lack of resources, the critical Pearl River bridge remained destroyed for over an entire year of the war, paralyzing Confederate logistical operations in central Mississippi before and long after the decisive Vicksburg campaign. For Johnston, the Grenada affair ended on his departure for Georgia in December 1863. Without regret over his mishandling of the Western railroads, he left Mississippi without rebuilding the Pearl River bridge or recovering the remaining serviceable rolling stock and railroad iron at Grenada. He thereby compounded and exacerbated his original blunder of miscalculation by his subsequent willful negligence and dereliction of duty.

The Grenada disaster, an event that dealt already declining Confederate military fortunes yet another devastating blow, scarcely disturbed Johnston with respect to his mismanagement of railway logistics or his needless sacrifice of rolling stock. He continued using the steadily deteriorating railroads of the Deep South for his military purposes, particularly for the strategic movement of troops. Even as critics excoriated Johnston in August 1863, events in Tennessee directed his attention to a different railroad problem at Morton, Mississippi. Late in the preceding June, Federal General Rosecrans had skillfully maneuvered the Army of Tennessee out of its strong position around Tullahoma and then driven Bragg's forces back to Chattanooga. There, by the middle of August, the formidable flood-swollen Tennessee River temporarily impeded Rosecrans's advance. At this juncture, Bragg desperately attempted to obtain reinforcements before the resumption of the Federal offensive. Since Confederate commanders could spare few troops from Atlantic seaport garrisons, Bragg called on Johnston for more soldiers. In complying, on August 22, Johnston sought War Department authorization to send reinforcements from Morton to Chattanooga. He needed this permission because, after the evacuation of Jackson in July, the War Department reduced his jurisdiction to certain parts of Mississippi and Alabama; he lost authority over middle Tennessee and east Louisiana. Shortly thereafter, Secretary of War Seddon approved Johnston's request to reinforce the Army of Tennessee with troops drawn from the "Department of Mississippi."

Johnston thereupon directed Major Barbour to urge Southern Railroad officials at Meridian to furnish the "necessary means of railroad transportation" for the movement of two infantry divisions. In making advance arrangements similar to those he had made in December 1862, when he attempted to hasten the movement of Stevenson's troops across the Deep South, he instructed Bragg to "give orders [to quartermasters] at Atlanta and West Point." Johnston neglected, however, to consider first the allocation of rolling stock in Mississippi. Since they maintained the bulk of the Southern's rolling stock at Meridian, the railroad officials could promise the arrival of trains at Morton only on August 23. Johnston's hope for a rapid troop movement from Morton to Chattanooga quickly vanished. Several hours into the transportation operation, he angrily complained to Bragg that "this road works so wretchedly that it will take five days, including yesterday, to get them [the troops] off."[40] Johnston probably witnessed an overconcentration of train traffic at Morton because that station lacked enough tracks and sidings for implementing such a large troop movement to Meridian. The congestion of railroad vehicles at Morton should not have surprised him, though, because in July Major Barbour had advised him from Morton that a protracted entrainment of numerous cars crowded with sick soldiers constituted a "disgraceful" situation that also impeded transportation of supplies between Meridian and Brandon.[41]

Ironically, Johnston's failure to rebuild the Pearl River bridge promptly the preceding June had prevented an even greater overconcentration of rolling stock at Morton. In mid-June Johnston had ordered Barbour, then at Jackson, to "learn the number of sleeping cars on the different Railroads leading to this place and have them collected at this point" for the transportation of sick soldiers. Although Barbour had concentrated Mississippi Central and New Orleans, Jackson & Great Northern and Southern Railroad equipment at Jackson, the lack of a railroad bridge across Pearl River had precluded the movement of that rolling stock to the Southern tracks east of Jackson. Consequently, only the Southern Railroad machinery running between Jackson and Meridian the previous May could later be employed in transporting sick troops from Jackson, Brandon, and Morton to Meridian and Mobile. Despite the continuing limitation on the total quantity of equipment available for use on the

Southern Railroad east of Jackson, Johnston still neglected to make arrangements with railroad managers to regulate the quantity of rolling stock moving toward Morton. As a result, most of the Southern Railroad's engines and cars continued to run from Meridian to Morton, considerably delaying the few troop trains at Morton already loaded and bound for Mobile. Because in Virginia Johnston had ordered the quartermaster agent Sharp to lengthen turnouts below Gordonsville to expedite troop train movements to Richmond, his neglect to carry out similar measures (including repairing badly dilapidated railroad tracks) in Mississippi delayed the reinforcement of Bragg.[42]

Notwithstanding the congestion at Morton, Johnston managed to strengthen Bragg's forces, and the Confederate army in Georgia soundly defeated the Union army at Chickamauga, whereupon Bragg besieged Rosecrans's demoralized troops at Chattanooga. Meanwhile, Johnston used the railroads of Mississippi and Alabama to reinforce garrisons at railroad centers threatened by Federal raiders in those states, again demonstrating his ability to mobilize his command and achieve strategic concentrations of force. Then, Johnston used his cavalry offensively to launch raids against Rosecrans's vulnerable railroad communications between Nashville, Tennessee, and Bridgeport, Alabama. Early in October Johnston instructed Major General Lee to "break the rail roads in rear of Rosecrans Army" and at "points on the rail roads where most injury can be done to them with least exposure of our troops," including the destruction of the "bridges over the branches of Duck river and of the Elk [River]."[43] Lee's raid succeeded brilliantly, although Johnston could not prevent Federal forces from quickly rebuilding the railroad to Bridgeport, below Chattanooga, and saving the beleaguered Union army from starvation or surrender. Having attacked Rosecrans's railroad communications in Tennessee, Johnston next attempted to improve the utilization of the Mobile & Ohio Railroad in northeast Mississippi. Preoccupied with the reconstruction and strategic use of railroads since his coming to Mississippi in May, Johnston had long neglected to exploit fully the potential of the Mobile & Ohio for supplying Confederate forces in Mississippi. Johnston demonstrated this lack of attention late in June 1863 when he failed to cooperate promptly with Mobile & Ohio president Milton Brown for a proposed rebuilding of the Okolona and Tupelo section of the Mobile & Ohio toward a recovery of commissaries from that productive agricultural region of the state, despite Brown's promise to repay after the war a $25,000 government loan needed to reconstruct his firm's tracks and trestles. Then, early in November, when a cavalry commander at Okolona ordered the use of troops to repair the railroad, Johnston sternly revoked the order. He then sent a message to Adjutant General Cooper, querulously inquiring, "has the War Department put any one in charge of the repair of railroads in this state? If so, what authority has he?"[44]

Johnston's inquiry prompted Quartermaster General Lawton later in November to appoint a Confederate officer to the position of general superintendent of railroads west of the Alabama River, but Johnston meanwhile refused to use his newly designated military superintendent of railroad transportation for the Department of Mississippi to make repairs to the Mobile & Ohio Railroad. On October 7, Johnston had departed from his usual practice of depending almost exclusively on his own staff quartermasters to handle railroad transportation and had appointed a quartermaster agent, Major George Whitfield, as his chief transportation officer. Johnston then supported the proposed rebuilding of the Mobile & Ohio, provided that the railroad company repay a government loan after the war. Instead of employing the energetic and efficient Whitfield (as Lieutenant General Polk later did) on the Mobile & Ohio, on November 19 Johnston merely advised Brown, "I understand from Mr. Fleming that you intended to repair your road to Tupelo. I hope that you will—transportation of supplies will make it pay well—the cost will be trifling." Rather than showing Johnston's improved appreciation of the logistical value of the railroad, this episode demonstrated his continued insistence that railroad officials should conduct repairs without direct military intervention—a disastrously inflexible and unenterprising policy in view of the military necessity of the work. Moreover, Johnston expressed a willingness to save supplies at a cost of $25,000 but showed scarcely any concern over the loss of rolling stock worth millions of dollars.[45]

While Johnston delayed in procuring the rebuilding of the Pearl River bridge at Jackson and the reconstruction of the Mobile & Ohio Railroad in northeast Mississippi, decisive events occurred farther north in Tennessee. After the assignment of Ulysses S. Grant to Tennessee late in November 1863, the Federal army broke Bragg's encirclement of Chattanooga in the battle at Missionary Ridge and drove the routed Confederate army into Georgia. Bragg then resigned his command, whereupon Lieutenant General Hardee temporarily led the Army of Tennessee until late in December. Finally, after naming Bragg as chief of staff for the Confederate armies, President Davis appointed Johnston as the new commander of the Army of Tennessee.[46] Before assuming his new command in Georgia, however, Johnston learned that Quartermaster General Lawton had appointed Major Thomas Peters, an officer acting under the authority and control of the War Department's Railroad Bureau, as military superintendent of railroad transportation embracing all the railroads west of the Alabama River. Lawton also designated Memphis & Charleston superintendent Tate as Peters's assistant. Early in December 1863 Tate assured Johnston that both he and Peters would endeavor to develop and implement a coherent and efficient transportation system designed to "rid you of any more serious troubles with the Rail Roads." Tate particularly wished to complete the railroad line that Alabama & Mississippi Rivers Railroad officials had partially constructed to connect Meridian, Mississippi, and Selma, Alabama. Indeed, under Bragg's orders in July 1862, Tate had assisted the railroad managers by furnishing them with materials and slave laborers to complete the whole line of the railroad except for a remaining four-mile gap between Demopolis and McDowell's Landing, points on either side of the unbridged Tombigbee River. Needing military assistance to close the gap, however, Tate urged Johnston to order the immediate impressment of black laborers for the laying of track, or to apply to the War Department for broad authority to impress.[47]

Tate's prompting proved unnecessary because Johnston also recognized the importance of completing the railroad connection at Demopolis. In November, he had urged President Davis and Secretary of War Seddon to prohibit Commissary General Northrop's agents in Alabama from impressing supplies that the railroad officials at Demopolis had previously purchased for railroad construction crews—a practice that threatened to delay the completion of the rail connection at Demopolis. Then in mid-December, in part to comply with Tate's request, Johnston provided the Alabama & Mississippi Rivers Railroad managers with slave laborers by preventing Major General Maury from impressing hands in Marengo County. Johnston's jurisdiction—that of the Department of Mississippi—included Demopolis, in Marengo County, and Selma and Montgomery, while the territory of Maury's Department of the Gulf remained largely confined to the southern portion of Alabama. Though Engineer Corps officers commanded and employed the "Mobile Negro Force," a group of specially assembled slave labor battalions, for work on the Gulf port's forts and fortifications, Maury resorted to impressing slaves in situations where slaveowners refused to hire out bondsmen to the Confederate government (usually for sixty days) for prices substantially below those offered by railroad officials. Consequently, when in December Maury announced his intention to impress slaves in Marengo County for work on the fortifications at Mobile, Marengo County slaveholders and Alabama & Mississippi Rivers president W. P. Bocock sent complaints to Johnston. Intervening on behalf of the aggrieved masters, Johnston ordered Maury not to seize black laborers in the Department of Mississippi. He thereby simultaneously placated slaveowners and railroad officials and satisfied Tate's request to have Mississippi or Alabama slaves sent to Demopolis. Since the railroad managers had ample funds to hire black laborers, Johnston prudently avoided impressing slaves and succeeded in procuring a sufficiently large slave labor force for temporary service under the railroad officials and military authorities at Demopolis.[48]

Though Johnston furnished Tate and the Alabama & Mississippi Rivers Railroad officials with slave laborers for a more expeditious completion of the railroad connection at Demopolis, he nevertheless failed to express concern over the delayed construction of a railroad bridge across the Tombigbee River west of Demopolis. In March 1863, while the Alabama & Mississippi Rivers managers struggled to lay tracks between Selma and Meridian, the Engineer Corps contracted with the Alabama & Mississippi Rivers firm to build the proposed Tombigbee River bridge; the War Department agreed to accomplish the work in return for eventual reimbursement by the railroad company. Accordingly, Engineer Corps officer and Lieutenant Colonel Minor Meriwether separately contracted with Anthony L. Maxwell, Jr., to construct the bridge in exchange for government compensation and continued exemption from military service. Although Maxwell had performed brilliantly by rapidly rebuilding burned railroad bridges for Bragg in East Tennessee, and in the spring of 1864 would also quickly construct duplicate trestles for Johnston in northwest Georgia, in Alabama in 1863 and 1864 Maxwell miserably failed to fulfill his obligations under the government contract. Maxwell's greed, negligence, and extravagance seriously delayed the construction of the Tombigbee River bridge after March 1863, prompting Meriwether to complain to Lieutenant General Richard Taylor about Maxwell's unreliability and wastefulness.[49]

Notwithstanding the continuing delay in completing the Tombigbee River bridge in his own jurisdiction, Johnston showed unconcern over the Engineer Bureau's loose supervision of the project and its tolerance of Maxwell's incompetence. It should have struck him, however, that the lack of a railroad bridge over the Tombigbee River largely nullified his efforts to procure the completion of the railroad connection at Demopolis: railroad officials could transport troops and supplies from Selma to Demopolis, but they then would have to forward soldiers and equipment by steamboat across the river. As with the Pearl River bridge, Johnston failed to understand that a destroyed, damaged, or even uncompleted railroad trestle could render a railroad line useless for military operations. Reluctant to approach President Davis or the War Department authorities to expedite the bridge-building project in Alabama, Johnston passed to his successor, Lieutenant General Polk, the power and responsibility for completing the railroad connection at Demopolis. As a result, Johnston contributed to further delays of railroad projects in Alabama. As late as May 1864, Polk still vainly sought broad impressment authority from the War Department, without which he could not finish closing the four-mile gap between Demopolis and McDowell's Landing.[50] Whatever Polk's mounting frustration and exasperation, Johnston left Mississippi on December 22. Four days later he had established headquarters at Dalton, Georgia, and promptly began rebuilding the Army of Tennessee in preparation for the spring campaign of 1864.[51]

The Grenada disaster, precipitated by Johnston's reckless unconcern for the safety of Mississippi rolling stock and his defiant disobedience of President Davis's orders to rescue that equipment by rebuilding the Pearl River bridge, was devastating to the Confederate transportation system in the Southwest. Moreover, the heavy losses of rolling stock and railroad iron at Grenada reflected Johnston's continued underestimation of the strategic and logistical value of the Southern railroads, an attitude he had previously demonstrated in Virginia and Tennessee. In Virginia, however, the War Department authorities and a number of influential railroad officials succeeded in controlling Johnston's tendency to abuse or destroy railway property, even if they failed to prevent his abandonment and destruction of enormous quantities of military supplies. In Tennessee and particularly in Mississippi, by contrast, neither the War Department authorities in Richmond nor a host of railroad managers stationed across the Deep South could restrain Johnston. Viewing Southern railroad equipment as an expendable resource, Johnston ultimately abandoned the Mississippi rolling stock at Grenada to implement his preconceived plans of defensive strategy following the fall of Vicksburg. A radically different situation, however, would shortly confront him in Georgia where he would have to use the state- owned and operated Western & Atlantic Railroad, a line closely managed and jealously guarded by Georgia governor Joseph E. Brown. Therefore, Johnston would need to deal with the War Department authorities and State Railroad officials in conducting military operations in Georgia; he would also have to contend with a powerful Confederate governor. These circumstances would severely test his ability to harmonize competing military, political, and commercial interests.

·{4}··

Politics, Logistics, and Supply in Georgia

PRESIDENT Davis's elevation of Johnston to the command of the Army of Tennessee late in December 1863 gave Johnston the enormous responsibility of protecting a substantial portion of the vitally important Confederate transportation system in the Deep South. A Federal army's invasion of northwest Georgia in November 1863 confronted the Confederacy's already seriously crippled railway network with the prospect of further dismemberment and disruption. The threatening situation occurred against the background of the Union reduction of Vicksburg the previous July, a strategic victory that severed the railway linkage connecting the trans-Mississippi Confederacy with the Gulf States. Worse for the Southern cause, the subsequent Federal occupation of Chattanooga in September 1863 broke railroad communication between the Atlantic coastal states and the heartland of the Confederate West. Georgia's railway network consequently assumed a crucial importance to the Confederacy's crumbling transportation system. Indeed, Atlanta served as the principal railroad center in the Deep South; from it radiated several railroads that maintained the linkage between the Gulf States and the Atlantic coastal states. A Federal military victory over the Army of Tennessee in northwest Georgia, either by crushing the Confederate army in battle or by forcing its retreat from that part of the state, could result in the capture of Atlanta and the rupture of those railroad connections. A subsequent march by the Union army to the Atlantic Coast or to the Gulf Coast would complete a second division of the Confederacy. Therefore, the Army of Tennessee had to protect Georgia's strategically pivotal railways. The greatest strategic difficulty was that the Confederate army could not

closely protect the East Tennessee & Georgia Railroad, which left
its spur line terminal at Dalton and extended northwest 110 miles to
its main terminal at Knoxville. The presence of Grant's army around
Ringgold and the Federal occupation of Knoxville limited the railroad's usefulness for Confederate military operations in northwest
Georgia and East Tennessee. The Army of Tennessee's single railway supply line—a feeder line critical to its maintenance as an effective fighting force—lay over a hundred-mile stretch of Western &
Atlantic Railroad track that connected Dalton and Atlanta. By contrast, the Rome Railroad, a Western & Atlantic spur line between
Kingston and Rome, Georgia, was of limited logistical value to the
Confederate army. A fifty-five-mile trackless gap between Rome and
the Alabama & Tennessee Rivers Railroad terminal at Blue Mountain, Alabama, broke direct railway connection between the Army of
Tennessee and the forces of Polk's Department of Alabama, Mississippi, and East Louisiana.[1]

The continued existence of this gap resulted partly from
Johnston's lack of concern and sound strategic judgment. Since the
making of a government contract in 1862, the War Department's Engineer Corps had sought to assist Alabama & Tennessee Rivers Railroad managers in building a thirty-seven-mile branch line between
Blue Mountain and the Georgia border in order to exploit the rich
reserves of grain and corn in that region for the supply of Confederate armies in the Deep South. By the summer of 1863, however, the
railroad officials had not yet begun the work because of delayed ap-
propriations of War Department funds and promised impressments
of railroad iron from shorter and relatively peripheral railroad lines in
Alabama and Florida. Johnston also bears much of the blame for the
failure to construct the proposed transportation link. In August 1863
he could have offered a strong endorsement of a recommendation of
the president of the Alabama & Tennessee Rivers Railroad to Secretary of War Seddon proposing in part an immediate impressment of
railroad iron in the Carolinas, states that presumably could have better afforded to sacrifice such property. Johnston failed to urge the
War Department to carry out the impressment of spare iron or to
offer his assistance in prosecuting the railroad-building project.
Rather, he expressed his recognition of the military importance of
completing the "railroad in question," but declared that he did not
stand "sufficiently well informed on the subject to be able to give an
opinion of the best mode of doing the work."[2] Johnston thus wasted

an extraordinary opportunity to strengthen the Confederate transportation system in the Deep South because of his culpable unfamiliarity with War Department railway policy, his indifference to the commercial interests of railroad managers, and his lack of strategic imagination and professional enterprise. Moreover, if Johnston in the fall of 1863 had removed railroad iron from Grenada and sent it to Alabama, railroad officials could have used that equipment to close the Blue Mountain and Rome gap—his failure also long delayed the completion of the four-mile Alabama & Mississippi Rivers Railroad connection between Demopolis and McDowell's Landing, points further separated by the unbridged Tombigbee River in western Alabama. Indeed, Johnston's failure to recommend the stripping of railroad iron from subsidiary lines represented essentially the same ignorance of and indifference to technical considerations affecting logistics and strategy that in the summer and fall of 1863 induced him simultaneously to neglect repairing the Pearl River bridge and delay removing irreplaceable Mississippi rolling stock and valuable scrap iron beyond the Alabama River.

Notwithstanding the incompleteness of the railroad network that connected eastern Alabama with northwest Georgia (owing in part to Johnston's unconcern), farther south and east from Dalton, Georgia, ran two feeder lines that linked Atlanta with the Atlantic seaports of Savannah and Charleston. The Georgia Railroad left Atlanta and ran east 140 miles to Augusta, Georgia, on the Savannah River along the Georgia and South Carolina border. Georgia Railroad freight trains could move southeast from Augusta and steam over two other connections to Savannah. At Augusta, Georgia Railroad rolling stock could also transfer onto the South Carolina Railroad at Augusta and go east to Charleston. The Macon & Western Railroad left Atlanta and extended south eighty miles to Macon. The Macon & Western linked Atlanta with Savannah and Albany by its connection with two other railways that met at Macon. The Central of Georgia Railroad left Macon and extended east to a branch line that connected it with Milledgeville, the Georgia state capital. The Central of Georgia then veered southeast and ran 140 miles to Savannah. The Southwestern Railroad left Macon and extended south ninety miles to Albany. The Southwestern's importance to the Army of Tennessee rested on its proximity to the fertile agricultural regions of central Georgia. The company's Albany terminal served as a convenient railhead from which quartermaster agents transported Florida beef cattle, previously driven north into Georgia, to Atlanta and Dalton.[3]

A third cluster of railroads promised Johnston considerable assistance in supplying his army at Dalton. The Atlanta & West Point Railroad left Atlanta and extended southwest forty miles to West Point on the Chattahoochee River along the Georgia and Alabama border; West Point was the terminal of eastern Alabama's Montgomery & West Point Railroad. Together, the two railroads formed the main line of transportation that joined the Gulf States and the Atlantic coastal states. Two other railroads strengthened the connections between Georgia and Florida. The Savannah, Albany & Gulf and the Atlantic & Gulf railroads ran consecutively across southern Georgia to Thomasville. The Thomasville terminal, though geographically remote, occupied a pivotal position in the Confederacy's Atlantic coastal railway network. Thomasville lay only twelve miles north of the Florida border and thus offered an even more advantageous railhead than Albany for the shipment of Florida cattle to Johnston's army at Dalton, although cattle cars would have to travel circuitously from Thomasville to Atlanta via Savannah and Macon rather than using the more direct line between Albany and Atlanta. Unfortunately, a proposed branch line connecting Lawton, Georgia, located on an extension of the Atlantic & Gulf Railroad, and Live Oak, Florida, a point on Florida's Pensacola & Georgia Railroad, remained uncompleted until March 1865. Notwithstanding the gap, commissary agents could drive Florida cattle north to Thomasville and Albany, and from those points quartermaster agents could transport the beeves to Savannah, Macon, and Atlanta and thence farther north to Dalton.[4]

Johnston's arrival at Dalton on December 26, 1863, and his enthusiastic acceptance by demoralized Rebel troops in Georgia encouraged army officers to believe that the Confederate army could prevent a Federal capture of Atlanta.[5] A few Army of Tennessee veterans, however, remained cautious in their assessment of Johnston. One officer at Dalton, reflecting the skepticism, confided to a fellow officer at Richmond that "Gen Johnson [sic] has assumed command, but whether his mighty powers can revive the old spirit in the ranks remains yet to be seen."[6] Johnston faced a problem in improving the Confederate army's morale, but to restore that army as an effective fighting force presented him with a more difficult undertaking.

Indeed, Johnston's recognition of the shattered condition of the Army of Tennessee at Dalton impressed on him the crucial role that Georgia's railroads would play in the resupplying of his army. The Confederate army's precipitate retreat from Chattanooga in November 1863 had resulted in heavy losses of clothing and accoutrements. Hundreds of unshod and ill-clad troops shivered in flimsily constructed cantonments around Dalton throughout December and endured the bitter cold without blankets. Doubting that the Quartermaster Department could soon remedy this deficiency, Johnston appealed to private firms and citizens in Atlanta to contribute shoes and blankets.[7] Complicating the supply problem, the army's field transportation had sustained equally severe losses in the disorderly retreat into Georgia. Nearly all the army's wagons and caissons lay strewn over the mountain roads southeast of Chattanooga. The horses and mules around Dalton subsisted on the verge of starvation; the unrelieved frigid weather during December killed many of the animals. Perhaps remembering his building and use of the Centreville Railroad to overcome supply problems in northern Virginia during the winter of 1862, Johnston turned to the Georgia railways for assistance in maintaining his troops and compensating for his army's lost field transportation. Immediately, however, he encountered a set of railroad problems that threatened to frustrate his efforts to rebuild the Army of Tennessee.[8]

The mismanagement of the state- owned and operated Western & Atlantic Railroad presented Johnston with his most serious railroad problem in the winter of 1864, a difficulty that had also complicated the operations of General Braxton Bragg. Only six weeks before Johnston assumed command of the Army of Tennessee, Bragg and Georgia governor Joseph E. Brown had had an acrimonious dispute over the alleged mismanagement of the State Railroad. Bragg had attributed the shortage of forage and subsistence stores accumulated at Chattanooga to the Western & Atlantic officials' commercial preoccupation, specifically to their determination to provide and maintain regular passenger train service in Georgia despite the critical Confederate military operations occurring in East Tennessee. In a series of indignant replies, Brown had categorically denied Bragg's charges, describing the manifold problems under which his railroad struggled to supply adequately the Army of Tennessee and simultaneously to maintain an essential level of private and public service. Brown had particularly emphasized the serious shortages of rolling

stock, wood for locomotive fuel, and railroad employees for the
Western & Atlantic's frequent inability to meet the Confederate
army's supply needs.

Although Johnston had not participated in the heated Bragg and
Brown debate, early in January 1864 he also concluded that Western
& Atlantic mismanagement largely accounted for the scarcity of forage and stores at Dalton. He complained to Governor Brown that the
State Railroad failed to "supply equal to daily consumption of army"
because of an inexplicable "want of supply of wood" and bluntly
warned Brown that unless Western & Atlantic management changed
"for the better, disaster will result."[9] In truth, Western & Atlantic
operations had steadily lost efficiency because of the lack of wood.
In accordance with past appropriation bills, the Georgia state legislature—by means of prearranged wood contracts with local timber-
harvesting firms—annually purchased thousands of dollars worth of
cordwood for use by the State Railroad. The legislature in 1861
alone appropriated $26,000 for the purchase of 14,000 cords of wood.
Because of the general wartime inflationary trend, however, the
price of cordwood rose each year. The Georgia legislature therefore
found itself progressively hard-pressed to keep Western & Atlantic
trains in regular operation. Moreover, the especially heavy demands
imposed on the State Railroad in the summer of 1863 for the maintenance of the Army of Tennessee nearly exhausted the wood supply for the entire year. Yet the Western & Atlantic managers had
contributed to the problem of scarcity by their earlier rejection of
wood contracts that, as the *Savannah Republican* charged, "any other
road in the State would have jumped at" in view of the favorable
terms and fair prices offered. Powerless to correct past corporate mis-
calculations, Governor Brown nevertheless dealt decisively with the
crisis: he called out the Georgia militia and ordered the troops to cut
wood for the Western & Atlantic Railroad.[10]

Forceful gubernatorial intervention thus enabled the Western &
Atlantic officials to maintain an adequate wood supply into the late
fall of 1863, but an acute shortage of locomotive fuel developed by
January 1864. For their part, the railroad managers struggled to ensure a sufficient supply of wood. The freight train locomotives that
steamed over the rugged, mountainous terrain between Atlanta and
Dalton traveled fewer miles per cord of wood than the engines that
moved over any other railroad in Georgia. The Western & Atlantic's
wood supply lay scattered along the entire hundred-mile stretch of

track between Atlanta and Dalton. The common practice required railroad officials to stack cordwood at the fourteen stations on the steeply inclined railroad line in northwest Georgia. Stationmasters were responsible for maintaining adequate reserves of locomotive fuel by either formally notifying the railroad officials of a dwindling supply of wood or by acting independently to replenish supplies. Pressed by other duties, they neglected to apprise Western & Atlantic managers of their rapidly diminishing fuel reserves late in 1863; and this, coupled with their failure to procure more wood by their own efforts, slowed train traffic to Dalton early in 1864. Consequently, by January 12, Johnston still did not recognize any appreciable improvement in the management of the Western & Atlantic. He again advised Governor Brown of the problem, informing him that quartermasters at Dalton complained of "great negligence in the management of the trains and great delay from want of fuel." In a message to President Davis, Johnston warned that "unless the management of the railroad from Atlanta is improved we shall be compelled to fall back" to Atlanta.[11]

Johnston's threat of a withdrawal of the Confederate army from Dalton dismayed Davis. The president immediately instructed Quartermaster General Lawton to advise Governor Brown of Johnston's complaints concerning defective railroad transportation in Georgia, while Lawton himself warned Brown that the "fate of Georgia may depend on that road" and an improvement in its military utilization. On January 17, Brown brusquely replied to Davis that "General Johnston's charge of want of efficiency in the management of the State road is without foundation" and declared that the War Department's previous impressment and diversion of Western & Atlantic rolling stock, exacerbated by a temporary deficiency of wood, accounted for the railroad's inability to supply the Army of Tennessee adequately. In this connection, Brown accused the government of having "taken from the State road" and "lost or destroyed on other roads over 200 cars and eight engines," and he demanded that the president promptly return the remaining equipment to Atlanta. Still seething, Brown also sharply rebuked Johnston, explaining that Western & Atlantic trains shipped to Dalton the forage and stores that Southwestern and Macon & Western trains had earlier transported to Atlanta. He flatly declared that the Western & Atlantic superintendent, John S. Rowland, had expressed the opinion that Johnston had been badly "misinformed" about the railroad officials' alleged mismanagement. Reproachfully, Brown added, "Your supplies at the time of the complaint went forward promptly as fast as delivered to us by connecting roads below" Atlanta, and that Western & Atlantic freight trains ran to Dalton on schedule.[12]

Rowland then resigned his position, apparently in protest against Johnston's charges, whereupon Brown quickly named George D. Phillips to succeed him. Acting decisively, although inadvisedly, Phillips, in an attempt to alleviate the scarcity of locomotive fuel, submitted a bold proposal to Johnston. He suggested "detailing men owning negroes, to cut wood for the use of the Rail Road," but Johnston prudently rejected the plan. Nevertheless, in carefully seeking to avoid controversy with Brown and the War Department over the question of forcing Georgia slaveholders to perform extraordinary military duty or impressing their slaves for railroad work to support Confederate operations, Johnston inadvertently prolonged the otherwise temporary shortage of wood. Then, in a message that compounded Johnston's frustration, Quartermaster General Lawton supported an argument of Governor Brown's original defense against Johnston's charges of railroad mismanagement. Late in January he explained to Johnston that although the Western & Atlantic's physical condition had indeed deteriorated as the war progressed—partly because of managerial neglect, but primarily because of heavy and constant use in support of Confederate armies in Virginia and Tennessee—the railroad's condition and efficiency still exceeded that of the Virginia Central Railroad that then continually struggled to supply Lee's Army of Northern Virginia.[13]

Brown's countercharges emphasized an important dimension of the whole issue of railroad mismanagement in Georgia: Confederate commanders could not attribute the difficulty entirely to civilian railroad officials. Rather, quartermaster agents at Atlanta and elsewhere in Georgia contributed heavily to the mismanagement of the railway supply traffic to Dalton, excluding the excellent service of Major John M. Hottle at Atlanta. Johnston, who initially considered the Western & Atlantic officials as those mainly to blame for the ineffective use of that railroad in supplying his army, early in January demanded Hottle's dismissal because of his alleged inefficiency. In seeking to dissuade Johnston, however, Lawton defended Hottle's record in handling military transportation and finally persuaded Johnston not to replace him. Yet both Johnston and Lawton otherwise underestimated the incompetence of the military management of railroad transportation in Georgia while exaggerating the degree of civilian mismanagement. A Confederate officer at Atlanta informed Major General Howell Cobb, also a former U.S. Senator from Georgia, that quartermaster agents at Atlanta and Dallas (possibly including Johnston's chief quartermaster, Lieutenant Colonel McMicken) bore heavy responsibility for the inefficient supplying of Johnston's army. The officer complained that Lawton's agents had allowed supply trains bound for Dalton to be detained at Atlanta for months because of their mishandling of railroad traffic and their inability to secure additional rolling stock from other Georgia railroads. Other reasons—including the government's use of engines and cars for cotton transportation in the Carolinas, the poor mechanical condition of Georgia rolling stock, and the shortage of railroad iron and skilled mechanics—complicated the operations of railroad managers and quartermasters in their efforts to supply the Confederate army at Dalton.[14]

Moreover, theft of supplies already loaded into freight cars at Atlanta contributed to the shortage of stores moving to Dalton. As late as April 1864, the Western & Atlantic superintendent Phillips complained to the War Department about the "constant losses by pillage" at Atlanta and urged that Johnston place guards on the freight trains. Quartermaster General Lawton advised Johnston of the problem early in May, recommending that Johnston assign military details to protect the supply trains to assist the railroad managers to "*prevent* such losses." Phillips sought assistance in vain. By April Johnston had drawn enough supplies from Atlanta to meet his army's needs for the coming spring campaign, and he took no extraordinary measures to protect exposed supplies. Previously, in Virginia and Mississippi, he had also neglected to provide military protection for freight trains; the rampant plundering in those states had provoked the protest of railroad officials and army quartermasters, who forwarded their complaints to the War Department.[15]

Notwithstanding the looting at Atlanta, Johnston continued to oversimplify his railroad problems and attribute railroad mismanagement almost exclusively to the alleged incompetence and negligence of Western & Atlantic officials. Indeed, he perceived other problems with Western & Atlantic management besides a scarcity of wood. Johnston therefore next attempted to alter the State Railroad's freight train schedules. Shortly after he sought Brown's and Davis's intervention for an immediate improvement in Western & Atlantic management, Johnston communicated with Major General Henry C. Wayne, Georgia's adjutant general and militia commander, about train schedules. Encouraging Wayne, then at Milledgeville, to prevail upon Governor Brown to change the schedules, Johnston complained that the railroad "seems to be entirely unmanaged. With abundant means it does not supply us." Further, Johnston rejected Brown's assertion that the railroad operated under competent management and criticized the railroad officials as "inefficient" while they "have produced and do not remedy this state of things." Johnston querulously wrote Wayne that "the chief commissary reports the average time of his train is thirty-six hours." Significantly, Johnston omitted a report by Chief Quartermaster McMicken, although the latter exercised principal responsibility for handling railroad transportation for Johnston. This limited use or deliberate neglect of McMicken apparently sprang from Johnston's preference for Major Barbour. Johnston had saved Barbour from dismissal in 1863 when Quartermaster General Lawton charged Barbour (correctly) with extravagance and inefficiency. Later, by early February 1864, Johnston succeeded in procuring Barbour's assignment to duty in Georgia. Barbour then superseded McMicken until recalled to Richmond in March for another official scrutiny of his accounts.[16]

Commissary chief Major William E. Moore's claim that Western & Atlantic freight trains consumed thirty-six hours (rather than the usual seven) in making the Atlanta and Dalton run was accurate, although obviously two conditions accounted for much of the delay. Western & Atlantic trains operated only during daylight hours, thus limiting the volume of freight train traffic on the railroad. Further delays caused by quartermaster agents at Atlanta increased the time that freight trains required for completion of the run to Dalton. Yet Johnston initially overlooked these important facts. Then, Wayne's failure to secure any improvement in Western & Atlantic management or change in its freight train schedules persuaded Johnston to suggest to Governor Brown the feasibility of establishing extended freight train schedules. He informed Brown on February 10 that one of his quartermasters, a man who had experience as "a railroad engineer," thought that the performance of the state railroad "might be greatly increased" by running freight trains at night. He also informed the governor that his quartermaster understood that the "trains from Dalton, after reaching Atlanta, remain there thirty-six hours, when twelve would be a sufficient time." In reply, Brown pleaded a labor shortage that prevented an acceleration of train traffic between Atlanta and Dalton and also precluded night operations.[17]

At this juncture, Johnston demonstrated his astonishingly inconsistent approach to the solution of railroad transportation problems. Having complained to Governor Brown and the Richmond authorities about Western & Atlantic mismanagement for much of January, Johnston suddenly concluded that the railroad officials had not caused, and therefore deserved no blame for, the supply shortages at Dalton. According to the *Atlanta Intelligencer,* Johnston discussed the problems of conducting the military supply traffic between Atlanta and Dalton with Superintendent Phillips after he failed to secure any railroad management improvement through Brown or Wayne. Impressed by Phillips's representations, Johnston "became satisfied that the State Road was not chargeable with the default attributed to it in the transportation of supplies, but that the default laid elsewhere." Johnston therefore identified a shortage of rolling stock on the Western & Atlantic as the fundamental cause of supply shortages at Dalton—a problem that he would increasingly address over the winter of 1864.

Johnston's abrupt reversal on the question of railroad mismanagement precipitated a sharp debate between two rival Georgia newspapers concerning the worsening supply crisis in northwest Georgia. The *Savannah Republican* accepted Johnston's carefully drawn distinction between the railroad's efficient management and its ineffective performance and, in frustrated exasperation, inquired, "Who is it that is starving out our army at Dalton?" Bluntly, the paper demanded to know the "name or names of the delinquent party" who continued to deprive the Army of Tennessee of necessary supplies. The *Macon Telegraph,* however, in depicting the *Republican* as an ill-informed accuser, admonished the *Republican* for "cocking his hat so fiercely over this business" of ineffective railroad transportation. Instead, the *Telegraph* blamed the "seriously crippled" Confederate transportation system as the ultimate source of the Army of Tennessee's supply crisis. The *Telegraph* identified several important contributions to the supply shortage: a lack of railroad iron, a deficiency of rolling stock and mechanical parts, large numbers of "rotting" crossties and defective stringers, and a shortage of railroad employees. The *Telegraph* advised the *Republican* to avoid "scolding about the inefficiency of the roads" and rather "urge upon Congress and

the government the necessity of remedial action." Unabashed at
these rebukes, the *Republican* continued to criticize the "very bad
order" of the Western & Atlantic and further accused it of having
diverted its "vast earnings of late years" into the Georgia "treasury
for political capital instead of being expended, in part, on repairs."
The Western & Atlantic had seriously failed, concluded the outspo-
ken *Republican*, to stockpile "crossties and fuel" for the task of supplying the Army of Tennessee.[18]

Whatever the Georgia editorial reaction to the railroad transportation crisis affecting the Army of Tennessee, and despite Governor
Brown's continued inaction on Johnston's specific proposals for
change, Brown succeeded in remedying the State Railroad's mismanagement. Johnston later recalled that the governor's "intervention"
in the middle of January produced a "better system" of forwarding
military supplies to Dalton. Besides ensuring an adequate reserve of
wood and water for freight train locomotives and promoting a cooperation between railroad officials and army quartermasters from Atlanta to Dalton, Brown secured from the War Department two
freight trains for operation on the Western & Atlantic Railroad. The
new supply trains and the more efficient joint efforts of railroad managers and army quartermasters swelled the volume of stores that
moved over the tracks to the Confederate army. Johnston, who had
previously denied that Western & Atlantic mismanagement caused
his supply problems, nevertheless advised President Davis on January 23 that the "management of the railroad is much improved since
my last letter; that is to say, we are much better supplied." On February 8, he assured Adjutant General Cooper that the "performance
of the railroads is greatly improved, especially that of the Western
and Atlantic." He found it necessary to add, however, "we do not
yet receive sufficient supplies of long forage to restore artillery
horses to the condition they lost on Missionary Ridge" in November
1863. Yet by early April even that shortage had disappeared, a favorable outcome encouraged in part by Johnston's sustained pressure on
Brown, but primarily because of Quartermaster General Lawton's
more effective and direct supervision of his agents in the Deep
South toward better supplying of Johnston's army and restoring its
field transportation.[19]

Johnston should have derived satisfaction from his efforts to improve the management of the Western & Atlantic Railroad. His persistent criticism of the State Railroad's mismanagement had forced

Governor Brown to take decisive measures to improve freight train service. Significantly, his conflict with Brown did not produce mutual antagonism or estrangement. Brown's belated cooperation with Johnston to improve the freight train service sprang from a self-serving motive: he sought to use Johnston as an ally against President Davis and the War Department to recover lost or diverted Western & Atlantic rolling stock. Indeed, Johnston's opposition to the Quartermaster Department's railway policy in Georgia would reflect and solidify their common effort to interfere with government cotton transportation traffic in the Carolinas in favor of State Railroad property and Confederate supply.

A second railroad matter that occupied Johnston's attention in the winter of 1864 concerned the shortage of rolling stock on Georgia's railways, a difficulty that he incorrectly perceived as the principal cause of his supply problems at Dalton. His efforts to secure more engines and cars for supply traffic to Atlanta and Dalton plunged him into controversy with the Richmond authorities. Johnston's first conflict with the War Department sprang from his defiant opposition to the Quartermaster Department's railway policy in Georgia, specifically that concerning the Wilmington cotton traffic. To pay for equipment for its armies, the Confederate Congress had authorized the Quartermaster Department to impress hundreds of thousands of bales of cotton throughout the South and transport them over the railroads to the Confederacy's seaports. The Richmond government vigorously promoted blockade-running and shipped to European ports enormous quantities of the cotton. In Europe, Confederate agents exchanged cotton for armaments and munitions. The Union navy's increasingly tighter blockade of Confederate seaports, however, drastically reduced blockade-running by late 1863. Largely restricted to a few Eastern ports, the War Department nevertheless continued the cotton trade with Europe chiefly through Wilmington, North Carolina, where blockade-running peaked in December 1863.[20]

The Quartermaster Department's impressment of Central of Georgia rolling stock for employment in the Wilmington cotton traffic formed the background of the controversy that developed between Johnston and Quartermaster General Lawton. Shortly after his arrival at Dalton, Johnston instructed Major Moore, chief commissary of subsistence for the Army of Tennessee, to submit a report on the general supply situation in Georgia and Florida, particularly

regarding the prospects of supplying the Confederate army over the
winter of 1864. Moore referred the matter to Major James F. Cummings, a Commissary Department agent, because Cummings had
had much experience as a collections agent in those states. Indeed,
late in 1863 he accumulated a considerable quantity of stores and
collected a large number of beef cattle at Albany, Macon, and
Atlanta. Moore forwarded Cummings's report to Dalton early in
January 1864. From that report, Johnston learned that the railroads
below Atlanta lacked a sufficient quantity of rolling stock. Previously, Cummings explained, he and his assistants found their "troubles" aggravated by quartermaster agents who appropriated many
engines and cars for the "transportation of Government cotton to
Wilmington."[21]

Failing to verify Cummings's information, Johnston exaggerated
the commissary agent's estimate of the quantity of railroad equipment commandeered in central and southern Georgia by also including rolling stock presumably removed from eastern and northern
Georgia railroads. On January 9, he explained to President Davis
that the "difficulty in supplying us comes from the employment of a
large number of cars in transporting Government cotton to Wilmington," while the diversion of an excessive quantity of Georgia rolling
stock to the railroads leading to Wilmington rendered it "difficult to
furnish daily rations" to the troops at Dalton. Davis immediately addressed the matter by ordering Quartermaster General Lawton to
submit a report on the Quartermaster Department's employment of
Georgia rolling stock in the Wilmington cotton traffic. Lawton
promptly conducted his own investigation and assured the president
that "only a portion" of Georgia's rolling stock regularly carried
government cotton to Wilmington. Then, on January 21, Lawton
denied Johnston's charges, asserting: "I am satisfied your army is
at this time better served with rolling stock than any other in
the Confederacy."[22]

Johnston, however, remained unconvinced that the War Department bore no responsibility for the reportedly severe shortage of
rolling stock operating upon the Georgia railroads. Governor Brown
soon furnished him with additional reason to dispute Lawton's claim.
Earlier, in the winter of 1862, Brown had offered Western & Atlantic
rolling stock to several railroad firms in Tennessee to support
Confederate military operations in that state. Although much of the
State Railroad's equipment safely returned to Georgia after the

evacuation of Nashville, Confederate quartermasters subsequently removed a large number of Western & Atlantic freight cars over the Mobile & Ohio Railroad into Mississippi during the evacuation of Corinth in April 1862. Thereafter, Bragg's retreat from Tullahoma in the summer of 1863 resulted in the displacement of other Western & Atlantic cars west of Huntsville, Alabama, on the Memphis & Charleston Railroad. Because of these repeated losses, in the fall of 1863 Brown strongly protested the Richmond government's continuing failure to indemnify the state of Georgia for the missing or destroyed Western & Atlantic property. Moreover, Bragg's retreat from Tullahoma to Chattanooga in the summer of 1863 resulted in the displacement of a considerable quantity of Tennessee rolling stock. Five Nashville & Chattanooga and East Tennessee & Georgia freight trains escaped Federal raiders by moving over the Western & Atlantic Railroad into Georgia. Brown, seizing the opportunity to use that equipment on the Western & Atlantic line in view of the War Department's failure or unwillingness to compensate the State Railroad for its loss of rolling stock, directed that the Tennessee freight trains be brought to Atlanta pending the safe return of the trains to Chattanooga and Knoxville.

Subsequently, though, quartermaster agents commandeered the displaced Tennessee railroad equipment and began employing the trains in the Wilmington cotton traffic. When apprised of this action in January 1864, Brown appealed to Johnston for assistance in locating and restoring the five trains to Western & Atlantic custody. In response, Johnston sent quartermasters to Savannah and Charleston to locate the Tennessee freight trains. On January 25, he informed Brown that the five trains ran east of the Savannah River and operated under the control of the War Department but that he had already "requested the Quartermaster-General to have them returned without delay." Lawton, however, rejected Johnston's request, an act doubtlessly reflecting his belief that the War Department had the right to impress and employ displaced rolling stock for its own military purposes anywhere in the Confederacy. Johnston's failure to recover the Tennessee rolling stock through Lawton persuaded him to approach General Beauregard, his former comrade in northern Virginia. Beauregard, from his headquarters at Charleston, commanded the Department of South Carolina, Georgia, and Florida, and he himself employed Central of Georgia engines and cars for the transportation of government cotton from Charleston to Wilmington.

From reports that his quartermasters submitted to him about the operation of the Tennessee freight trains east of the Savannah River, Johnston discovered the full extent of Beauregard's cooperation with quartermaster agents at Charleston in conducting the Wilmington cotton traffic. On February 8, he therefore requested Beauregard to "permit rolling-stock of the Savannah and Macon road to be used to bring much-needed supplies from Macon" to Dalton. Beauregard agreed to divert rolling stock to the Western & Atlantic Railroad for supplying Johnston's army. Dutifully, however, he notified Major General Gilmer of the Engineer Bureau of his action, apparently expecting Gilmer to inform Lawton of the diversion.[23]

Despite Brown's assistance, Johnston's efforts to place more rolling stock on the Georgia railroads for employment in the supply traffic to Atlanta and Dalton showed serious errors in judgment. Understandably, he sought to secure more railroad equipment to increase the number of supply trains running to Dalton. Yet he mistakenly accused the Quartermaster Department of having conducted a wholesale removal of Georgia rolling stock for use in the Wilmington cotton traffic. His cotton traffic charge also evidenced a remarkable ignorance about the military significance of that traffic, the enormous importance of the Confederacy's cotton trade with Europe for the equipping of Confederate armies, including the Army of Tennessee. Clearly, Johnston's implied charge that the Quartermaster Department illegally employed Tennessee railroad equipment in the cotton traffic showed an inaccurate interpretation of War Department railway policy. He ignored the government's right, especially in case of military necessity, to employ displaced rolling stock anywhere in the South and for whatever purposes defined by the War Department. Johnston erred concerning another matter. Contrary to his belief, the Central of Georgia Railroad equipment that Beauregard's quartermasters and Lawton's agents employed along the Atlantic coast formed only a small portion of the total quantity of rolling stock then operating in Georgia.

The controversy over the allegedly severe deficiency of rolling stock on the Georgia railways increasingly revolved around the Western & Atlantic's reported shortages of engines and cars. Johnston's determination to place a greater quantity of rolling stock on the Western & Atlantic Railroad induced him to offer his services to Governor Brown for the relocation and restoration or replacement of the State Railroad's lost and destroyed property. He fulfilled his pledge in the middle of January when he sent Major Goodwin, formerly Bragg's and more recently his own military superintendent of railroads, to Mississippi to search for those missing Western & Atlantic cars presumably operating on the Mobile & Ohio Railroad. By early February Goodwin had found on the railroad, and brought south to Mobile, twenty-five Western & Atlantic cars; he then ordered the cars sent north to Blue Mountain, from which point teams of draft animals hauled the cars across northeast Alabama to the Western & Atlantic spur line terminal at Rome, Georgia. Despite his success, Johnston should have felt some guilt or regret when the State Railroad cars reached Atlanta and joined freight trains in the supply traffic to Dalton. His inaction in the matter of recovering rolling stock in the summer of 1863, justified in part by his view that Mississippi-based locomotives and cars could never reach the East because of the trackless gaps in Alabama's railway system, resulted in the costly loss of railroad equipment around Grenada.[24]

The recovery of the Western & Atlantic freight cars encouraged Johnston to attempt to secure the placement of still more rolling stock on the State Railroad. He thereupon assumed the role of advocate for Governor Brown against President Davis in the dispute over the government's alleged responsibility for the displacement or destruction of Western & Atlantic property. Johnston's preoccupation in January with the issue of railroad mismanagement prevented him from actively supporting Brown's case against the government. The marked improvement of the State Railroad's freight train service early in February, though, provided him with an opportunity to intervene in behalf of the Georgia governor. On February 10, Brown belatedly acknowledged Johnston's letter of January 5 that had pledged Johnston's intervention for the prompt restoration of displaced Western & Atlantic equipment. The governor expressed his gratitude for Johnston's "offer to do all in your power to have part of our Engines and Cars returned to the Road." Yet Johnston, entirely ignorant of the running controversy between Brown and the Confederate government, allowed the Georgia governor to perpetrate an outrageous deception upon him.[25]

Ironically, the War Department had already discovered the extent of Brown's exploitation of Johnston's credulity. Stung by Johnston's criticism of the Quartermaster Department's allocation of rolling stock for the Wilmington cotton traffic, in mid-January Quartermaster General Lawton ordered Lieutenant Colonel Sims, the Railroad

Bureau chief and a former Georgia railroad executive, to investigate the Western & Atlantic Railroad's alleged shortage of rolling stock. Promptly, Sims communicated with the East Tennessee & Georgia Railroad president Campbell B. Wallace and sought this close friend's views on the transportation question in Georgia. Wallace and his son Charles, the general superintendent of the East Tennessee & Georgia, operated a "Refugee Office" in Athens, Georgia, and established company headquarters and shop facilities in Augusta. The two men and their employees maintained a substantially reduced fleet of rolling stock on the Georgia Railroad between Athens and Augusta, besides permitting the War Department to use four of their trains in the Wilmington cotton traffic. In replying to Sims, Wallace criticized the Western & Atlantic Railroad officials and Johnston's subordinates, while he strongly suggested that economic expediency motivated the Western & Atlantic managers in their search for additional rolling stock. Specifically, Wallace advised Sims that Johnston's army at Dalton required only fifty to sixty carloads of supplies each day, or only three trains. He further explained that the Western & Atlantic Railroad—a company that operated upward of sixty engines and seven hundred cars at the start of the war—had since 1861 lost some cars "*but not an Engine*," while the state-owned railroad also maintained superior machine shop facilities between Atlanta and Dalton.[26]

Indignantly, Wallace complained that, despite their abundance of rolling stock, State Railroad officials continued to "cry out for help" and to call upon him for engines but that he refused to entrust them with his property. Charging that the Western & Atlantic officials sought to protect their rolling stock from hard use by employing East Tennessee & Georgia equipment, Wallace warned that "if Genl Johnson yeilds [*sic*] to their trickery and impresses ours it will be a hard day for his army before he succeeds." Wallace refrained, however, from accusing Governor Brown of encouraging a fraudulent appropriation of East Tennessee & Georgia property. He informed Sims that Brown had earlier advised E. B. Walker, the Western & Atlantic's master of transportation, that Johnston's army *"has to be supplied and that the W & A R Rd has the work to do at all Hazards,"* a prompting that Wallace believed would discourage further attempted encroachments upon his property. Besides censuring the Western & Atlantic officials, Wallace also criticized Johnston's interference with the Wilmington cotton traffic and his arbitrary impressment of East Tennessee & Georgia rolling stock. Wallace advised Sims that in mid-January Major Cummings, Johnston's commissary chief, arrived in Augusta and "demanded seven of my Engines to run for Govt. west of Atlanta." Cummings commandeered the East Tennessee & Georgia equipment, Wallace complained, even though "Macon & Western trains [are] running east of Augusta and when the Central Road (over of the So Western) has stock in abundance standing idle." Wallace declared that "there is something wrong in Rail Road matters" in Georgia, but that he intended to defend vigilantly East Tennessee & Georgia interests.[27]

After studying Wallace's letter and on completing his investigation of the alleged diversion of Western & Atlantic rolling stock to other railroads in the Deep South, Sims reported to Lawton on January 29 that "I am compelled to think His Excellency is laboring under great apprehension in regard to this loss" of equipment and that Brown erred "in supposing this road incapable of supplying General Johnston's army." Sims assured Lawton on February 9 that Western & Atlantic officials possessed "plenty of cars" if any "degree of energy is exhibited in loading and unloading and moving them promptly." Moreover, unknown to the governor, the War Department also learned that late in 1863 Brown had contracted with A. K. Seago and Palmer Company, an Atlanta-based saltworks firm, to supply Georgia with salt. The contract had required Brown to put a heavy locomotive (the Texas) and eight freight cars on the railroads between Richmond and Atlanta in order to ship Virginia salt to Georgia—a diversion of rolling stock that Brown never revealed to Johnston or to the War Department.

Having clear and convincing evidence of Brown's duplicity and Johnston's gullibility, Lawton referred Sims's reports to President Davis, giving him cogent evidence with which to deny Brown's extravagant claims for indemnification. In a serious miscalculation, on February 20 Johnston rashly widened the breach, petitioning Davis to "order the restoration" to the Western & Atlantic Railroad of the "engines and cars taken from it by officers of the Confederate Government." Davis spurned Johnston's petition. He instructed Adjutant General Cooper to require Johnston to show "when, where, and by whom the rolling stock was taken, the amount, and the authority under which it was done," and, if Johnston could determine its location, "let that fact also be communicated."[28] Cooper's message of February 23 persuaded Johnston to stop supporting Governor Brown and to avoid antagonizing Davis further over the vexed question of the Confederate government's responsibility for a shortage of rolling stock on the State Railroad. It probably struck Davis that Johnston's blatant partisan alliance with Brown against the government to secure more equipment for the Western & Atlantic represented renewed insubordination, especially in view of Johnston's earlier refusal to cooperate with the War Department authorities or with Mississippi railroad officials for the removal of irreplaceable rolling stock from Grenada.

The Western & Atlantic's unwillingness to employ more of its railroad equipment complicated the Army of Tennessee's supply problems beyond the shortage of forage for the army's horses and mules. The shipment of cattle from Atlanta to Dalton substantially reduced the volume of stores that moved over the Western & Atlantic to the Confederate army early in January. In preceding years Confederate quartermasters had transported cattle by railroad a good deal. In the fall of 1862, Confederate troops in Virginia and Tennessee exhausted the supply of beef produced in the Carolinas, Kentucky, and Tennessee. The disappearance of that source of meat forced the Commissary Department to exploit other sources of beef in Florida and Texas. Since the Southern railroads so laboriously and constantly transported Confederate troops and armaments, the department made arrangements in 1862 and 1863 to "bring cattle from those states and put them on the grass lands of Virginia and Tennessee." Such efforts soon demonstrated, however, the impracticability of long cattle drives across the South and compelled the department to abandon further attempts because of a "want of good grass" in different regions of the Confederacy. Moreover, the Federal reduction of Vicksburg and Port Hudson and the earlier interdiction of the Red River supply route cut Rebel armies off from the Confederacy's trans-Mississippi cattle supply. Thus, Florida provided the Commissary Department with its last major source of beef after the summer of 1863. Even earlier, though, beginning in 1862, commissary agents annually purchased 25,000 head of cattle and shipped the beeves over Florida railroads to the Atlantic & Gulf spur line on the Georgia and Florida border. The agents also hired drivers to move the cattle overland from stations on the Pensacola & Georgia to Thomasville and Albany. From the Thomasville railhead, quartermaster agents transported the beeves over the Atlantic & Gulf, the Savannah, Albany & Gulf, and other Atlantic coastal railroads to the Army of

Northern Virginia. Farther north, from Albany, Lawton's agents shipped other cattle to the Army of Tennessee over the Southwestern, Macon & Western, and the Western & Atlantic railroads.[29]

Commissary agents purchased so many Florida beeves after the fall of 1862, however, that by the end of 1863 they had virtually depleted the state's cattle supply. At this point, Major Cummings's report of January 1864 informed Johnston of the increasingly serious cattle shortage in Florida. Cummings pointed out that he had directed the driving of "large numbers of beef cattle" from Florida to Atlanta, but that the remaining supply fell considerably short of his needs for 1864. He also reported that the "people in Florida complain that cattle are becoming scarce" while "few more beeves can be expected until next summer." Cummings further informed Johnston that what few "poor" cattle remained in Florida would surely perish if driven north to Atlanta "as the grazing season is past" and "pasturage and forage so scant on the long route to this place that they could not be driven." Cummings neglected to advise Johnston, however, that although he had supervised the driving of hundreds of beeves to Atlanta, he had left a considerable number of cattle at Albany and Macon for shipment to Atlanta. The Southwestern and Macon & Western officials transported the beeves to Atlanta in stock cars. Since the Western & Atlantic Railroad lacked stock cars and because Governor Brown had no authority to transfer privately owned rolling stock onto the State Railroad, quartermaster agents at Atlanta employed Western & Atlantic boxcars to forward the cattle to Dalton. The shipment of cattle to Dalton in boxcars, coupled with the State Railroad's unwillingness to employ more rolling stock early in January, considerably reduced the Western & Atlantic's ability to transport stores to the Army of Tennessee.[30]

Johnston should have viewed the unloading of beef cattle at Dalton early in January 1864 with approval. He had observed the operation of a completely different system of supplying Confederate troops with beef at Chattanooga in February 1863. At that time commissary agents slaughtered cattle at Atlanta and Chattanooga, pickled the cuts in brine, and then shipped and distributed the preserved meat to the Army of Tennessee at Tullahoma. Johnston firmly opposed that system as a waste of meat. He complained to Secretary of War Seddon on February 25 that "our troops have not the means of boiling meat, and therefore throw away the greater part of this except when pressed by hunger." He also warned Seddon that the "Commissary Department continues to salt beef here. Beef salted after this will not be saved." His complaints and threats resulted in the adoption of a different system of supplying Army of Tennessee troops with meat. Johnston's departure from Tennessee for Mississippi early in May 1863 prevented him from observing the implementation of that system. The Commissary Department halted butchering and brining operations at Atlanta and Chattanooga, and quartermaster agents instead transported Florida cattle over the railroads from Albany and Macon to Tullahoma.[31]

Despite his earlier recommendation for transporting cattle by rail, ironically, Johnston expressed his later opinion of the shipment of cattle from Atlanta to Dalton in contrary and querulous terms. On January 2, he complained to President Davis that the "practice of transporting beef cattle by railroad has made it impossible to accumulate stores here." He declared to Davis his intention "to have the cattle driven, but the change will require time." Johnston scarcely considered the impracticability of cattle drives from Atlanta to Dalton. Although he received Major Cummings's cattle supply report several days later, a report that referred to the scarcity of grass between Florida and Atlanta, he should have known that the hundred-mile stretch of mountainous and pine-forested country between Atlanta and Dalton lacked sufficient grass for the continued fattening or even bare subsistence of hundreds of beeves amidst a harsh winter in northwest Georgia.[32]

Johnston's preoccupation with Western & Atlantic mismanagement prevented him from implementing his cattle drive scheme early in January, but the continuation of the Quartermaster Department's system of transporting cattle to Dalton by rail finally exhausted his patience. In preparing to introduce change, he reluctantly communicated with Commissary General Northrop, the man whom he held responsible for his difficult logistical problems in northern and central Virginia in 1861 and 1862. Despite his hostility toward Northrop, on January 6 Johnston advised him that "our beeves are very lean, so that the ration, three-fourths of a pound, gives very little meat." Northrop quickly replied that "the meat ration under the present exigencies must obtain everywhere in the Confederate States this side of Mississippi River." Dissatisfied, on January 14 Johnston again complained to Northrop that "our beeves are brought long distances in cars, losing flesh and health," and he suggested that "they be butchered when driven to the railroad." He pointed out that a cattle slaughter at Atlanta "would save three fifths in transportation and much in the quality of meat. Transportation is a very serious question." Johnston apparently based his charges on the complaints of commissary officers at Dalton that quartermasters kept the animals aboard boxcars on the railroad between Atlanta and Dalton for four or five days without providing the beeves with food or water. In urging a change in Commissary Department policy in Georgia, Johnston reversed his previous position on the slaughtering of cattle at Atlanta. He recognized that the necessity of supplying the army had turned fresh beef from ordinary fare into a luxury. Unfortunately, the unsavory taste and inedible condition of the pickled beef that nauseated Bragg's soldiers in February 1863 would soon provoke complaint and waste among the troops at Dalton.[33]

The proposal that commissary agents slaughter cattle at Atlanta sprang from Johnston's recollection of the same method that Northrop's agents so efficiently practiced in Atlanta during the winter of 1863. Atlanta offered those agents extensive facilities for butchering and brining Florida cattle. Georgia, like most of the other seceded Southern states, struggled from the outbreak of the war to maintain an adequate supply of salt for public consumption. Indeed, Governor Brown contracted with A. K. Seago and Palmer Company of Atlanta in 1863 to ship Virginia salt to Atlanta by using Western & Atlantic rolling stock. The railroads that radiated from Atlanta enabled the Seago and Palmer firm to distribute salt throughout the state, and the railways established Atlanta as Georgia's principal salt depot. Confederate War Department commissary agents at Atlanta also purchased large quantities of salt from Seago and Palmer; they usually bought one and a quarter bushels of salt to preserve a freshly butchered five-hundred-pound steer or cow.[34] In any event, Johnston's proposal to butcher cattle at Atlanta reflected a continuation or renewal of past practice.

Meanwhile, as Commissary General Northrop prepared orders for the resumption of butchering at Atlanta, Johnston received Governor Brown's letter of January 16 that denied his charges of Western & Atlantic mismanagement. Brown's missive also contained information about the cattle transportation question, informing Johnston that Superintendent Rowland could not have shipped larger numbers of cattle from Atlanta to Dalton over the Western & Atlantic early in January because he, Rowland, lacked stock cars to carry more of the beeves to the Confederate army. Brown suggested that, if Johnston would "impress a few stock cars from some of the roads below Atlanta and place them on the State Road," it would greatly "facilitate the business" of shipping cattle to Dalton. Brown's letter explained to Johnston why Rowland permitted quartermaster agents to employ boxcars for the transportation of cattle to Dalton, as well as why the beeves reached the Confederate army in such an emaciated condition. More important, Brown's proposal for an impressment of Southwestern and Macon & Western stock cars presented Johnston with a serious dilemma: he could either risk violating the War Department's punctiliously observed railway policy by arbitrarily seizing stock cars and yet increase the numbers of possibly healthier cattle shipped to Dalton, or else pursue his contemplated policy of having the cattle slaughtered at Atlanta and risk encouraging the waste of meat by his own troops. He decided he could not order the impressment of privately owned rolling stock without express authorization from the War Department. In this regard, Johnston prudently avoided infringing on the commercial rights and interfering with the carrying trade of the railway firms or invoking a doubtful military necessity to justify appropriation of private property. Yet he should have more carefully weighed the practical considerations in favor of Brown's plan.[35]

Despite its raising the possibility of controversy over an unwarranted military seizure of stock cars, Brown's proposal for the impressment and employment of that equipment presented Johnston with an otherwise effective solution to his cattle transportation problem. The operation of stock cars on the Western & Atlantic would have freed a number of the State Railroad's boxcars for use in transporting stores and forage to Dalton. The employment of stock cars would also have ensured a more balanced flow of cattle and stores over the tracks to the Confederate army. From studying Brown's letter, Johnston should have realized that numbers of beeves still remained in Atlanta stockyards steadily losing condition. A thirty-six-hour train trip from Atlanta to Dalton could not have appreciably attenuated a fully fattened cow or steer. Clearly, Johnston could not have expected Western & Atlantic officials to assume responsibility for the subsistence and growth of feeder cattle. Brown gave Johnston another seemingly compelling reason to order an immediate impressment of stock cars. He tried to dissuade Johnston from attempting a series of cattle drives. The governor drew Johnston's attention to the rugged terrain of northwest Georgia and expressed the well-founded apprehension that Johnston's commissary officers would not "find it easy to procure food for them [beeves] on the way through the country from Atlanta to Dalton." Ignoring Brown's counsel, however, Johnston prepared to execute his plan.[36]

Johnston's decision not to implement Governor Brown's impressment proposal coincided with the recommencement of the butchering operations at Atlanta. Commissary General Northrop, an ardent supporter of President Davis and a bitter enemy of Johnston, perhaps derived satisfaction in complying with Johnston's request for the resumption of cattle butchering operations at Atlanta—operations that Northrop had originally initiated and continued until Johnston's and Bragg's complaints to the War Department resulted in their suspension. Thereafter, commissary agents resumed slaughtering cattle at Atlanta and practiced the usual method of saline preservation when they "cut up [the beeves] & put [them] in barrels of very salt brine" before quartermaster agents shipped the pickled beef to Dalton in boxcars. Then, on January 25, Johnston replied to Governor Brown's letter of January 16 and stated his settled views on the cattle transportation question. He refused to impress stock cars for employment on the Western & Atlantic Railroad and instead defended the reasoning of his originally proposed, albeit untested, scheme that commissary officers direct the driving of beeves to Dalton. He informed the governor that, as a result of his success in having the cattle butchered at Atlanta, he had "partially succeeded in relieving the road of their transportation," adding that the slaughtering operations at Atlanta permitted Lawton's agents "to transport in two cars an amount of beef that before required five."[37]

The butchering operations at Atlanta so strongly recommended by Johnston undoubtedly had immediate advantages. The slaughter of the cattle preserved what edible flesh the beeves still retained after their long drive from Florida and their confinement at Atlanta pending shipment to Dalton. The butchering operations also eliminated the prolonged hunger and thirst that impaired the condition of the cattle transported to Dalton in boxcars early in January. Moreover, Johnston recognized that the War Department would, at most, have provided him with temporary and strictly limited authorization for an impressment of stock cars, in view of his opposition to the Quartermaster Department's appropriating Georgia rolling stock for the equally important Wilmington cotton traffic. Yet, Johnston's decision against Brown's impressment proposal entailed adverse consequences. The rancid taste and inferior quality of the pickled beef that revolted Bragg's troops in February 1863 created pervasive dissatisfaction in Army of Tennessee ranks around Dalton in January 1864. Indeed, one private grumbled over the foul "blue beef" ration that commissary officers irregularly issued to the troops. The soldier confided to his journal that "I fear the cattle came near starving to death before they were slaughtered" at Atlanta. For want of the necessary cooking utensils, he found the meat "so poor and tough."[38] The shipment of cattle to Dalton in stock cars might have brought leaner beeves to the Confederate army, but their arrival by rail would have furnished the troops with fresh and palatable beef.

Furthermore, Johnston requested Northrop to order the butchering of beeves in Georgia without knowing how many head of cattle still remained at Atlanta. He apparently believed that the beeves crowded Atlanta's stockyards. Johnston perhaps expressed surprise when informed late in January that commissary agents had completed the butchering and brining operations. On February 1, he advised President Davis that Major Cummings reported that he could "procure no meat but a thousand cattle promised from Mississippi. This army has no country to supply it." He noted that when Cummings depleted the Mississippi cattle supply, the Army of Tennessee would "have to depend for meat, which Southern men think a necessary of life, upon an exhausted country, the mountainous part of Georgia and Alabama." Johnston exaggerated the gravity of the supply situation. In mid-January he had publicly commended a meat-packing firm in Georgia for selling 50,000 pounds of bacon to Confederate commissary agents at Dalton at half the regular price, while the company sold another 25,000 pounds of bacon at the lower price in February. The purchases alleviated the meat shortage considerably, whatever the problems of transporting beef by rail. Then, early in February, Lieutenant General Polk in Mississippi sent to Georgia the thousand head of cattle that Cummings had designated for Johnston's army. Polk authorized a commissary officer at Columbus, Mississippi, to "impress fifteen (15) negroes to drive beeves to Atlanta, the negroes to be returned to their owners as soon as this work is accomplished."[39] Ultimately, the ability to transport beef proved less important than the lack of supply, although the supply crisis steadily abated and Johnston increasingly turned his attention to developing strategic plans for repelling a threatened deeper Union invasion of northwest Georgia.

Johnston's disputes with Governor Brown and the Richmond authorities resulted from his more direct, though still fundamentally inconsistent, approach to railroad problems over the winter of 1864. Fortunately, his initial conflict with Brown over the issue of Western & Atlantic mismanagement led to the formation of a strong alliance between him and Brown that produced a substantial improvement in the State Railroad's freight train service, even if Johnston's actions alienated Western & Atlantic superintendent Rowland and East Tennessee & Georgia officials. Suppressing his hostility and opposition after President Davis defeated his and Brown's attempts to interfere with Confederate railway policy, Johnston thereafter communicated more fully with the War Department authorities, particularly with Lawton and Northrop, for steadily more effective utilization of the Georgia railroads. His cooperation scarcely sprang from a growing sense of soldierly duty or submission to superior authority; it reflected a belated recognition of the Army of Tennessee's increasing dependence on the railroad and expressed his need for the War Department's assistance in solving his railroad problems. In this regard, the Army of Tennessee's acute supply problems in the winter of 1864 finally forced Johnston to deal more directly with railroad transportation questions, while he also more effectively used quartermasters, commissary officers, and a military superintendent of railroads to overcome his difficulties with rail transport. Johnston seriously erred, however, by mixing politics with logistics in Georgia. His cooperation with Brown brought pressure on the War Department to send additional rolling stock to Atlanta, but the forced diversion of that equipment to Georgia further strained relations among President Davis, Governor Brown, and Johnston. Rivalry and acrimony notwithstanding, Johnston finally ceased quarreling with Brown and the Richmond authorities and prepared to use the Western & Atlantic Railroad to help defend Atlanta from Federal attack and capture.

··{5}··

The Atlanta Campaign

THROUGHOUT the winter of 1864 Johnston succeeded in rebuilding the Army of Tennessee by a generally effective use of the Georgia railroads. His achievement showed significant growth in his ability to manage railroad transportation for purposes of Confederate supply, as compared to his frequently incompetent use of the Virginia, Tennessee, and Mississippi railroads to feed and equip his troops. Johnston's grateful troops praised their commander's efforts. A Confederate officer advised Lawton late in April that "Genl Johnson [*sic*] has performed wonders with the soldiers, we seem almost a new creation and firmly believe we will be successful in the next fight." Another Rebel commander agreed, assuring a fellow officer in South Carolina that "Genl Johnston has the confidence of the whole army and they are willing to follow him any where."[1] Notwithstanding the solution of his most difficult problems in utilizing the Western & Atlantic Railroad and the increased confidence of his army at Dalton, Johnston recognized that he would encounter serious problems in using that railroad to defend Atlanta against an anticipated deeper Federal invasion of northwest Georgia. In foreseeing the strategic as well as the logistical importance of the Western & Atlantic Railroad in the coming campaign, Johnston demonstrated dramatic, though still sporadic and erratic, improvement in his military use of railroads and railroad equipment.

Reflecting his growing understanding and ability and his continued limitations, Johnston late in February employed Western & Atlantic rolling stock to transport three thousand Army of Tennessee troops from Dalton to West Point on the Georgia and Alabama border. This marked the first step in his effort to reinforce Polk's command in the Department of Alabama, Mississippi, and East Louisiana. In executing the operation, however, Johnston failed to order his quartermasters to coordinate advance transportation arrangements with railroad officials and with Colonel Moses H. Wright, the commanding officer of Confederate troops at Atlanta. Wright, to whom Johnston had assigned the duty of forwarding Confederate forces from Dalton to West Point, on February 20 sought Johnston's authorization to ship the troops directly from Atlanta to West Point aboard Western & Atlantic cars to avoid the delay of a transfer of soldiers to Atlanta & West Point cars. Wright complained to Johnston's chief of staff, Brigadier General William W. Mackall, that "conflicting instructions come to different agents" while the Western & Atlantic's principal agent refused "to allow the cars to pass through [Atlanta] without the Genl.['s] approval, for fear he might fall short of demands made on his road." Johnston, who (ironically also on February 20) complained to President Davis about a shortage of rolling stock on the State Railroad, authorized the direct transportation of troops from Dalton to West Point via Atlanta, the soldiers traveling aboard Western & Atlantic cars on Atlanta & West Point tracks. Consequently, on February 22 Wright, in Atlanta, assured Mackall that "everything moves on firmly—No delay here."[2] Commendably, Johnston promptly reinforced Polk by employing Western & Atlantic rolling stock to transport troops over two different Georgia railroads to West Point, although he understood that his action would temporarily impede the supply traffic between Atlanta and Dalton. In achieving this limited strategic objective, however, Johnston also demonstrated that he indeed commanded a sufficient quantity of rolling stock to support his army from its rearward base at Atlanta, notwithstanding his and Brown's assertions to the contrary.

Although Johnston recognized the abundance of rolling stock operating in the rear of his army at Dalton, he addressed the problem of an insufficiency of railway equipment running on the railroads in front of his forces in northwest Georgia. His appreciation of this difficulty sprang from his formulation of strategic plans for the coming spring campaign against Sherman's army northwest of Dalton. Toward late March 1864, Johnston considered the possibility of launching offensive operations against Union forces at Knoxville or Chattanooga. He recognized, however, that he would have to return locomotives and cars to the East Tennessee & Georgia Railroad, despite the threat of Federal cavalry raids on the equipment, to support Confederate operations north of Dalton. Consequently, as East Tennessee & Georgia president Wallace advised Lieutenant Colonel Sims (rather querulously, in view of Johnston's arbitrary impressment of his property in January), "now we are ordered by Genl Johnson [sic] to send a portion of our stock to Dalton to be used in East Tennessee."[3] Subsequently, though, Johnston abandoned his partially formed plans to undertake offensive campaigning in East Tennessee and kept Wallace's equipment in reserve in Georgia.

More important, Johnston's successful effort to secure replacement bridges to carry the Western & Atlantic line over broad rivers in northwest Georgia also illustrated his definite, albeit unsteady, growth in understanding the military uses of the railroad. He sought to have the War Department assist him in accumulating duplicate trestles to replace those that Federal cavalry or Confederate troops might damage or destroy during operations between Chattanooga and Atlanta. Johnston offered an imaginative, though certainly not an unprecedented, proposal. Unlike Union armies that usually included an auxiliary railroad reconstruction corps, Confederate armies depended principally upon the War Department's Engineer Bureau for the reconstruction of railroads and bridges in different theaters of the war. Previously, in December 1863, the Confederate Congress required the formation of a pioneer company for each division within the several Confederate armies, and Johnston ordered the formation of such a unit in the Confederate army in Mississippi before his assignment to Georgia. Yet Bragg failed to create pioneer companies within the Army of Tennessee before his resignation from command, and Johnston, preoccupied with problems of railway supply, thereafter neglected to form such companies in the Confederate army at Dalton, choosing instead to use Engineer Corps officers stationed at Dalton and Atlanta and the army engineers who served on his staff to supervise railroad reconstruction work. Consequently, Johnston belatedly sought a large quantity of prefabricated bridge apparatus from the War Department to compensate for his earlier failure to create and equip a mobile railroad reconstruction force in Georgia.

Indeed, apparently chagrined over his egregious failures to provide prompt, effective military assistance to railroad officials in their efforts to repair strategically important railroad bridges in Tennessee, Mississippi, and Alabama in 1863, Johnston decided in the spring of 1864 to procure duplicate bridges for the Western & Atlantic.

This would avoid delays in transporting supplies or troops between Atlanta and Dalton as well as save whatever rolling stock that Federal cavalry attacks on railroad bridges might isolate behind the Confederate lines. Therefore, in contrast to his previous failure to cooperate with the War Department authorities and the Tennessee and Mississippi railroad managers to complete railroad repairs, late in April 1864 Johnston ordered Major Stephen W. Presstman, the acting chief engineer of the Army of Tennessee, to advise the Engineer Bureau that "the Comd'g General desires that all the principal bridges on the W & A R.R. between Atlanta & Chattanooga should be duplicated." Presstman also informed Major Rives, the acting Engineer Bureau chief, that the Western & Atlantic superintendent Phillips had advised Presstman that an Engineer Corps officer at Atlanta, Captain Lincoln P. Grant, already had "duplicates of one or two of the smaller bridges," while the foundry firm of A. L. Maxwell, Jr., and Co., having previously removed its shops from Knoxville to Atlanta, offered duplicates of the larger trestles.[4]

Acting on Johnston's request, Rives ordered Grant to "assist the commanding General of the Army of Tennessee as far as you are able in the matter of bridges" and advised him that the War Department would provide funds to defray the cost of furnishing duplicate trestles. Finally, Rives assured Presstman that he had ordered Grant to provide such duplicate bridges "as may be considered most important to the public service." He also recommended that Presstman cooperate with both Grant and another Engineer Corps officer who remained stationed in Alabama, the commissioner of removal of railroad iron Lieutenant Colonel Minor Meriwether, in constructing alternate trestles. Increasing Meriwether's responsibility, the Engineer Bureau had recently assigned him to superintend the building of a railroad between Blue Mountain, Alabama, and Rome, Georgia. This included the same branch line about which Johnston had revealed an ignorance of procurement and construction methods in 1863. Meriwether had previously acted as an agent for the Confederate government, by contracting with Anthony L. Maxwell, Jr., to build bridges in northwest Georgia and a railroad bridge over the Tombigbee River in western Alabama. Johnston independently recognized the need for spare trestles and therefore specifically requested the War Department to provide him with prefabricated bridges (actually the individual truss members, or interchangeable timbers, that on assembly would form the new trestlework) for use on the Western & Atlantic Railroad; but the Engineer Bureau originally initiated bridge-building projects in Alabama and Georgia and then modified its contract with Maxwell's firm to provide duplicate bridges for Johnston. Moreover, while Johnston exercised responsibility for procuring and using the bridges, Rives coordinated efforts to secure the trestles without the closer involvement of Johnston or Presstman. In short, Johnston showed a substantially improved appreciation of the military importance of railroad bridges, but he continued to depend excessively on staff officers and insufficiently on War Department officials to ensure the successful building and maintaining of railroad trestles. Johnston's negligence or loose supervision notwithstanding, Presstman and Engineer Corps officers collaborated with Maxwell's timber agents and furnished Johnston with the duplicate bridges he requested, although this work prevented Maxwell from devoting his exclusive attention to the Tombigbee River bridge project in Alabama. Grant performed especially ably on this project, and consequently Rives called on him again in August 1864 to cooperate with the Army of Tennessee's chief engineer to complete similar work on the Central of Georgia Railroad—work undertaken and accomplished, however, after Johnston's command in Georgia had abruptly ended in July.[5]

Shortly after Johnston ordered the construction of duplicate bridges to carry the railroad over rivers between Dalton and Atlanta, he addressed the problem of badly deteriorated trestles at Dalton. Those had undergone severe strain by the constant running of heavy freight trains over the Western & Atlantic Railroad since the fall of 1862. Johnston therefore instructed Inspector General J. P. Jones to order the Dalton post commander to "send an Officer to examine the Bridges around, & in Dalton, and where they found out of repair, you will please give the necessary orders, & have them immediately repaired."[6] Johnston understood that he could not practically use duplicate bridges for the railroad below Dalton in supporting his army if the trestles around Dalton were dangerously defective and could collapse under the weight of freight trains heavily loaded with troops and ordnance amidst the crisis of battle; such a disruption of railroad communications would temporarily cut off his army from its supply base at Atlanta.

Having prepared to replace vital railroad bridges in northwest Georgia, Johnston also took measures to protect the Western & Atlantic Railroad in anticipation of Federal General William T. Sherman's operations against the Confederate army at Dalton and its railway connections with Atlanta. Even earlier, in January, Johnston had instructed Brigadier General Danville Leadbetter, the Maine-born Engineer Corps officer who had supervised fortifications work at Mobile, to make an initial "tour of observation to the several RR crossings being fortified in rear of the army" at Dalton. Having received favorable reports from Leadbetter about the progress of the fortification work over the winter of 1864, Johnston then moved to protect—in this situation quite inadequately—the railroad bridge over the Chattahoochee River at West Point; the structure connected the Atlanta & West Point and Montgomery & West Point railroads. The two railways were strategic lines of transportation that linked the Confederate army with its principal source of food supply in Alabama. Failing to recognize the need for special military protection of the trestle, early in March Johnston ordered a special detail of only twenty Georgia militiamen to guard the bridge constantly to prevent its destruction by Federal cavalry or Unionist saboteurs. In April, Johnston deployed two regiments of Georgia's reserve forces near the three trestles (those for which he also made duplicate bridges) that bore the Western & Atlantic line over the Oostenoula, Etowah, and Chattahoochee rivers. On May 4 he also ordered a part of a cavalry division encamped near the Etowah River to move to Resaca to reinforce the Georgia militiamen already entrenched around the Oostenoula railroad bridge.[7]

Then, two days later, Lieutenant General Polk advised Johnston that President Davis had ordered his command of nearly fourteen thousand infantry and cavalry to Dalton to reinforce the Army of Tennessee. Promptly, Polk mobilized his army at Demopolis and sent his forces by rail to Selma, commencing the first stage of a massive troop movement to Georgia. Despite Polk's quick action, the transportation of troops to Selma progressed slowly. On May 7 a disappointed and impatient Polk sent a message to Johnston, explaining, "regret we have not as much rolling stock as we could use." Johnston's responsibility for the heavy losses of railway equipment at Grenada contributed to Polk's transportation problems at Demopolis. Apparently unmindful of that connection, however, on May 8, Johnston suggested to Polk that, if Polk could spare a cavalry brigade from his command, "its presence near Kingston would be most valuable in giving security to our communications."[8]

Major General William T. Sherman, Johnston's antagonist in the Atlanta Campaign.

Polk agreed to detach a part of his command and informed Johnston that Brigadier General Samuel W. Ferguson's brigade would guard Kingston as soon as it could reach that strategically located railroad junction. The rest of Polk's command then boarded cars at Selma and moved over the Alabama & Tennessee Rivers Railroad to Blue Mountain. The troops traveled by rail a part of the distance to Georgia and then marched swiftly across country to the Western & Atlantic spur line at Rome. Lieutenant Colonel Meriwether, who had previously assisted Johnston in the procuring of duplicate bridges, had only partially completed the railway connection between the two points. Nevertheless, Polk reached Rome in advance of his infantry and asked Johnston for further instructions. Johnston foresaw the need for rolling stock with which to transport Polk's fourteen thousand infantry and cavalry from Rome to Dalton in stages and directed Brigadier General Mackall to request the Western & Atlantic officials at Atlanta to send cars for two thousand men to Rome. The State Railroad managers complied promptly and hurried their trains to Rome. Polk entrained his first troop contingent at Rome and then went to Kingston. He smoothly supervised the successive troop movements from Rome to Dalton and finally left Kingston, heading farther north to Resaca on May 12. Thus, despite the extended break between Blue Mountain and Rome, the Confederate railroads proved capable of moving a large unit quickly when effectively used by Johnston and Polk. Polk fell at Pine Mountain during a break in the bloody battles for Atlanta; his death deprived the Confederacy of its most enterprising and successful railroad general.[9]

Having been substantially reinforced by Polk, Johnston now considered the critical strategic situation that confronted him. He fully expected the Federal army to assault directly the Confederate positions north of Dalton and scarcely considered the possibility that Sherman could execute a flanking movement around the Army of Tennessee through Snake Creek Gap. He designed his preparatory measures, including the construction of duplicate bridges and the deployment of militia, to maintain and protect the Western & Atlantic line below Dalton in the event of Federal cavalry raids. Startled by word on May 9 that an entire Federal infantry corps had debouched at the southern end of Snake Creek Gap, Johnston hurriedly began reinforcing the garrison at Resaca, a point sixteen miles south of Dalton. Skillfully, he ordered an immediate emptying

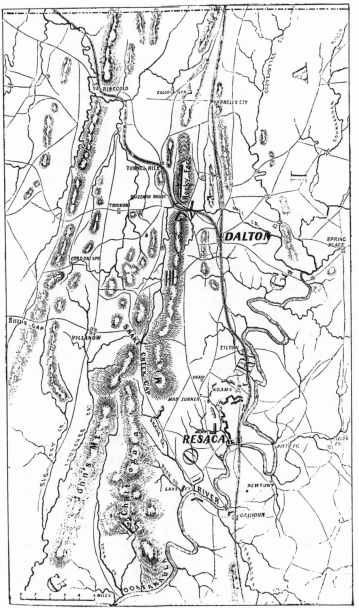

Johnston used the Western & Atlantic line to move troops quickly from Dalton to Resaca to cut off Sherman's flanking movement. From John William Draper, *History of the American Civil War* (New York, 1870), 3:273.

of supply trains at Dalton and loading of troops aboard the cars. Union soldiers who confidently expected to capture Resaca without a struggle suddenly faced the unnerving prospect of a fierce and bloody battle—anticipated by the "loud rumbling noise made by the trains, and the unusual shrieking of the locomotives on the road between Dalton and Resaca." Having quickly mobilized some units and moved the rest of his forces to Resaca by May 12, Johnston disposed his army so as to shield the 620-foot-long Oostenoula River railroad bridge. Federal gunners positioned opposite the town trained their batteries on the bridge and shelled its trestlework, setting it aflame, and the "Rail Road Station buildings were fired by their shells." Confederate troops then hastily passed over the burning and smoking railroad bridge and over pontoon bridges, crossed the river, and on May 15 marched toward Calhoun and Adairsville. Johnston's cavalry covered the retrograde movement, protecting his engineers who demolished the bridge's yet unburned trestlework before the Federal army occupied the town.[10] In this situation the duplicate bridge over the Oostenoula served no useful purpose: only a Confederate counteroffensive could make effective use of the spare trestle that quartermasters evacuated with other property of the Rebel forces. A counterattack never occurred, though, because Johnston failed to stop Sherman's movements around Adairsville, and the Confederate retreat continued to Kingston.

The Army of Tennessee reached Kingston, the strategic railroad junction forty-one miles south of Dalton, early on May 18, completing a thirty-five-mile withdrawal in three days. The rapid retreat afforded Johnston's troops little time to tear up tracks on the Dalton and Kingston portion of the Western & Atlantic Railroad. After the Union occupation of Kingston on May 19, one Federal private wryly observed, "the railroads have all been left intact by the retreating army. They undoubtedly expect to return and have use for them hereafter." Sherman later recollected that his railroad reconstruction crews spent only "a few days to repair the railroad, which had been damaged but little, except the bridge at Resaca." Nevertheless, before evacuating his army from Kingston later on May 18, Johnston accomplished an essential objective in railroad transportation. Demonstrating a remarkable concern over preserving railway property, he protected rolling stock that supported his army at the front. Acting decisively, Johnston ordered that "eleven engines and trains, under Confederate control" at Kingston be "moved south with the army," and the railroad equipment thereafter continued to support Confederate military operations north of Atlanta. In Virginia and Mississippi Johnston had either destroyed or allowed Union cavalry to destroy entire fleets of rolling stock that the Confederacy needed. In Georgia, by contrast, Johnston exhibited a proper appreciation of the value of Southern rolling stock and therefore saved it, but he probably would have sacrificed the equipment at Kingston if it had not served his immediate purposes. The Union army's close pursuit of the Confederate forces also prompted Johnston's decision to remove the rolling stock; he and his cavalry simply lacked enough time to make preparations to destroy the equipment. Indeed, in approaching Kingston, Sherman almost overtook Johnston by boldly sending his railroad trains directly to the front. The Federal commander's action encouraged his troops, so that gloating soldiers at Kingston facetiously boasted that "General Johnston traveled on a train just in advance of General Sherman and that the former kept his train flagged to keep Sherman from running into him!"[11] At Kingston, therefore, the Confederate rolling stock narrowly escaped capture or destruction.

Johnston's timely removal of the trains from Kingston, besides showing his appreciation of the value of rolling stock for logistics also emphasized the coordination of effort between railroad managers and army quartermasters. The Western & Atlantic officials effectively cooperated with commissary and quartermaster agents at Atlanta and satisfied the Army of Tennessee's supply requirements during this part of the Atlanta campaign. Their joint efforts represented a particularly critical collaboration because the Confederate army's shortage of field transportation compelled Johnston to depend heavily on the railroad for the subsistence of his troops below Resaca. Yet the railroad officials met the challenge and stockpiled a sufficient quantity of stores at Kingston. An escaped Federal officer rejoined Sherman's army near Kingston on May 21 and informed one soldier that Johnston's troops had drawn rations there for "seventy-thousand men." Since the Confederate army only mustered about sixty thousand infantry and cavalry, the Western & Atlantic officials' efficiency offset the army's limited ability and opportunity to collect supplies from the country. The energy and good management of the railroad officials proved crucial because the army's retreat to the Etowah River led to its renewed dependence on the railroad. As one Federal commander later recalled, Johnston maneuvered so as to "make the largest use of the railroad to move his baggage and supply his troops" at Kingston "for wagon trains were not overabundant with the Confederates."[12]

The Army of Tennessee's movement toward the Etowah River, eleven miles south of Kingston, initiated the second phase of the Atlanta campaign. Johnston now desperately attempted to disrupt Sherman's railroad communications in Georgia, despite President Davis's decision not to support Johnston (or to appease an indignant Governor Brown) by sending the cavalry forces of Major General Nathan Bedford Forrest against Sherman's more vulnerable rail supply lines in Tennessee. Johnston sent five successive cavalry expeditions against the Federal army's railroad connections below Dalton, but, as anticipated, all failed because they were too weak. Moreover, Johnston had to deploy most of his ten-thousand-man cavalry force behind the Confederate lines for the protection of the Western & Atlantic line below Allatoona from raiding Union cavalry. Having preserved his railway communications in Georgia and Tennessee, Sherman conducted a movement around the Army of Tennessee south of Kingston, forcing another Rebel retreat. Sherman's maneuver quickly prompted Johnston to abandon further concern for the safety of Confederate railway property.

Acting precipitately, he destroyed a quantity of rolling stock and then permitted his cavalry to burn the large trestle over the Etowah River near Cartersville. According to a member of Johnston's staff, on May 20 Confederate troops burned the "railroad bridge by mistake," although Johnston had ordered them to destroy adjacent pontoon bridges and wagon train trestles over the Etowah. Regardless of any failure in communication, Johnston bore heavy responsibility for the destruction of the Etowah River Bridge because he had adopted careful measures to preserve a duplicate bridge for the Etowah (a fully assembled "one railroad bridge" well guarded by Confederate cavalry on the river's south bank) for possible use in conducting a retreat toward Allatoona. Oblivious to his blunder, Johnston hastily withdrew his forces from Cartersville. Shortly thereafter, Federal troops entered the abandoned town and observed raging fires still consuming the Etowah River "railroad bridge and a number of cars."[13]

Then, in a remarkable series of decisions and events, Johnston again demonstrated his inconsistent and confused approach to the military use of railway property. In April, he had recognized the

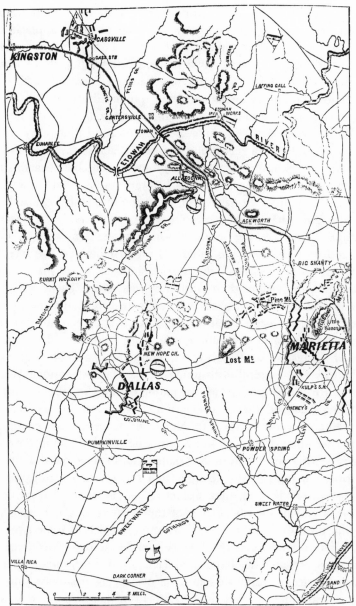

Sherman's continued flanking movement toward Atlanta prompted
Johnston's orders for the destruction of portions of the Western & At-
lantic line. From John William Draper, *History of the American Civil
War* (New York, 1870), 3:278.

potential value of duplicate bridges, but after the commencement of the Atlanta campaign he failed to make practical application or effective use of a single replacement trestle. Later, after allowing the destruction of the Etowah River railroad bridge, Johnston withdrew his army south of the river toward Allatoona Pass. When Sherman halted to regroup his forces and then temporarily retired to his advance bases at Kingston and Cassville, Johnston decided to recross the Etowah and possibly mount an attack on the Union army. Therefore, the "timbers for rebuilding the bridge across the Etowah River went up" quickly on May 22 and Johnston sent both wagon trains and railroad trains north of the Etowah for a possible offensive against Sherman. Two days later, Johnston suddenly reversed himself, deciding that he had established too vulnerable an advanced position. As a *Charleston Mercury* war correspondent near Allatoona reported on May 24, "the railroad bridge being reconstructed, all trains are sent south of the Chattahoochee as a precautionary measure."[14] Johnston then withdrew his army back across the Etowah and totally destroyed the duplicate bridge that he had just raised. Since Johnston briefly contemplated and then abruptly foreclosed the possibility of a counterattack on Sherman and a reoccupation of Kingston or Cassville—a contradictory course of action marked by the wasteful destruction of the duplicate bridge over the Etowah River and his second evacuation of the Confederate army to Allatoona Pass and thence to Marietta—the costly preparation of a replacement trestle for the Etowah proved to be a futile exercise.

Johnston then determined to hinder Sherman's forward movement by devastating the Western & Atlantic Railroad below the Etowah. His troops first stripped the iron from the tracks running immediately south of the river, then uprooted long sections of track on the Allatoona and Ackworth portion of the Western & Atlantic, and finally, farther south, "the rebels tore away the rails of some two miles of the railroad between Big Shanty and Marietta." Encouraged by Johnston's obvious vacillation and lack of aggressiveness, Sherman moved his army southward, and, on occupying Allatoona, immediately issued orders to "repair the railroad bridge forward from Kingston to Allatoona, embracing the bridge across the Etowah River." Sherman's rapid progress stunned Johnston. The Confederate commander had mistakenly assumed that the total destruction of the thirteen-mile section of track between the Etowah River and Marietta would delay the Federal advance for several weeks. Therefore,

Double tracks at Allatoona Pass in northwest Georgia, a critical point
on Johnston's supply line over the Western & Atlantic Railroad, 1864.

he had employed his troops in thoroughly breaking up the railroad
below the river to impede the Federal march and disrupt Sherman's
communications. Unfortunate irony: this policy glaringly contrasted
with his obstinate refusal to use soldiers for railroad repairs in
Mississippi in the summer of 1863. Johnston's decision had paralyzed Confederate transportation operations around Jackson for five
months and resulted in the costly loss of rolling stock around
Grenada, but the destruction of the railroad between Allatoona and
Marietta only briefly delayed the Federal advance. By June 11 the
Union army reached Johnston's strongly fortified position. Sherman's
railroad reconstruction crews swiftly erected another trestle over the
Etowah River, and, as Sherman later proudly recalled, "the railroad
was repaired up to our very skirmish-line, close to the base of Kennesaw" Mountain.[15]

Meanwhile, Western & Atlantic officials supplied the Army of Tennessee during its operations below the Etowah River more effectively than they had supported the Rebel forces during the campaign north of the river, an accomplishment facilitated by that army's steady retreat to its principal supply base at Atlanta. The railroad officials again cooperated with quartermaster agents at Atlanta and shipped to Allatoona such a great quantity of stores that the army operated "twenty miles from the railroad" and "with no baggage" during the fierce and heavy fighting along Pumpkin Vine Creek near Dallas, the site of another Confederate supply depot. Further, the Confederate army's defense of strongly fortified positions in the mountains around Marietta provided the railroad managers with the opportunity to accumulate even greater quantities of supplies at Marietta. Soon, however, Johnston received complaints from quartermasters at Marietta that Western & Atlantic freight cars brought unbalanced cargoes of corn and bacon from Atlanta. Johnston responded by instructing Lieutenant Colonel McMicken, then stationed at Atlanta, to ascertain the cause. McMicken, who had replaced Major Barbour as chief quartermaster early in March (because of Quartermaster General Lawton's recalling of Barbour to Richmond to settle a set of disputed accounts), concluded that the unbalanced supply shipments sent from Montgomery, Alabama, to Atlanta accounted for the disproportionate cargoes carried from Atlanta to Marietta. Johnston thereupon advised Lawton on May 30 to "please order your transportation quartermaster at Montgomery to divide the cars for supplying this army in proportions" that McMicken specified "from time to time." Johnston's direct intervention proved decisive; the Confederate army resumed drawing an evenly distributed stock of rations. Indeed, by the middle of July, the *Charleston Mercury* reported that "General Joe continues to feed his men well" because of his effective direction of army quartermasters and his efficient use of the Alabama and Georgia railroads.[16]

Johnston's handling of the unbalanced supply shipments from Montgomery represented a more realistic recognition of the limitations of his authority over quartermaster agents. As supreme commander of the Department of the West in March 1863, he possessed authority over Pemberton's quartermasters in Mississippi and East Louisiana. He exercised that power when he instructed Pemberton to direct quartermasters at Vicksburg to ship balanced proportions of corn and sugar to Mobile. In Georgia, however, Johnston lacked authority to order Lieutenant General Lee, acting commander of the Department of Alabama, Mississippi, and East Louisiana, to execute instructions regarding the operations of quartermaster agents at Montgomery. His respect for Lawton's jurisdiction in Alabama sharply contrasted with his previous opposition to Lawton's railroad policy in Georgia and the Carolinas, and specifically to Lawton's right to impress and employ displaced Tennessee rolling stock in the Wilmington cotton traffic in the winter of 1864.

Having solved the problem of unbalanced supply shipments from Montgomery, Johnston returned his attention to the military situation and shortly thereafter repelled Sherman's determined but unsuccessful frontal attacks against Confederate positions at Kennesaw Mountain. The Union army's bloody repulse on June 27 persuaded Sherman to swing his army around the Confederate's army's left wing below Marietta, a movement that necessitated still another Army of Tennessee retreat toward Atlanta. Johnston's troops evacuated the entrenchments at Kennesaw Mountain on the night of July 2, followed the Western & Atlantic tracks southward to a new defensive line below Marietta, and on July 4 marched to prepared positions north of the principal Chattahoochee River railroad bridge. The Rebel forces also protected Johnston's duplicate bridge for the Chattahoochee north of Atlanta, but for a third time such a replacement trestle proved impracticable and wasteful. Johnston's delaying tactics above the Chattahoochee proved equally useless. The Federal army's swift pursuit prevented retreating Confederate troops from completely destroying the twelve-mile section of track between Kennesaw Mountain and the river. As an Illinois veteran later recalled, "but little more than three miles of track had been torn up by the enemy below Marietta." Consequently, the removal by Johnston's soldiers of railroad iron from the Western & Atlantic tracks failed to delay or seriously impede Sherman's steady advance toward Atlanta. On July 6 Sherman advised the chief of staff Henry W. Halleck that Johnston had left "two breaks in the railroad—one above Marietta and one near Vining's Station," but that "the former is already repaired and Johnston's army has heard the sound of our locomotives."[17]

This phase of Johnston's retreat toward Atlanta again demonstrated his continuing inconsistency in the military exploitation of railway property. He salvaged the railroad iron that his troops uprooted above Marietta to repair tracks elsewhere in Georgia (and as one Union veteran later declared, "to prevent General Sherman from riding into Marietta in triumph"), ordering the loading of the rails on a "train of cars" at Marietta and having them removed on July 3 to Atlanta. Yet later, when Johnston ordered the uprooting of rails near Vining's Station, below Marietta, he permitted his soldiers to discard that equally valuable stock of iron. A surprised group of Union troops, then reconnoitering near the railroad tracks above the Chattahoochee River at a point only fourteen miles north of Atlanta, discovered that "a quantity of iron rails had been taken up by the rebels and pitched down a hill, just as if the 'Yankees' could not very soon place them on the track again" for use against the Confederate army.[18]

Repeated breaks in the railroad having failed to retard Sherman's movement toward Atlanta or the subsequent crossing of the Chatta-hoochee River by units of Sherman's army, Johnston withdrew his army to the south bank of the Chattahoochee. On the night of July 9, he ordered the evacuation of Lieutenant General Hardee's corps, which had guarded the main railroad bridge over the river. Hardee obeyed Johnston's instructions, "burning the bridge behind him" as he retreated. Johnston's action threw Atlanta into an uproar and prompted dismayed and exasperated Georgia railroaders to serve private interests over Confederate military purposes: Macon & Western and Georgia Railroad officials thereafter assigned priority to accommodating importunate and panic-stricken citizens in removing private property to Macon and Savannah.[19] Yet even before the mass evacuation of Atlanta, Johnston's failure to make advance arrangements with the War Department authorities resulted in confusion and conflict over the removal of hospital equipment and ordnance stores from the city. Early in June, Johnston assured Colonel Wright, the commanding officer of Confederate troops at Atlanta and the head of the Ordnance Department's Atlanta arsenal, that the Army of Tennessee "would be kept in front of Atlanta." Johnston's confidence of success persuaded Wright to delay making preparations to remove arsenal stores to Macon and Augusta, but in a letter to Colonel Josiah Gorgas, the Ordnance Bureau chief, Wright also expressed his fear that premature action on his part "might produce a *panic*" among the citizens of Atlanta.

Forgetting his earlier assurances to Wright, however, on July 5 Johnston ordered the immediate removal of ordnance stores from Atlanta. Wright promptly obeyed, but soon encountered opposi-

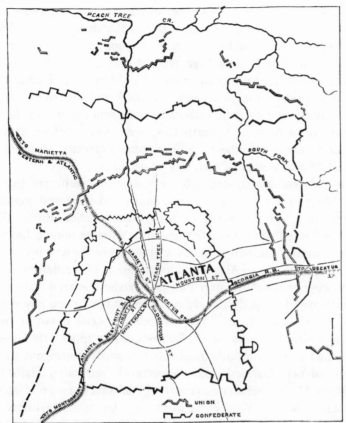

Atlanta railroad lines and fortifications around the city. From Benson J. Lossing, *Pictorial History of the Civil War in the USA* (Hartford, 1868), 3:384.

tion from quartermaster agents and Macon & Western managers. He discovered that Quartermaster General Lawton had ordered the removal of hospital equipment before the evacuation of armory machinery. Complicating the situation, the railroad officials not only refused to furnish Wright with additional freight cars but threatened to unload the cars bound for Macon that Wright's subordinates had already laboriously loaded. Dismayed, Wright sought Brigadier General Mackall's intervention. The arsenal commander complained of the interference and opposition posed by quartermaster agents and railroad officials and explained that the War Department could more easily replace "bunks and old Hospital furniture" than it could restore "our valuable machinery, guns & other ordnance stores."

Forcefully reminded of his promises to Wright, Johnston quickly procured a War Department order resolving the difficulty, and Wright completed the shipment of arsenal property to Macon and Augusta.[20] Johnston might have averted this situation by determining what constituted the Quartermaster and Ordnance Departments' evacuation priorities in June, although the War Department authorities had not prepared more elaborate contingency plans for the catastrophic loss of Atlanta. Nevertheless, instead of coordinating efforts between Confederate officers and the railroad officials, Johnston contributed to the conflict of authority at Atlanta.

While Wright hastily evacuated the arsenal machinery from Atlanta, Sherman's relentless advance southward increased Johnston's concern over the protection of the Chattahoochee River railroad bridge at West Point on the Georgia and Alabama border, the structure connecting the two railroads that together formed his only remaining supply line to Alabama. His attention to the defense of that bridge arose particularly after Provost Marshal General Benjamin J. Hill informed him early in July that the bridge lacked any military guard. In March, Johnston had ordered a special detail of twenty Georgia militia troops to guard the bridge, but apparently Governor Brown had since arbitrarily removed the small contingent to help protect Atlanta. Alarmed, Johnston urgently requested Major General Jones M. Withers, commander of Alabama's reserve forces, to send state troops to West Point to protect the trestle. Withers complied on July by sending eleven militia companies from Montgomery to West Point. On July 11, however, Withers suddenly recalled the militia forces to Montgomery to defend central Alabama from a Federal cavalry raid launched by Major General Lovell H. Rousseau. Confused by Rousseau's movements, on July 12 Withers informed Johnston of his decision to send the state troops to Mobile, a point Withers mistakenly believed to be the ultimate objective of the Union raid. Withers then notified Major General Maury, the commanding officer of Confederate forces at Mobile, about the Federal raid but neglected to advise Maury of his intention to send reinforcements to the Gulf port. Nevertheless, Maury urged Johnston to send to Montgomery eleven companies of infantry for the defense of Alabama's railroad connections with Georgia. Johnston clearly appreciated the logistical importance of the Montgomery & West Point Railroad. The unrelenting Federal pressure on his lines below the Chattahoochee, however, prevented him from detaching the infantry units, while he further advised Maury that the "Alabama reserves which I had at West Point are ordered to Mobile."[21]

Complicating this confusing situation, on July 16 Maury decided to send to Montgomery to repel the Union cavalry raid the militia companies that Withers previously dispatched to Mobile. The chaotic mishandling of troop movements by rail—largely caused by Withers's and Maury's incompetence—would not have occurred if Johnston, in cooperation with Brown, had earlier deployed and retained larger numbers of Georgia militia troops or Confederate cavalry at West Point. The failure in Confederate command enabled Rousseau to destroy much of the Montgomery & West Point Railroad in central Alabama. Johnston's removal from command of the Army of Tennessee on July 17, an action taken urgently by President Davis in response to Johnston's failure to stop Sherman's advance north of the Chattahoochee, therefore also coincided with the Confederate army's loss of its principal railway supply line to Alabama.[22]

Jefferson Davis's enmity toward Johnston had an important influence in his decision to appoint a new army commander in Georgia. Yet he also feared that Johnston's habit of constant retreat posed a potentially catastrophic blow for the Confederacy's Atlantic coastal railway network. Johnston's sheer indifference to the massive destruction of Mississippi railroad equipment around Grenada in 1863 persuaded Davis that Johnston attached no great military importance to preserving the Atlanta railway nexus. The president therefore appointed Lieutenant General John B. Hood to the command of the Army of Tennessee, confidently believing that Hood would resolutely hold "Atlanta, and the railroads, threatened with destruction," and especially defend the lines which transported "indispensable supplies for the armies" in the Carolinas and Virginia. Relieved from command, Johnston left Atlanta on August 8 and went to Macon pending further War Department orders.[23]

The overcautiousness and lack of aggressive spirit that characterized Johnston's approach to field command appeared prominently in his handling of the Western & Atlantic Railroad during the Atlanta campaign. Johnston's preoccupation with defensive strategy accounted for his construction of duplicate railroad trestles, his fortification of railroad crossings, and his protection of supply trains and salvaging of railroad iron before and during the battles in northwest Georgia. These defensive preparations to an extent represented Johnston's prudence, but, because he failed to exploit them effectively, his railroad arrangements proved to be wasteful diversions of precious military resources. Moreover, his army's dependence on the Western & Atlantic confirmed his opinion that the railroad formed primarily a logistical resource, an instrument of war with limited strategic value for theater operations. Johnston did, however, use the Western & Atlantic skillfully to reinforce his army with Polk's forces at the outset of the Atlanta campaign and later to rescue the garrison at Resaca when Sherman outflanked the Confederates at Dalton. Unfortunately, Johnston thereafter resorted to his practice of destroying rolling stock, trestles, and tracks in a futile and misguided effort to cripple an invading Union army. Instead of using the Western & Atlantic to support a sustained counteroffensive against Sherman, Johnston allowed his adversary to exploit the same railroad to facilitate the Federal army's invasion of northwest Georgia and ultimately its capture of Atlanta. Johnston therefore prepared to sacrifice the Deep South's most important railroad center after two months of offering feeble opposition to Sherman's advance, although he had earlier used all the railroads of Georgia for four months to rebuild the Army of Tennessee toward the destruction of the Union army. On being restored to command, Johnston would have one final opportunity to demonstrate a more consistent and coordinated exploitation of Confederate railroads. In North Carolina he would have to use the railroad as an important military resource in his attempt to halt Sherman's triumphant march through the Carolinas toward Richmond.

·{6}·

Chaos and Capitulation in North Carolina

THE fall of Atlanta in September 1864 marked the first of a succession of military disasters that threatened utterly to destroy the crumbling Confederacy. Hood's evacuation of Atlanta and the Army of Tennessee's retreat into Alabama led to Sherman's devastation of the Atlanta railway nexus and the Federal army's triumphant march across Georgia to the Atlantic coast, tearing up railroads in its path. The Army of Tennessee sustained crippling losses at the battle of Franklin, Tennessee, late in November, and in December Federal General George H. Thomas's victorious army hurled Hood's defeated forces from Nashville into northeastern Mississippi. Concurrently, Sherman's army besieged Savannah, and on December 21 the Confederate garrison evacuated the Georgia seaport. The Federal army then marched into South Carolina and thoroughly destroyed the railway lines below Columbia. The Union army captured Columbia on January 17, 1865, and then marched toward Charlotte, North Carolina. The Confederate War Department clerk, John B. Jones, noted that the inhabitants of Richmond appeared "stunned and sullen" over the fall of Columbia and he predicted consequences "calamitous beyond calculations." Amidst the worsening military crisis, Southern newspaper editors and prominent citizens clamored for the reappointment of Johnston to independent command. Politicians and military commanders also demanded his return to duty, but President Davis steadfastly refused.[1]

To justify his decision, on February 18 the president prepared a statement for the consideration of the Confederate Congress in which he set forth cogent arguments against the reinstatement of Johnston. Davis reviewed Johnston's record from Harpers Ferry to

Atlanta and condemned his incompetence as an independent field commander. Although the president's arguments rested heavily on exaggerations and distortions of the truth, Davis accurately denounced Johnston's blunder in Mississippi that had resulted in the massive destruction of railway equipment around Grenada. He contended that Johnston's evacuation of Jackson, Mississippi, in July 1863, much like his withdrawal from Centreville, Virginia, in March 1862, "was marked by one of the most serious and irreparable sacrifices of property that has occurred during the war" and a loss for which he believed "no sufficient explanation has been given." Davis specifically referred to the irreplaceable rolling stock that railroad managers removed to Grenada before the Federal capture of Jackson and Sherman's burning of the Pearl River railroad bridge in May 1863. He censured Johnston on the ground that "with over 20,000 men [he] suffered this gap to remain without an effort to fill it, although the work could with little difficulty have been completed in a manner" so as to have removed over six hundred locomotives and cars to safety beyond the Alabama River. Davis rancorously declared that the Confederacy had never "recovered from the injury to the transportation service occasioned by this failure on his part." Ultimately, however, he decided to withhold his message from the Congress. The president believed that Robert E. Lee, whom Davis had recently appointed as general in chief of the Armies of the Confederate States, could restrain Johnston's tendency to destroy railroad property. Consequently, the president permitted Lee to appoint Johnston commanding general of the Army of Tennessee on February 21, 1865. Southern papers in the Confederate East generally supported Davis's decision and Lee's action. The *Richmond Dispatch*, for example, favored Johnston's restoration despite having serious doubts about his capacity for conducting aggressive military operations. Closer to the front, the *Raleigh Conservative* more optimistically declared that "General Johnston will neither wantonly expose the property of our people or the territory of our country to unnecessary hazard" in opposing Sherman's invasion of North Carolina.[2]

Johnston, however, hesitated to accept renewed command. He had resided in virtual seclusion in Macon, Georgia, and Columbia, South Carolina, in the months after Hood assumed command of the Army of Tennessee and had gone to Lincolnton, North Carolina, shortly before the fall of Columbia. Then, on February 22, both Adjutant General Cooper and General in Chief Lee notified Johnston about his new command. Johnston instantly sent a message to Lee, frantically protesting that he could not concentrate troops capable of repelling Sherman because the "remnant of the Army of Tennessee is much divided." Reluctantly, though, he assumed command. The ubiquitous Southern diarist, Mary Boykin Chesnut, recalled that "he said he was very angry at being ordered to take command again," while she expressed disenchantment with the popularly styled "God of War" because of his lack of patriotic fervor.[3]

Notwithstanding his resentment, Johnston dealt with a critical military situation confronting the Confederacy. He would have to accomplish four major objectives in North Carolina. First, he would have to use what remained of the Confederate railway system from Mississippi to North Carolina to concentrate forces of the Army of Tennessee at strategically located points within the Tarheel State. Second, Johnston would need to use the North Carolina railroads to provide logistical support to those assembled forces. Then he would have to coordinate the tactical use of railroad transportation with the War Department authorities, other top-ranking Rebel commanders in North Carolina, and the railroad officials. Finally, Johnston would need to protect the rolling stock of North Carolina, South Carolina, and Virginia carriers—railroad officials having moved much of that equipment into the Tarheel State to avoid its capture or destruction by Federal cavalry. In short, Johnston would have to exploit all his accumulated experience with the Southern railroads if he expected to use the North Carolina railroads effectively in a desperate effort to avoid a Confederate defeat and surrender in that state.

Whatever he thought of these objectives, Johnston boarded a train at Lincolnton on February 25 and traveled thirty miles to General Beauregard's headquarters at Charlotte. Beauregard, who had served under Johnston in Virginia in 1861 and who had aided him by sending rolling stock to Atlanta, Georgia, in 1864, recognized Johnston as his successor and yet retained nominal command of the Military Division of the West. Johnston conferred with Beauregard on the strategic situation in South Carolina and learned more about Beauregard's earlier unsuccessful effort to halt the Federal army's advance on Columbia. After consulting with Beauregard, Johnston advised Lee that "your order to me to concentrate all available forces and drive back Sherman" reflected an unrealistic assessment of the strategic situation. Because of the shortage of field transportation in North Carolina, he feared that the Army of Tennessee would have to depend principally on the railroad for supplies. Johnston explained to Lee that his troops had "only the means of transporting cooking utensils" and consequently "cannot operate far from railroads."[4]

Johnston's lack of confidence about achieving a swift concentration of force sprang from his knowledge of the scattered locations of the forces that constituted his newly assigned command. He already knew about the Army of Tennessee's earliest movements from Mississippi to South Carolina. Previously, the Federal army's prolonged occupation of Savannah provided Beauregard (then at Charleston) with the opportunity to draw reinforcements from the Army of Tennessee. Beauregard sent Major Edward Q. Willis, his chief quartermaster, to Tupelo, Mississippi, to exercise a general supervision over what became the last major railway troop movement across the Confederacy. Thereafter, a number of troop contingents took trains at Tupelo and went by the Mobile & Ohio Railroad to Meridian and Mobile. From those points, the troops traveled over several Alabama railways to Montgomery, the state capital. From the Alabama capital, Montgomery & West Point trains transported the soldiers farther east to Columbus, Georgia. Boarding cars at Columbus, the Army of Tennessee veterans took the Southwestern Railroad to Macon and then Central of Georgia cars from Macon to Milledgeville, the Georgia capital. The troops detrained at Milledgeville marched twenty miles to the Georgia Railroad terminal at Mayfield and then went by rail to Augusta. Despite repeated delays on its journey, Major General Carter L. Stevenson's division reached South Carolina in time to oppose the Federal army's crossing of the Edisto River below Columbia. Stevenson's troops then marched under Beauregard's orders to Charlotte.[5]

Alternatively, despite the radically changed military situation, the forty-five-mile section of the Charlotte & South Carolina Railroad between Chester and Charlotte could get Army of Tennessee troops more quickly to Charlotte, sparing the soldiers a final and forced march across South Carolina territory to reach the Tarheel State. On February 25, Beauregard told Johnston that by early March he expected another six thousand Army of Tennessee troops to reach Chester, from which point they would go by rail to Charlotte. Johnston also learned from Beauregard of the fall of Charleston and about the movement by rail to Cheraw of Lieutenant General Hardee's eleven thousand infantry troops. From other sources, he knew of the operations of Lieutenant General Wade Hampton's six-thousand-man cavalry force below Charlotte and of Hampton's slowing the Federal march toward Chester. Farther east, General Braxton Bragg, who had resumed field command after serving as military adviser to President Davis in Richmond, commanded fifty-five hundred troops at Kinston. Bragg's forces opposed a Federal infantry corps positioned near New Bern on the Atlantic coast. Although Beauregard acted as Johnston's subordinate, Johnston would not exercise direct authority over Bragg until early March.

The extensive railroad destruction in Georgia and South Carolina complicated moving Army of Tennessee troops from Georgia to North Carolina. Sherman's devastation of the Georgia railways in the last months of 1864 precluded any rapid or unimpeded movement of troops from West Point to Atlanta or from Columbus to Augusta. Confederate Engineer Corps and Railroad Bureau officers promptly mobilized slave labor forces and completed track repairs on the Atlanta & West Point Railroad by the middle of January 1865, but damaged portions of both the Central of Georgia Railroad and the Georgia Railroad presented those officers with much more formidable undertakings. Extensive sections of both lines remained in disrepair for three more months. The South Carolina railway system offered Johnston even fewer lines on which to move Army of Tennessee troops from Georgia to North Carolina. Beauregard's earlier evacuation of South Carolina spelled ruin for the state's principal railways. Federal troops struck the South Carolina Railroad near the Edisto River and uprooted long segments of track between Augusta and Charleston. Sherman later recollected the efficiency with which his troops "set to work to tear up the rails, to burn the ties and twist the bars." The soldiers also dismantled the broad-gauged Charlotte & South Carolina Railroad north of Columbia, severely damaging the fifty-four-mile section of track between the state capital and Black Stocks Depot. One of Sherman's staff officers noted that "the destruction has been made even more complete than usual" because the rails "have been easily twisted into kinks, bows, and corkscrews."[6] Other South Carolina railroads escaped such devastation, but they had slight value for Johnston's military operations in North Carolina. From Charleston, the Northeastern Railroad and Cheraw & Darlington Railroad lines consecutively ran north 135 miles to Cheraw. Johnston recognized the strategic advantage that those railroads had afforded Hardee in his previous troop movement to Cheraw, but he also understood that Hardee could not travel by rail toward North Carolina beyond Cheraw.

Although limited in what he could accomplish in accelerating Army of Tennessee troop movements to North Carolina from the Deep South, Johnston might have considered the more favorable prospects for a swift concentration of his scattered forces at some point within North Carolina. The North Carolina Railroad departed from Charlotte and extended 223 miles across the state to its eastern terminal at Goldsboro. Johnston possessed a railroad that closely followed an interior line of strategic defense; over this railroad he could move Army of Tennessee troops and concentrate them at different points along Sherman's front between Charlotte and Goldsboro. The Western North Carolina Railroad ran eighty-four miles from Salisbury to its western terminal at Morganton. Johnston could not use the railroad to move troops to eastern North Carolina, but he could employ Western North Carolina rolling stock in transporting troops from Salisbury to points farther east on the North Carolina Railroad. The Piedmont Railroad directly linked Virginia and North Carolina. Though running for only forty-five miles, the Piedmont Railroad (completed earlier in the war as a military measure) connected the Richmond & Danville Railroad at Danville with the North Carolina Railroad at Greensboro. The Piedmont Railroad's four-foot-eight-and-one-half-inch gauge matched that of the North Carolina Railroad. The Richmond & Danville firm, however, used track five feet wide in conformity with southern Virginia's three other broad-gauged lines. The difference in gauge between the Richmond & Danville and Piedmont railroads prevented transfers of rolling stock between Virginia and North Carolina over the Piedmont line. Nevertheless, the Piedmont company employed its rolling stock (much of it actually owned by the North Carolina Railroad) between Greensboro and Danville in an effort to supply Lee's Army of Northern Virginia, then besieged by Grant at Petersburg. From Raleigh, the North Carolina capital, the Raleigh & Gaston Railroad extended north nearly ninety miles to Weldon, North Carolina, where it connected with Virginia's Petersburg Railroad and Seaboard & Roanoke Railroad lines. The Wilmington & Weldon Railroad ran south from the Weldon railway nexus to the port of Wilmington on the Atlantic coast. The Federal reduction of Wilmington on February 22 deprived Johnston and Bragg of the Wilmington and Goldsboro segment of the railroad, but the Goldsboro and Weldon portion of the line remained a practical and important line of transportation as long as Bragg maintained his position at Kinston. The Federal capture of Wilmington rendered its southern connecting roads useless for moving Hardee's forces northward from Cheraw.[7]

Two apparent cases of railroad mismanagement in South Carolina increased Johnston's difficulty in effecting swift shipment of his scattered commands to North Carolina. The advance elements of Lieutenant General Alexander P. Stewart's corps reached Chester on February 25 and boarded cars bound for Salisbury. Acting on Quartermaster General Lawton's authorization, Beauregard had ordered the widening of the narrower-gauged North Carolina Railroad between Charlotte and Danville to permit the transfer of South Carolina rolling stock onto the North Carolina line. Despite the completion of this work, delays in the movement of troop trains northward occurred. Stewart's troops first moved slowly over the Chester and Charlotte section of the Charlotte & South Carolina Railroad. His command then left Charlotte and traveled even more slowly over seventeen miles of the widened North Carolina track toward Salisbury. Major William F. Avent, one of Stewart's quartermasters at Concord, a station north of Charlotte, on February 27 complained to Johnston about the bad management of the railroad. Avent declared that it had taken Stewart's troops thirty-eight hours to reach Concord. He also warned Johnston that an overaccumulation of idled rolling stock between Chester and Concord, without military orders to move, threatened further delays.

Johnston may have shared Avent's exasperation, but he carefully avoided compounding the problem at Concord by sending more rolling stock there. He had traveled over the stretch of track between Chester and Concord three times since December 1864 and each time had taken the usual four hours. Though quartermasters and railroad officials between Chester and Salisbury largely created Avent's predicament by their mishandling of troop train traffic, Johnston understood that the difficulty did not result from an insufficient quantity of rolling stock. As Johnston had learned, Beauregard brought to Chester and Charlotte in February from the railway lines north of Columbia upward of 185 boxcars and scores of locomotives. Indeed, the South Carolina Railroad company owned more than forty engines in 1863, and most of those locomotives escaped to Chester before Sherman's troops captured Columbia. Johnston recognized that quartermasters and railroad managers had collected a considerable quantity of South Carolina railway equipment at Chester; he also knew that the railroad officials commanded a sufficient number of trains for the transportation of Stewart's troops from Chester to Salisbury. Then, as Sherman's army relentlessly moved northward, railroad managers sent increasing quantities of South Carolina and North Carolina rolling stock farther north to more distant points on the North Carolina Railroad. The action should have struck Johnston as similar to the precautionary measure that the Mississippi railroad officials took before the fall of Jackson and Vicksburg in the summer of 1863. Indeed, not since his command in Virginia did Johnston have so much rolling stock to use for military operations in a single Confederate state. Perhaps he remembered his over-concentration of rolling stock at Manassas Junction in northern Virginia in 1862. Therefore, Johnston judiciously decided temporarily to leave the South Carolina rolling stock below the North Carolina border. Moreover, he expected the early arrival at Chester of the rest of Stewart's corps and the whole of Lieutenant General Benjamin E. Cheatham's corps, and he reasonably anticipated the active employment of idled rolling stock between Chester and Concord for the shipment of those forces to Salisbury. In not overreacting to Avent's charges of railroad mismanagement, Johnston showed prudent restraint in his effort to expedite Army of Tennessee troop movements from Chester to Salisbury, even if he could not more closely control locally stationed quartermasters.

Another incident that tested Johnston's forbearance about railroad mismanagement arose in consequence of word from Hardee on February 28 on the slow shipment of his troops and equipment over other South Carolina railroads. On the evacuation of Charleston on February 18, Hardee marched most of his infantry toward Greensboro, while Northeastern Railroad and Cheraw & Darlington Railroad trains started carrying the rest of his troops and his command's equipment to Cheraw. The troops that marched overland from Charleston reached Cheraw before the bulk of Hardee's other troops and baggage came north by rail. Meanwhile, the Federal army abruptly turned away from the Charlotte & South Carolina Railroad and began marching toward Cheraw, imperiling Hardee's troops. Fearing that Federal forces might yet intercept that part of his command still bound for Cheraw, Hardee angrily advised Johnston that "this road, like all the others in the Confederacy, is wretchedly managed. With proper management, I ought to have had everything here by now." Hardee admitted, however, that a series of derailments had occurred on the tracks below Cheraw and delayed the arrival of the trains. In this situation Johnston could not help Hardee, although the latter succeeded in moving his forces into North Carolina without opposition from Sherman.[8]

The difficulties of railroad transportation at Concord and Cheraw coincided with the development of another railroad problem that more seriously threatened to delay Army of Tennessee troops from joining other Confederate forces in the Tarheel State. The problem stemmed from North Carolina governor Zebulon B. Vance's opposition to widening of North Carolina Railroad tracks between Salisbury and Danville. Early in February, Quartermaster General Lawton instructed Beauregard to remove to Chester and Charlotte all available South Carolina rolling stock in an effort to save the machinery from Federal capture. Beauregard obeyed but remained concerned about the continued safety of the railroad equipment that he had brought to Chester and Charlotte. On February 21 he advised Lawton from Chester that the rolling stock lay exposed to capture or destruction by Sherman's cavalry "unless the gauge of the road from Charlotte to Danville be widened" and he sought orders to begin the work immediately. Lawton authorized Beauregard to widen the tracks above Charlotte but failed to obtain Governor Vance's permission to undertake the project—quite a failure, because the state of North Carolina owned three-fifths of the North Carolina Railroad company's capital stock.[9]

Meanwhile, Beauregard's engineers and troops swiftly widened the narrower-gauged North Carolina Railroad tracks above Charlotte, extending the work to Concord by the time Johnston arrived at Charlotte on February 25. Johnston approved of the project, and the troop details completed the work to Salisbury by the beginning of March. At Salisbury, however, the track widening abruptly stopped because North Carolina Railroad officials opposed any continuation of the work toward Danville. Governor Vance, belatedly apprised of the project, peremptorily demanded information from Johnston as to who had authorized the work. In complying, Johnston erroneously assumed that Secretary of War John C. Breckinridge, who had replaced Secretary of War Seddon on February 6, had specifically authorized the widening of tracks. He therefore advised Breckinridge on March 12 that Governor Vance "objects to alteration of gauge" of the railroad northeast of Salisbury, as Vance did not "wish connection

broken with the road west of that place. What are your wishes?"
Breckinridge informed Johnston that he had not issued orders to undertake the project but that he would seek an explanation from General in Chief Lee. Shortly thereafter, Lee advised Johnston that he
had notified Vance that "the Quartermaster-General and I deem
very important that the widening of the gauge should continue to
Danville if possible." Not satisfied with Lee's reply, Johnston immediately conferred with Beauregard to determine who originally ordered the commencement of the railroad project and then informed
Vance that he discovered that "not the War Department but General
Beauregard ordered the widening of the railroad." This was accurate, but neither he nor Beauregard further explained to Vance that
Lawton had authorized Beauregard to undertake the work. Nevertheless, Johnston advised Vance that "I consider the extension of the
work to Danville a military necessity." Unconvinced, Vance forbade
the extension of track widening beyond Salisbury.[10]

Johnston's recommendation that Beauregard's troops should continue the gauge-change work to Danville rested on sound and urgent
considerations, but he should have more carefully explained to
Vance the military necessity that required the work. Vance complained to Secretary of War Breckinridge later in March that he had
"asked various officers for reasons" justifying the project but had not
received a sufficient explanation. Breckinridge then sent Vance a letter in which he identified and fully described the military advantages flowing from a continuation of the project.[11] Vance received
Breckinridge's missive after the fall of Richmond in April, and by
then he had entirely abandoned the project. Furthermore, where
Beauregard sought to procure the implementation of track-widening
work to save Confederate rolling stock for subsequent military use in
North Carolina and Virginia, Johnston understood the work primarily
as a method of increasing the number of supply trains running over
the Piedmont Railroad to Lee's army in Virginia. Johnston did perceive that keeping the rolling stock could facilitate his immediate
strategic concentration of troops at Charlotte and Salisbury, but he
underestimated the importance of preserving the equipment for
equally important strategic and logistical uses within the Tarheel
State. Moreover, Johnston supported Beauregard's use of troop details to execute the gauge-change project because of its military
necessity complicated by an apparent shortage or lack of available slave
laborers. In Tennessee, Mississippi, and Alabama, Johnston had re-

fused to use Confederate troops for necessary railroad work, even though the War Department authorities repeatedly urged him to employ both troops and slave laborers to accomplish railroad repair work in those states.

Otherwise, Johnston's communication with Vance marked a noticeably improved approach to a Confederate governor over his use of Southern railroads. He avoided antagonizing Vance as he had earlier angered Governors Shorter of Alabama and Brown of Georgia. Departing from his confirmed tendency to depend excessively on quartermasters in handling railroad problems, he obtained from Beauregard information surrounding the gauge-change project, even though he failed to persuade Vance of its military necessity. Johnston also demonstrated greater willingness to cooperate with the War Department over a matter concerning the Confederate railroads— in sharp contrast to his hostility and opposition to the Richmond authorities when dealing with his railroad problems in the West and in Georgia.

Meanwhile, the Federal army's movement toward Cheraw in divided columns offered the Rebel commanders in North Carolina the opportunity to concentrate their scattered forces and crush one of Sherman's isolated commands. On March 1, Beauregard urged Johnston to designate Smithfield as the point of convergence for the commands of Hardee and Bragg as well as for the forces of the Army of Tennessee. He reasoned that South Carolina trains at Chester and Charlotte could transport Army of Tennessee troops to Salisbury, while North Carolina Railroad trains could ship those troops from Salisbury to Smithfield, a station on the North Carolina line between Raleigh and Goldsboro and north of Fayetteville. Johnston accepted Beauregard's proposal and ordered quartermasters to assemble rolling stock for the railway shipment to Salisbury of Major General Stevenson's division of Lieutenant General Stephen D. Lee's corps. The arrival at Chester of the rest of Stewart's corps and the whole of Cheatham's corps on March 3 confirmed the feasibility of Beauregard's plan.[12] Johnston boarded a train at Charlotte on March 4 and later advised General in Chief Lee from Salisbury that "I am on my way to Hardee via Fayetteville," while the forces of Lee, Stewart, and Cheatham would follow him from Chester. Beauregard remained at Charlotte to protect the railroads between Charlotte and Danville and continued to direct troop train movements between Chester and Smithfield under Johnston's supervision.

Johnston reached Smithfield on March 5 and then went to Fayetteville to direct the movements of Hardee's infantry and Hampton's cavalry. Sherman's capture of Cheraw on March 3 and the Federal army's subsequent march toward Fayetteville, however, coincided with Federal General John M. Schofield's advance on Kinston. The latter movement prompted Bragg to request that Johnston send reinforcements to Kinston. Johnston authorized Bragg to send trains from Goldsboro to Smithfield for the transportation of Major General Daniel H. Hill's 1,950-man contingent of Lee's corps to Kinston. Moreover, the concurrent movement of Stewart's brigades over the rails between Salisbury and Raleigh gave Johnston the opportunity to reinforce Bragg with additional troops. Johnston ordered Colonel Archer J. Anderson, his assistant adjutant general, to notify Major Charles S. Stringfellow that the latter should convey, to officers commanding all troops reaching Raleigh, Johnston's orders to proceed immediately to Goldsboro. Anderson instructed Stringfellow to "see that quartermasters make necessary railroad arrangements." At this juncture three of the Confederacy's highest ranking generals— Johnston, Beauregard, and Bragg—proved incapable of coordinating railroad transportation in North Carolina to achieve a critical strategic objective, although Johnston bore principal responsibility for failing to supervise effectively the combined tactical movements of rail transport. Sheer chaos on the North Carolina railroads followed, a wild disorder marked by a succession of commands and countermands. [13]

The confusion began on March 7 when Johnston, planning to reinforce the Confederate forces at Kinston, ordered Hill to support Bragg in the event of battle. He further instructed Hill to "keep your cars and return the moment it is over." Johnston then discovered that the trains that brought Hill's troops to Smithfield had already returned to Raleigh. He therefore instructed Hill to "ascertain if General Bragg can command cars to transport your troops at a moment's notice," an order Hill obeyed. Shortly after issuing revised instruction to Hill, though, Johnston decided that Hill should remain at Smithfield where he could either reinforce Bragg at Kinston or Confederate forces at Fayetteville. Therefore, Johnston advised Bragg that both Hill's and Stewart's "Tennessee troops should remain at Smithfield until you have an opportunity to fight; then join you by railroad." Acting precipitately, Bragg instead directed Colonel John B. Sale, his assistant adjutant general at Goldsboro, to instruct his military superintendent of railroads at Raleigh, Colonel Francis S. Parker, to send Stewart's troops to Kinston. Bragg also instructed Major Harold R. Hooper, his chief quartermaster at Raleigh, to forward Stewart's forces to eastern North Carolina. Although uninformed of Bragg's action, Johnston again reversed himself by deciding on a concentration of Army of Tennessee troops at Kinston. He therefore commanded the assistant adjutant general Anderson to inform the Army of Tennessee's inspector general at Raleigh, Colonel Edwin J. Harvie, that quartermasters should immediately send forward to Kinston all troops passing through Raleigh. Johnston also solicited the aid of the North Carolina railroad superintendent Thomas J. Sumner, advising him that Johnston required his assistance in moving the troops to Kinston. Ironically, Sumner's help in accelerating Stewart's and Cheatham's troop movements to Kinston increased the danger of a transportation crisis between Raleigh and Kinston, a desperate situation worsened by the outbreak of battle. Bragg's reinforced command attacked Schofield's corps on March 8, and his troops drove the Federals beyond Kinston. Overconfident, Bragg then instructed the assistant adjutant general Sale at Raleigh to stop further troop trains bound for Kinston and to halt them at Smithfield. Bragg then decided that he would need Stewart's whole corps for another battle. He countermanded his previous order and instructed Sale to "let all troops ordered here by General Johnston be pressed forward to this point." Sale then urged Harvie to "hurry forward all troops to Kinston. Operation there not closed." Despite the breakdown of communication and coordination of effort between Johnston and Bragg, all of Stewart's brigades reached Kinston in time to participate in Bragg's second assault on Schofield's corps on March 10. Failing to crush Schofield and fearing a Federal counterattack, Bragg withdrew his troops to Goldsboro after heavily damaging the Neuse River railroad bridge.[14]

While Bragg attempted to overwhelm Schofield, Sherman's army continued its steady advance toward Fayetteville. Alarmed at the prospect of a junction of Sherman's and Schofield's forces at Goldsboro, Johnston considered abandoning the Raleigh & Gaston Railroad if Sherman should force his evacuation of eastern North Carolina. Johnston proceeded circumspectly, however, by inquiring of General in Chief Lee on March 11 if possession "of the road by Raleigh is necessary for the subsistence of your army." Johnston may have perceived the Raleigh & Gaston as possibly vulnerable to

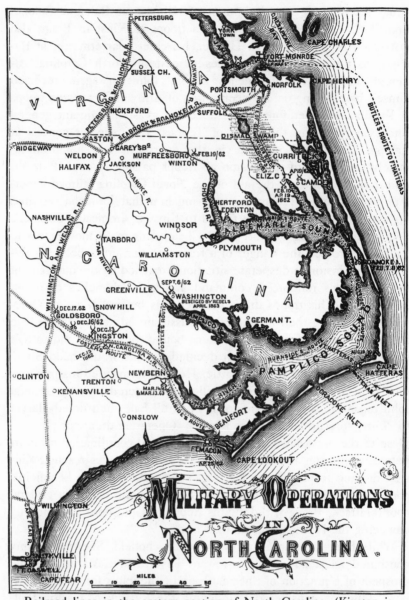

Railroad lines in the eastern section of North Carolina. (Kinston is misspelled Kingston on the map.) From Benson J. Lossing, *Pictorial History of the Civil War in the USA* (Hartford, 1868), 3:182.

attack in view of the Federal seizure of the Wilmington & Weldon below Goldsboro, but he should have recognized that the Army of Northern Virginia critically depended on all the North Carolina railroads. Previously, on March 5, Lee cautioned Johnston that "in moving troops on North Carolina Railroad please do not interrupt transportation of supplies to this army." Forgetting or ignoring Lee's message, Johnston on March 12 again suggested to Lee the abandoning of the Raleigh & Gaston. Johnston viewed the situation as one involving either the destruction of his army or the loss of Lee's most important supply line. He therefore asked Lee whether protection of the Raleigh & Gaston made it "proper to give battle with the chance of winning against us?" Lee, whose army remained under heavy siege by Lieutenant General Ulysses S. Grant at Petersburg, forcefully rejected Johnston's proposed abandonment of the Raleigh & Gaston by reminding his subordinate that "if you are forced back from Raleigh, and we be deprived of the supplies from East North Carolina, I do not know how this army can be supported."[15]

While Johnston contemplated the adverse consequences of abandoning the Raleigh & Gaston, Beauregard advised Johnston of renewed railroad transportation difficulty at Salisbury. The bulk of Cheatham's infantry and field transportation arrived at Salisbury on March 10. Beauregard learned, however, that Cheatham's command lacked transportation to Smithfield because of Johnston's and Bragg's employment of North Carolina Railroad trains between Raleigh and Kinston. He then requested Johnston to order trains returned to Salisbury as quickly as possible, particularly because of the 185 carloads of troops, wagons, and ordnance equipment that continued to await shipment to Greensboro. Johnston sent no trains to Salisbury. Instead, he completed preparations to defend Fayetteville, one of the Confederacy's most important manufacturing centers and the site of an extensive ordnance arsenal. On the approach of a part of the Federal army, however, Johnston decided to abandon Fayetteville and sacrifice its factories, armories, and machine shops rather than to risk a crushing defeat in battle. He returned to Smithfield after ordering Hampton to cover the Confederate withdrawal by burning the railroad bridge over Cape Fear River. Hampton's troops saturated the bridge's trestlework with rosin and ignited the timbers. Quickly, the bridge became "enveloped in flames, and fell with a crash that resembled the roar of artillery."[16] Federal troops then occupied

Fayetteville on March 11, further scattering Hardee's and Hampton's commands at the Battle of Averysboro on the thirteenth.

Farther east, the Federal advance on Goldsboro persuaded Johnston to evacuate Bragg's forces to Smithfield. Not certain whether North Carolina Railroad trains could be located at Goldsboro, Johnston asked Bragg whether the railroad could help him in reaching Smithfield. Bragg replied that he could not secure railroad transportation and that he expected to march his troops twenty-two miles to Smithfield, a movement completed on March 16. Although Bragg advised Johnston that he could not find trains at Goldsboro, Johnston neglected to instruct quartermasters at Raleigh to return to Salisbury the North Carolina Railroad trains at the capital. A six-day delay ensued before any trains moved to Salisbury to ship Cheatham's corps to Smithfield. By then, Beauregard had already gone to Raleigh to join Johnston for a conference of war. Meanwhile, Johnston designated Raleigh & Gaston trains for the transportation to Richmond of over nine hundred Federal prisoners at Raleigh. He ordered quartermasters to ship the prisoners from Raleigh to Gaston and then march them under guard to a point on the Richmond & Danville Railroad for transportation to Libby Prison at the Confederate capital. The Union prisoners reached Richmond a few days later and remained imprisoned there until Federal forces liberated them after the Confederate evacuation of the capital in April.[17]

However successful the shipment of Federal prisoners to Richmond, the poorly executed but finally completed junction of the troops of Hardee, Hampton, and Bragg with the forces of the Army of Tennessee at Smithfield failed to offset the greatly superior numbers brought against them by the combined commands of Sherman and Schofield. Recognizing the Federal advantage, Johnston positioned his smaller army to the east of Smithfield and within an area formed by the intersection of the North Carolina and Wilmington & Weldon railroads. There he planned to intercept Sherman's columns if the Federal army either marched west toward Raleigh or moved north toward Weldon. Pending Sherman's movement, Johnston desperately attempted to obtain additional reinforcements from Salisbury. He denounced the mismanagement of the North Carolina Railroad by railway officials and stationmasters and sought assistance to overcome the problem. On March 17 he complained to General in Chief Lee that "this railroad, with its enormous amount of rolling stock, has brought us only about 500 men a day." He then querulously advised Governor Vance that "the railroad has brought us in the past thirteen days but some 500 men a day." Johnston explained to Vance the problem of large numbers of troops, wagons, and teams piling up at Salisbury as a result of the poor management of the North Carolina Railroad, and he urged the governor to "use your influence to improve its working for our benefit." Unknown to Johnston, however, railroad agents at Chester, South Carolina, and Raleigh, North Carolina, contributed to the delayed troop movements to Smithfield. In complaining to the *Raleigh Conservative*, an Army of Tennessee veteran urged Johnston to "correct the fault" of ticket agents who insisted that soldiers either submit Confederate vouchers during regular office hours or else pay full fare for transportation to Smithfield—a policy that prevented the troops from promptly reaching the front. Johnston's appeal to Vance apparently remedied this as well, although he refrained from directly addressing the soldiers' grievances.[18]

Soliciting Lee's and Vance's aid to accelerate Army of Tennessee troop movements to eastern North Carolina and to improve the railroad officials' management of train traffic between Salisbury and Smithfield again showed Johnston's growing reliance on higher military and political authority for solving his railroad problems. He may have expected that Lee would divert to Smithfield some of the North Carolina Railroad rolling stock then employed in the supply traffic between Salisbury and Danville. His appeal to Governor Vance stood in sharp contrast to his initially antagonistic approach to Governor Brown over Western & Atlantic mismanagement. Johnston's more diplomatic approach did not simply arise from his knowledge that the state of North Carolina virtually owned the North Carolina Railroad: he had understood that the state of Georgia totally owned the Western & Atlantic. Rather, Johnston probably remembered his self-defeating course of action toward Brown and wisely decided that cooperation, and not confrontation, would more effectively ensure Vance's intervention in the existing transportation crisis. Finally, Vance's influence resulted in considerably reducing the excessive quantity of rolling stock operating on the North Carolina Railroad between Charlotte and Goldsboro. Vance issued orders diverting much of the spare equipment to railroad yards and sidetracks. His action relieved the railroad of much congestion and expedited the movement of troops and supplies. Consequently, Cheatham's corps left Salisbury on March 19 and arrived at Smithfield on March 20.

Notwithstanding Vance's action under Johnston's pressure, Johnston contributed little to the partially successful movement of Army of Tennessee troops to Smithfield in the first two weeks of March. The conception and implementation of troop movements to Smithfield sprang from Beauregard's sound grasp of logistics and his superior strategic judgment—the same combination of qualities he had shown in Virginia when he provided rolling stock to hasten Johnston's troop movement to Manassas Junction after the outbreak of the battle of Bull Run. Yet Johnston should have ordered Beauregard to remain at Charlotte or Salisbury; Beauregard's decision to remove his headquarters to Raleigh thereafter deprived the Confederates of steady and effective direction of rail transport in western North Carolina. Not having the assistance of Major Barbour or Lieutenant Colonel McMicken in North Carolina, Johnston also failed to maintain close communication with quartermasters who employed trains between Salisbury and Kinston. Moreover, he lost control over troop train movements and permitted Bragg to operate independently, even though Bragg's transportation orders frequently contradicted his own. Then, while he belatedly coordinated train traffic with Bragg, he neglected to direct Beauregard at Charlotte. Recognizing his mishandling of railway logistics, Johnston turned to the Confederate Railroad Bureau's supervisor of military transportation at Raleigh for assistance in coping with all further matters of railroad transportation in North Carolina. Despite this, Johnston continued to attribute his railroad problems chiefly to the alleged incompetence of Southern railroad officials. Convinced that railroad managers had again complicated and frustrated his military operations in the South, Johnston avoided further communication with North Carolina Railroad Superintendent Sumner, a decision that hindered his last attempts to use the railroad to defeat Sherman or to save his army in the Tarheel State.

While Johnston and Beauregard endeavored to press reinforcements forward from Salisbury to Smithfield, the Federal army's march toward Goldsboro in widely divided columns offered Johnston an opportunity to attack Sherman's isolated left wing, which by then approached the Neuse River. The Confederate army struck the Federal column at Bentonville on March 19, but Union reinforcements from Sherman's right wing repelled the Rebel assaults. The defeat forced the Confederate forces to withdraw to Smithfield, where they met the last arriving detachments of Cheatham's corps. At Raleigh,

Beauregard learned of the outcome of the battle at Bentonville. Fearing the imminent capture of the North Carolina capital, on March 22 he asked Johnston what he should do with Raleigh & Gaston and Wilmington & Weldon supply trains on the railroads between Raleigh, Weldon, and Tarboro. Beauregard assumed that Johnston understood that the rolling stock occupied an imperiled position, particularly if the Federal army continued its march toward Raleigh. Johnston responded to the threat by instructing the assistant adjutant general Anderson to order Captain John R. Robinson, a Railroad Bureau officer at Raleigh and the former superintendent of Virginia's Seaboard & Roanoke Railroad, to remove all trains west of Raleigh if Sherman's forces started to march on the capital from Goldsboro. Anderson assured Robinson that "you will have at least two days time after notice" to remove the trains to Company's Shops or Greensboro, points located west of Raleigh. Johnston then asked Beauregard, "rolling-stock you mention can still be used for General Lee's benefit, can it not?" Beauregard replied to Johnston's inquiry on March 25, expressing his opinion that if the Federal army "be moving toward Goldsborough, rolling stock referred to may be still used for Lee's army, but should be ordered west of here as Sherman shall resume his line of march." Thus far Johnston had shown remarkable restraint in not precipitately ordering a wholesale destruction of threatened Confederate rolling stock—as he had disastrously failed to do in Virginia and Mississippi.[19]

Despite the Confederate reverse at Bentonville, Beauregard's fear of the imminent fall of Raleigh proved unjustified. After the Battle of Bentonville, Sherman moved to join his forces with the units of Schofield at Goldsboro, a point where the Union commanders met on March 23 to reorganize their combined forces of eighty thousand troops before launching a crushing offensive against Johnston's army of 13,500 poorly equipped Army of Tennessee veterans. The break afforded Johnston the opportunity to remove to Greensboro the enormous quantity of subsistence stores that lay in depots along the railroads of eastern North Carolina. He first instructed Beauregard to order a curtailment of supply shipments from Greensboro to Raleigh. Johnston specified that "stores not needed for immediate use should not be accumulated above the quantity that can be removed in two days." As the Federal occupation of Goldsboro continued, Johnston decided to remove to Greensboro the stores accumulated in depots along the Raleigh & Gaston and Wilmington & Weldon railroads. Yet he also insisted that Raleigh & Gaston and Wilmington & Weldon trains should still carry to Weldon the supplies in Lee's depots around Raleigh, Gaston, and Tarboro. In Johnston's judgment, quartermasters could conduct the two operations simultaneously without conflict. Shortly thereafter, though, he decided that the trains should stop making further shipments to Weldon and should instead move to Raleigh the supplies just previously transported to Weldon. Assistant Adjutant General Anderson advised Captain Robinson that Johnston directed him to "remove supplies on Goldsborough and Weldon and Raleigh and Gaston Railroads as fast as possible with your trains." Previously, Robinson had begun removal operations, although he labored under a shortage of rolling stock, particularly heavy freight train engines for hauling supplies south to Raleigh. He therefore asked Anderson if "the North Carolina engines can stop hauling to Greensborough, in whole or in part, and aid in removing to Raleigh."[20]

Robinson's assessment of the prospects for a rapid removal to Raleigh of the stores in the depots at Gaston, Weldon, and Tarboro prompted Anderson to obtain from Johnston revised instructions for Robinson about the removal operations. In issuing another set of instructions, Johnston authorized executing Robinson's proposal to employ North Carolina Railroad locomotives on the railroads north of Raleigh, but he also ordered Robinson to transport supplies from Raleigh to Greensboro "only so fast as they can be carried on from Greensborough. This will give you additional trains in Eastern North Carolina." Thereafter Robinson and army quartermasters moved to Greensboro most of the supplies in the depots around Gaston, Weldon, and Tarboro, but a great quantity of stores still remained around Raleigh when the Federal army marched on the capital in April. Nevertheless, Johnston deserves substantial credit for the successful conduct of removal operation in eastern North Carolina. Although he failed to act promptly after the Confederate defeat at Bentonville, he correctly designated the supplies around Tarboro, Weldon, and Gaston for removal to Greensboro. Initially, he oversimplified the difficulty of Robinson's and the quartermasters' operations, but he correctly decided that a curtailment of the removal operations between Raleigh and Greensboro and a placement of North Carolina Railroad equipment on the Raleigh & Gaston would accelerate moving to Raleigh the more exposed supplies around Gaston and Weldon. The removal operations marked a substantial growth in Johnston's ability to supervise complex railway logistical operations, particularly compared to his poor performance during the evacuation of northern and central Virginia in the late winter of 1862.[21]

Johnston's attention to the removal operation in eastern North Carolina coincided with his consideration of an entirely different transportation question, railroad reconstruction in Georgia. The extensive damage sustained by the Central of Georgia and Georgia Railroad lines in the wake of Sherman's march across that state late in 1864 further depleted the Confederacy's dwindling supply of railroad iron for the repair of the two fragmented tracks. Confederate Engineer Corps officer Lincoln P. Grant predicted in January 1865 that shortages of laborers and iron would delay completion of repairs on the Georgia Railroad until the middle of April. Grant subsequently secured a slave labor force and supervised the reconstruction of long sections of Georgia Railroad track east of Atlanta, but by late March the company's roadbeds between Madison and Augusta still remained stripped of iron. Johnston, who had demonstrated gross neglect in rebuilding railroads in Tennessee, Alabama, and Mississippi, grew increasingly impatient over the continuing delay because he needed to accelerate Army of Tennessee troop movements across Georgia in a larger effort to take those forces to North Carolina. He informed Major General Gilmer, the Engineer Bureau chief, on March 27 that "Major General [Howell] Cobb has been assigned to command in Georgia and instructed to direct construction of railroad." Johnston meanwhile assured Cobb that "nobody has the right to direct impressments of railroad iron except department commander." In truth, Cobb had no power of impressment. In January 1863 the Engineers Bureau's "Iron Commission" divested army commanders of the right to impress private railroad company iron and granted only its members the power of seizure.[22]

Then Johnston again displayed his unfamiliarity with War Department railroad policy. He showed an ignorance of one part of it as early as March 1863, when Gilmer advised him of the availability of a subsidy for the Central Southern and Tennessee & Alabama Central railroads if the firms agreed to undertake the repair of their tracks and trestles between Columbia, Tennessee, and Decatur, Alabama. Johnston did not know that the War Department made available such aid to railroad companies that lacked sufficient funds to repair their own facilities. His lack of knowledge of this practice of

government assistance should have prompted him to acquire a
clearer understanding of the War Department's railway policy as
formulated by both the Quartermaster Department and the Railroad and Engineer bureaus. Moreover, Johnston refused to cooperate
with Gilmer in August 1863 in the proposed employment of army
engineers and troops for the repair of the Pearl River bridge at Jackson, Mississippi, in an effort to move the highly valuable rolling
stock and scrap iron around Grenada to Meridian or Mobile. Similarly, he failed to remain informed of the Engineer Bureau's chang-
ing iron impressment policy while serving in the West and in
Georgia. This indifference and negligence ultimately resulted in his
issuing invalid orders to Cobb, and it further delayed railroad reconstruction in Georgia.

Johnston remained concerned over the reconstruction of the Georgia Railroad, however, because the completion of that work promised
more rapid Army of Tennessee troop movements across Georgia.
Since early February, Lieutenant General Lee at Augusta had supervised the mobilization of the troops arriving in Georgia from Mississippi. In March, he forwarded the veterans, including Stewart's and
Cheatham's corps, across South Carolina to Chester. Later, word
from Lee that several thousand Army of Tennessee troops had left
Augusta in a single group for Chester prompted Johnston to instruct
Beauregard on March 24 that "on reaching railroad march should be
continued by those not taken up at Chester until they meet trains."
Then, in displaying improved ability to control more directly troop
train movements over the North Carolina Railroad, Johnston again
invoked the aid of Governor Vance. On March 29 he urged Vance to
employ all available rolling stock, or the "whole force of the North
Carolina road," to transport the troops from Chester and Charlotte to
Raleigh. Johnston again solicited the governor's "whole influence
and authority over railroad officials in aid" of executing the troop
movements. Although Johnston recognized that he had concentrated
much of North Carolina's rolling stock in eastern North Carolina to
conduct troop movements and remove supplies, he also understood
that enough rolling stock remained around Raleigh for service in the
western part of the state. Therefore, Governor Vance encountered
no difficulty in having trains sent to Salisbury to collect Lee's first
detachments that began arriving from Chester. An unexpected Federal cavalry raid into western North Carolina, however, threatened to
disrupt the smooth flow of troops between Chester and Smithfield.

Major General George Stoneman's raid against the North Carolina Railroad forced Lee's troops to defend the railroad between Charlotte and Greensboro. On March 30 Johnston advised General in Chief Lee about the raid and then inquired of Beauregard if "we can not put on the road troops enough to protect all chief places on it?" In particular, he ordered Brigadier General James G. Martin, who commanded two cavalry regiments, to "co-operate with troops on railroad near Salisbury against Federal raid." Johnston also mobilized an artillery company at Hillsboro and sent the battery aboard boxcars west toward Salisbury. The threat to Salisbury passed, however, when Stoneman's forces returned to Virginia. Johnston then ordered the artillery unit stopped at Greensboro and instructed quartermasters to resume the direction of troop train movements from Salisbury to Raleigh.[23]

The renewed movement of Army of Tennessee troops to Smithfield early in April coincided with Johnston preparing for the evacuation of eastern North Carolina. His most significant decision rested on a serious strategic miscalculation: he concluded that Sherman's anticipated advance on Raleigh necessitated the destruction of a portion of the rolling stock under Confederate control. To retard the Federal march and ensure continuation of the removal of supplies from Tarboro to Raleigh, Johnston also concluded that he should destroy the Wilmington & Weldon and North Carolina Railroad tracks north and west of Goldsboro. He therefore instructed Hampton on April 6 to "tear up both railroads as near the enemy as possible." Having completed this work, Johnston ceased to believe that the North Carolina and Raleigh & Gaston rolling stock between Raleigh and Weldon stood in jeopardy. Accordingly, he expected Robinson to remove to Raleigh and thence to Greensboro that equipment in the event of a Federal march on the capital. In contrast, he reasoned that Wilmington & Weldon trains between Tarboro and Weldon occupied a perilous position. Should Sherman's cavalry threaten them, Johnston recognized that he could not safely send the equipment north of Weldon because Grant both besieged Petersburg and controlled the railroad that ran directly south to the North Carolina border above Weldon. Nor could he send the rolling stock south of Tarboro toward Goldsboro because Sherman occupied that point. Consequently, on April 7 Johnston ordered Hampton to instruct Brigadier General Lawrence S. Baker, then at Weldon, to "keep the trains on Wilmington and Weldon road, hauling supplies

long as practicable, and in case they are cut off to destroy them."
Johnston also instructed Hampton's subordinate, Major General
Joseph Wheeler, to "destroy any rolling-stock which would otherwise
fall into enemy's hands."[24]

Johnston's orders for the destruction of Wilmington & Weldon
property manifested glaring errors of judgment. First, he neglected
to notify Robinson about the instructions that authorized the destruction of the railway equipment between Tarboro and Weldon.
Anderson had sent Robinson Johnston's orders concerning the dispo-
sition of Raleigh & Gaston trains between Raleigh and Weldon and
the Wilmington & Weldon trains between Weldon and Tarboro in
the event of a Federal advance on Raleigh. Anderson assured Robinson that quartermasters at Gaston, Weldon, and Tarboro would
have two days after notice to remove the rolling stock of both companies to Raleigh. Johnston then abruptly concluded that neither
Robinson nor Baker could, within two days, remove to Raleigh the
Wilmington & Weldon trains between Tarboro and Weldon. He
therefore decided to sacrifice the rolling stock when he could no
longer use the machinery to save supplies, but he overlooked the
equally important strategic value of the railroad equipment to the
remaining Confederate armies in the east if Robinson could bring
the locomotives and cars to Raleigh from Tarboro and Weldon. Further, he failed to consider ordering a series of delaying operations
north of Goldsboro to protect a removal of the trains, even though
Hampton's mounted command nearly equaled in strength Federal
General Judson Kilpatrick's cavalry force.[25]

Besides this, Johnston authorized the massive destruction of rolling stock, not knowing how many locomotives and cars actually remained in service between Tarboro and Weldon. Robinson had
informed Beauregard only three weeks before that he regularly employed 19 engines and 150 cars (that equipment also included Petersburg and Seaboard & Roanoke property) around Weldon alone. In
any event, Johnston also decided that destruction of the trains on the
railroad between Tarboro and Weldon could hinder a Federal march
from Goldsboro on Weldon and into Virginia. He recognized that
Sherman used a limited quantity of rolling stock on the Atlantic &
North Carolina and Wilmington & Weldon railroads below Goldsboro, and he clearly perceived the vulnerability of Sherman's communications to the Atlantic coast. Yet he should have understood
that Sherman could easily have established another supply base on

the Atlantic coast (possibly Norfolk or Portsmouth) even if the Federal commander abandoned his base at Goldsboro because of a shortage of rolling stock in northeastern North Carolina or southeastern Virginia. Moreover, Sherman depended on field transportation, not the railroad, as the principal means of his army's overland mobility and supply in North Carolina—a masterful application of conventional resources that Johnston never fully appreciated.[26]

While the fate of the railroad equipment remained uncertain, the Federal army left Goldsboro on April 10, and Sherman's columns marched north toward Weldon. Johnston learned from Beauregard, then at Greensboro, that Federal cavalry again threatened the North Carolina and Piedmont railroads. Johnston responded to the imminent attacks on his and Lee's communications by ordering Beauregard to "stop troops of Army of Tennessee at threatened points on railroad." Those troops, however, had already reached Greensboro; consequently, the railroad center at Salisbury, farther to the rear, lay exposed to devastation. Having adopted measures by which he believed he could protect Salisbury, Johnston used "his railroad to lighten up his [wagon] trains" and then withdrew his army toward Raleigh, leading his soldiers over the roads to Smithfield. Union soldiers found the Neuse River railroad bridge at Smithfield "burned by the rebels," but they crossed the river on pontoons and resumed their march on Raleigh. Meanwhile, the Confederate army reached Raleigh on April 11, and Johnston undertook one final removal operation at the capital. He ordered Beauregard to "send us immediately 100 cars to remove stores from here. We can afterward remove them from Greensborough." Beauregard quickly promised Johnston "all the cars practicable." Ten heavy freight trains steamed away from Greensboro and arrived at the capital late that night. Johnston's quartermasters used the equipment effectively and they directed the loading of stores before the Army of Tennessee retreated to Hillsboro.[27]

In this effort Johnston assumed responsibility for removing supplies, again demonstrating his improved supervision of the type of logistical operation which in Virginia and Georgia he assigned to railroad officials and inexperienced army quartermasters. Yet Johnston did not understand the necessity of preserving both supplies and rolling stock in eastern North Carolina, and that failure of judgment largely nullified the usefulness of his removal operation at Raleigh. For although neither Baker nor Wheeler destroyed the rolling stock between Tarboro and Weldon—railway property that Sherman's movement against Raleigh threatened to cut off from the state capital—Johnston effectively abandoned that equipment, which he should have brought earlier to Raleigh over the Raleigh & Gaston Railroad. Ironically, he decided against removing the machinery to safety because he believed it more prudent and advantageous to avoid interfering with temporary removal operations on that railroad.

Despite the loss of the Wilmington & Weldon equipment, at Weldon Robinson obeyed Johnston's earlier orders and succeeded in removing to Raleigh the bulk of the rolling stock on the Raleigh & Gaston Railroad. Rebel troops, retreating from Weldon to the state capital, reached Ridgeway and "found the track filled with cars which had been withdrawn from both ends of the road, including those with our own stores of provisions and ammunition." Johnston thus deprived Sherman of a rich prize in captured rolling stock, but this success scarcely compensated for his failure to protect exposed Rebel property in western North Carolina. Johnston had no sooner finished removing supplies and withdrawing the Confederate army from Raleigh to Hillsboro than Federal cavalry again threatened to destroy the principal railway connections between Salisbury and Danville. From Greensboro on April 11, Beauregard advised Johnston that Federal raiders had struck both railroads, causing extensive damage between Greensboro, Salisbury, and Danville. He explained in more encouraging terms, however, that the attacks on the North Carolina Railroad below Greensboro had ended, while he expected to repair promptly damaged sections of the railroad. Beauregard miscalculated. Stoneman's brigades struck Salisbury the following day. Overcoming weak resistance, Federal cavalrymen scattered the railroad center's defenders (including Lieutenant General John C. Pemberton), burned over 250 tons of military supplies, and left the junction's railway facilities a smoking shambles. Beauregard preserved the Yadkin River railroad bridge at Salisbury, but Federal cavalrymen "destroyed fifteen miles of railroad and the bridges toward Charlotte." Farther north, Union cavalry attacking the Piedmont Railroad also demolished the Reedy Fork River bridge, thereby breaking railway connection between Greensboro and Danville for several days.[28]

While Union cavalry reduced Salisbury to ruins, Johnston conferred with President Davis and Secretary of War Breckinridge at Greensboro on April 12. At that meeting Davis confirmed the fall of

Richmond and Lee's surrender to Grant at Appomattox earlier in April. Davis authorized Johnston to communicate with Sherman about establishing an armistice in North Carolina. On April 14 Johnston returned to Hillsboro, where he resumed command of the Army of Tennessee. At Hillsboro Johnston ordered Hampton, whose cavalry covered the army's retreat from Raleigh, to "destroy all railroad bridges" of any "importance to the enemy" to delay the Federal army's close and dogged pursuit.[29] Hampton demolished few trestles on the railroad between Raleigh and Hillsboro. The Haw River bridge served as strategically the most useful trestle between Smithfield and Greensboro, but that bridge lay fifteen miles west of Hillsboro.

While Hampton's rear guard action covered the Confederate retreat to Hillsboro, Johnston found his supply problems complicated by a problem other than Lee's use of much of North Carolina's rolling stock to supply the Army of Northern Virginia. The Army of Tennessee's shortage of field transportation forced Johnston to use and protect the North Carolina Railroad as he had utilized and defended the Western & Atlantic Railroad in Georgia during the Atlanta campaign. Fortunately, Johnston's commissaries had established depots in North Carolina—depots holding five months' supplies for sixty thousand men; so despite the later loss of stores at Salisbury, the Confederate army suffered no food shortage during its retreat from Smithfield to Hillsboro. Ironically, Johnston issued orders to destroy and finally abandon Wilmington & Weldon rolling stock in eastern North Carolina to impede Sherman's advance and to gain time to save supplies around Raleigh—food that Lee's defeated army could not use for active campaigning and supplies that Johnston's retreating forces did not need while conducting delaying operations. Still, the "Rebel forces could not leave the line of the railroad and subsist." Johnston could solve the problem of an excessive dependence upon the railroad if his forces could reach the supply depots at Greensboro. Recognizing this, Johnston led his army across Haw River on April 15 toward Greensboro. Leaving Hampton at the Haw River bridge, Johnston assured him that "corn can be sent to you by railroad" from Greensboro.[30]

At Greensboro Johnston surrendered his army to Sherman. In his opinion, one Army of Tennessee veteran considered Johnston's action as justified because it had appeared "fruitless to continue the strife with armies practically all around us, railroads torn up, and bridges burned." A veteran of Lee's defeated Army of Northern Virginia who returned home through the devastated Carolinas recalled that in April 1865 the North Carolina "railroad tracks were in a shocking condition where they could be used, and the freight cars were equally bad."[31] Having decided to surrender, Johnston wished to provide additional food for his troops as they prepared to disband and march south through the Carolinas, and he had also to turn over to Sherman all the railroad property and ordnance equipment under his authority at Greensboro. Johnston therefore requested Sherman late in April to furnish the Confederate army with 250,000 rations, mostly fresh meat that the supply depots at Greensboro lacked. Sherman responded by offering the use of the railroad between Raleigh and Morehead City, advising Johnston that "if you send trains here, they may go down with our trains and return to Greensboro" with the needed rations. Accordingly, Johnston ordered Major Samuel R. Chisman, a quartermaster at Greensboro, to instruct Superintendent Sumner to send to New Bern thirty-five cars to collect the supplies. Johnston, however, proudly refused to accept Sherman's generosity without first offering and making payment in kind. He therefore purchased the supplies by sending to New Bern an additional thirteen cars loaded with valuable Confederate cotton. Having provided his army with food, Johnston ordered a concentration of all the rolling stock under his control at Greensboro and handed the equipment over to Sherman on May 2. As one Federal veteran later recalled, the "switches and sidings of the railroads were packed with locomotives and cars." In the aggregate, Johnston surrendered "two hundred and forty-five locomotives, and more than one thousand cars, with an immense amount of commissary and ordnance stores" at Greensboro. Johnston's forces then disbanded; he himself returned to his native state of Virginia, where he had originally used the Confederate railroads.[32]

Johnston's use of the North Carolina railroads showed his continued pattern of inconsistency in handling military transportation. Strategically, he proved incapable of fully exploiting those railroads in concentrating Confederate forces in the state because he failed to develop a coherent strategic plan and because he invoked the assistance of Governor Vance and railroad managers only in a critical or desperate situation. Without Beauregard, Johnston would have failed to assemble an organized fighting force against Sherman in the Tarheel State. From a logistical standpoint, Johnston showed improvement in the handling of supply operations and particularly in his removal of accumulated stores from advanced areas. He therefore demonstrated less skill than before in using Confederate railroads to achieve strategic objectives but more competence than previously in using them to accomplish logistical operations. Yet in North Carolina Johnston also demonstrated his one consistent approach to Southern railroads: he never hesitated to order the destruction of rolling stock or other railroad property. He controlled an abundance of rolling stock in North Carolina but, instead of protecting it for further Confederate military use, he prepared to destroy it to deprive Sherman of increased mobility—overlooking the substantial contribution of Sherman's superior field rail transportation to the rapid Union march through the Carolinas. Finally, Johnston proved unable to coordinate the tactical movements of rail transport with the War Department authorities, Governor Vance, and the railroad officials or with Generals Lee, Beauregard, and Bragg. His inability to conduct more effective railroad-supported military operations in the Tarheel State hastened the Confederate surrender at Greensboro.

Conclusion

EXAMINATION of Johnston's use of the Confederate railroads supports the position that Civil War historians have exaggerated his ability as a strategist and logistician. Because
Johnston never recognized or admitted the crucial importance of the
railroad to his military operations, his continual mishandling of the
railroad contributed significantly to the successive failures of his
strategic and logistical operations in different quarters of the Confederacy. Inconsistency and contradiction characterized Johnston's
exploitation of the railroads, and this erratic approach adversely
affected his relations with War Department authorities and Confederate governors concerning railroad policy, his use of Confederate
commanders and army quartermasters in solving railroad problems,
and his relations with Southern railroad company managers. Concep-
tually, early in the war Johnston appreciated the Confederacy's strategic advantage in its possession of a railway network that formed a
system of interior lines of transportation. He perceived that advantage in Virginia after his unanticipated but decisive Manassas Gap
Railroad troop movement during the first Battle of Bull Run. For
the rest of the war he steadily, although extremely unevenly, grew in
the ability to achieve strategic concentrations of force throughout the
Confederacy. Despite this increasingly skillful utilization of the
Southern railroads in conducting offensive and defensive operations,
Johnston attached slight importance to the maintenance of railroad
tracks and trestles. He failed to commence promptly railroad reconstruction operations in Tennessee, Alabama, and Mississippi, and his
negligence complicated or paralyzed Confederate transportation operations in different parts of those states for much of the decisive

182

year of 1863. In this regard, Johnston oversimplified the problems of conducting mobilized strategic and logistical operations and underestimated the difficulties of repairing and reconstructing stripped roadbeds and burned bridges. His lack of sound military judgment and incorrect technical assessment sprang principally from his intellectual inflexibility, lack of imagination and enterprise, and an indifference to the necessity of establishing and maintaining an effective mechanized Confederate transportation capability.

Johnston showed equally uneven growth in his use of the Confederate railroads in logistical and supply operations. His construction of the Centreville Railroad in 1862 marked his first significant and accurate perception of the railroad as a superior means of supplying an army, particularly under conditions where he could not employ effectively conventional field transportation. Immediately following this impressive accomplishment, however, he disastrously mishandled railroads in implementing the removal of food supplies and ordnance equipment from northern and central Virginia. Later, in middle Tennessee in 1863, he failed to obtain an abundance of supplies from Alabama for the Army of Tennessee because of his negligent supervision of Bragg, who bore immediate responsibility for directing the Central Southern and Tennessee & Alabama Central reconstruction project. The Army of Tennessee's renewed supply shortages in Georgia early in 1864 finally compelled him to confront his railroad problems. In the course of his controversies with Governor Brown and the Richmond authorities, he acquired an improved appreciation of the complex management and technical problems that had hindered his logistical operations in Virginia. He showed a firmer grasp of railway logistics in North Carolina through his support of Beauregard's gauge-change project and by his effective supervision of the removal operations in the eastern part of that state.

Through a combination of indifference and neglect, Johnston utterly failed to understand the goals and apply the rules of the War Department's policy toward a more successful military exploitation of the Southern railroads. He infrequently communicated with the War Department authorities about his railroad problems and consequently displayed a reprehensible ignorance of the Engineer and Railroad bureaus' activity in the development of that policy. He evinced an equally culpable ignorance of the Quartermaster Department's activity in the formulation of that policy, as exemplified by his interference with the Wilmington cotton traffic in the winter of

1864. He appreciated gubernatorial assistance in solving his railroad problems only after his clash with Governor Brown in Georgia; subsequently, he cooperated effectively with Governors Brown and Vance in addressing and solving those problems. Yet Johnston never attempted to make a successful adjustment to Confederate railroad policy relating to the Southern railway firms. Initially, in 1861, he irregularly observed the government's laissez-faire policy covering the companies' commercial interests and property rights. His reckless abuse and destruction of several Virginia railroad firms' property (besides the Baltimore & Ohio Railroad's) represented his most flagrant violation of War Department policy. After his involvement in the corn order controversy that Pemberton precipitated in 1863, however, he scrupulously respected the firms' private carrying trade and property prerogatives. Ironically, the War Department, in recognizing the increasingly deteriorating military situation as the war progressed, gradually adopted a more liberal policy with regard to government intervention in railroad company commercial activity. Indeed, after 1863 Johnston's punctilious observance of largely disregarded formalities of formerly prescribed government railroad policy contributed to his failure to supervise the rebuilding of the Central Southern and Tennessee & Alabama Central railroads and the Pearl River bridge in Mississippi. In those critical situations he at first obstinately denied and then belatedly offered railroad officials and military commanders the slave labor and technical assistance they required to repair tracks and trestles in an attempt to save desperately needed supplies and irreplaceable railroad property.

Besides this, as ranking general Johnston failed to improve the effectiveness of the Confederate high command that served under him as an important channel of communication between the War Department and the Southern carriers. Particularly in the Western states and in North Carolina, he and his immediate subordinates—Bragg, Pemberton, and Beauregard—failed to interpret properly and communicate clearly War Department railroad policy to Southern railway companies. The breakdown in communication led to a more serious breakdown in transportation. Worst of all, Johnston never accurately appraised the value of the South's rolling stock to the Confederate war effort. From Harpers Ferry to Raleigh, he indiscriminately destroyed or threatened to destroy railroad equipment. He resorted to that course of action because he constantly overestimated the usefulness of rolling stock to Union generals invading the South, erroneously convinced that Federal commanders—particularly Patterson, McClellan, Rosecrans, Grant, and Sherman—critically depended on rail transport in prosecuting successful offensive operations in Confederate territory. Without the advantage of captured Southern railroad property, Johnston incorrectly reasoned that Federal generals and their armies could not conquer the South, even when supported by Northern rolling stock, the Union navy, a steadily improving cavalry force, and a superior organization of field transportation. Yet he simultaneously underestimated the value of that same property to Confederate armies, equally mistakenly persuaded that Southern generals could win the war without the railroad by employing superior theater strategy and by utilizing a sufficiently well-maintained conventional field transportation capability. To Johnston, the railroad was an auxiliary—not an essential—resource of modern war.

Apropos of his use of staff quartermasters and other Confederate generals in handling his railroad problems, Johnston seriously erred by delegating responsibility to poorly qualified officers for the management of railroad transportation. His choice of Major Barbour as chief quartermaster was injudicious because of Barbour's inability to coordinate large-scale railroad transportation operations effectively. Although Johnston extensively used Quartermaster Agent Sharp in Virginia and employed Engineer Corps officers and quartermasters to help him overcome railroad problems in Mississippi and Georgia, he failed to appoint a permanent military superintendent of railroad transportation, except for his brief and limited use of Majors Whitfield and Goodwin in that capacity late in 1863 and early in 1864. Other Confederate commanders, including Bragg and Pemberton, designated army engineers or experienced railroad officials such as Goodwin and Tate as military superintendents of railroad transportation. By contrast, Johnston usually used staff quartermasters, and, when a crisis arose, he employed seasoned railroad men such as Sharp for temporary and extraordinary duty. Nor did Johnston obtain effective aid from other Confederate commanders to solve his railroad problems. He seldom collaborated with Robert E. Lee to use the railroads of northern and central Virginia and eastern North Carolina in moving or saving supplies in 1862 and 1865, although he cooperated with Lee in transporting troops to Richmond in 1862. In Tennessee, Alabama, and Mississippi Johnston allowed Bragg and

Pemberton seriously to complicate his railroad problems, while he proved unable or unwilling to prevent Bragg (and to some extent Beauregard) from badly mismanaging railroad transportation in North Carolina.

Undoubtedly, too, Johnston generally manifested contempt for the Confederacy's railroaders. He rarely deferred to a railroad company president and usually communicated with railway executives, chief engineers, and general superintendents through quartermasters. Johnston's suspicion of and disdain for the Southern railroaders, many of them of Northern birth, created and perpetuated a mutual estrangement. This deprived him of their complete cooperation in a full military utilization of the railroads. Finally, Johnston's personality defects contributed to his decidedly ineffective use of the Confederate railroads. He isolated himself from President Davis and the War Department authorities and attempted to overcome unprecedented railroad problems on the basis of his prewar training and experience as a topographical engineer. The product of stubborn pride and flagrant defiance, this miscalculation caused him to blunder with the railroads and inevitably to hasten the Federal conquest of the Southern heartland. The worst result of this combination of profound self-delusion, pride, and defiance was the staggering loss of Southern rolling stock in the summer of 1863. In truth, Johnston's Grenada blunder resulted from an act of blatant insubordination that exacerbated the already strained relationship between him and Davis while it irretrievably harmed the Confederate transportation system.

Notes

Introduction

1. For a more thorough analysis and discussion of the relationship between the Confederate War Department, individual leaders of the Rebel high command, and the Southern railroads, see Frank E. Vandiver, *Rebel Brass: The Confederate Command System;* Robert C. Black, *The Railroads of the Confederacy;* George Edgar Turner, *Victory Rode the Rails,* 109–10, 233–46; Richard D. Goff, *Confederate Supply;* Charles Ramsdell, "The Confederate Government and the Railroads"; and Edward Hagerman, *The American Civil War and the Origins of Modern Warfare: Ideas, Organization, and Field Command,* 34–35, 105–7, 130–31, 288–89.

2. Gilbert E. Govan and James W. Livingood, *A Different Valor: The Story of General Joseph E. Johnston, C.S.A.,* 1–28; Ezra J. Warner, *Generals in Grey: Lives of the Confederate Commanders,* 161.

3. Scott's remark, variously phrased, is quoted in *Richmond Examiner,* June 4, 1862; and Robert M. Hughes, *General Johnston,* 28.

4. Johnston to Abert, Dec. 1, 1851, Feb. 16, 29, May 8, 1852, and Swift to Abert, Mar. 26, 1852, Letters Received, I–J, 1838–1853 (Letters Received, 1838–1853), Topographical Engineers, National Archives Microfilm Publication M506, roll 36, Records of the Office of the Chief of Engineers, Record Group 77 (Record Group hereafter cited as RG); National Archives, Washington, D.C. (hereafter cited as NA); Abert to Johnston, Jan. 2, 1852, Letters Issued, vol. 16, Apr. 22, 1853–Dec. 5, 1853 (Letters Issued, 1853), Topographical Bureau, M66, RG 77, NA; Abert to Johnston, Mar. 29, 1852, Letters Issued, vol. 14, Aug. 1851–Aug. 1852, Topographical Bureau, M66, RG 77, NA. See also William H. Goetzmann, *Army Exploration in the American West, 1803–1863,* 226–27; and Earl F. Woodward, "Internal Improvements in Texas in the Early 1850s," 169–70.

5. Govan and Livingood, *Johnston,* 11–41; Mark Mayo Boatner, *The Civil War Dictionary,* 441. See also Robert Garnett to Johnston, Apr. 26, 1861; Miscellaneous Letters and Orders Received at General J. E. Johnston's Headquarters, 1861, chap. 8, vol. 238, M998, roll 7, Records of the Virginia Forces, 1861, War Department Collection of Confederate Records, RG 109, NA. In August 1860, Quartermaster General Johnston ordered that payment be made to a New York City–based railroad company for its transportation of army recruits to Fort Leavenworth, Kansas, despite

allegations raised by officers that the firm had seriously mismanaged the entire operation. This experience failed to impress on Johnston the difficulty of conducting troop movements by rail under principally civilian direction, as his Manassas Gap Railroad operation in July 1861 would show. See Henry E. Wayne to D. D. Tompkins, Aug. 30, 1860, Letters Sent by the Office of the Quartermaster General, Main Series, 1818–1870, M745, roll 35, Records of the Office of the Quartermaster General, RG 92, NA.

6. Cooper to Johnston, May 15, 1861, Records of Command Headquarters, Registered Letters and Telegrams Received, May 13–29, 1861, M998, roll 3, Records of the Virginia Forces, 1861, RG 109, NA. See also U.S. War Department, *The War of the Rebellion: A Compilation of the Official Records of the Union and Confederate Armies,* series 1, 2:844–45, 929 (hereafter cited as *OR;* all references are to series 1 unless otherwise noted); and Joseph E. Johnston, *Narrative of Military Operations Directed during the Late War between the States,* 13–15.

7. James W. Silver, ed., *A Life for the Confederacy: The Diary of Private Robert A. Moore,* 110.

8. *Louisville Courier,* June 15, 1861, quoted in *Baltimore Sun,* June 28, 1861.

9. *Richmond Examiner,* June 4, 1862; David P. Conynghan, *Sherman's March through the South,* 385.

1. Victory and Evacuation in Virginia

1. For a contemporary analysis of the strategic advantages of Harpers Ferry, the Gibraltar of Virginia, see *Charleston Courier,* June 21, 1861. See also *OR* 2:924, 940, 977; 51:788, 790–91, 802–3, 977; 2:44–49, 51–52, 802–3, 874. Johnston, *Narrative,* 17–18; Angus J. Johnston, *Virginia Railroads in the Civil War,* 5, 21–24; G. F. R. Henderson, *Stonewall Jackson and the American Civil War* 1:118–19.

2. Lee to Johnston, May 27, 1861, Records of Command Headquarters, Letters Sent, Apr. 24–Nov. 4, 1861, M998, roll 3, Records of the Virginia Forces, 1861, RG 109, NA; *OR* 2:881; John D. Imboden, "Jackson at Harpers Ferry in 1861," 111–18; William E. Bain, ed., *B & O in the Civil War,* 30–37; *Washington Evening Star,* May 17, 1861; Turner, *Victory Rode the Rails,* 73–75; *OR* 2:806; Johnston, *Narrative,* 21–22, 28–29.

3. *Washington Evening Star,* June 6, 1861; William L. Clark (president, Winchester & Potomac Railroad) to Judah P. Benjamin, Feb. 9, 1862, Letters Received by the Confederate Secretary of War, 1861–1865 (Letters Received, 1861–1865), M437, roll 28, Feb. 1862, RG 109, NA. See also Angus J. Johnston, *Virginia Railroads,* 9, 11; and Turner, *Victory Rode the Rails,* 43.

4. Johnston, *Narrative,* 28–29; Johnston to Abert, Dec. 1, 1851, Letters Received, 1838–1853, Topographical Engineers, M506, roll 36, RG 77, NA; Abert to Johnston, Jan. 2, 1852, Letters Issued, 1853, Topographical Bureau, M66, RG 77, NA. Regarding the heavy and constant military use of his company's property by Jackson and Johnston at Harpers Ferry, Winchester & Potomac president Clark recalled that after April 1861 the "Confederate Government absolutely *took possession of the road"* and he demanded indemnification from the War Department toward the repair of damaged Winchester & Potomac rolling stock and tracks. See Clark to Benjamin, Feb. 9, 1862, Letters Received, 1861–1865, M437, roll 28, Feb. 1862, RG 109, NA.

5. *Baltimore American and Commercial Advertiser,* June 15, 17, 22, 1861; *Baltimore Sun,* June 17, 28, 1861; *Washington Evening Star,* June 14, 15, 17, 21, 1861; *Charleston Courier,* June 26, 1861.

6. Myers to Sharp, June 11, July 2, 8, 1861, Letters and Telegrams Sent by the Confederate Quartermaster General, 1861–1865 (Letters and Telegrams Sent, 1861–1865), M900, roll 1, Mar. 25–Sept. 4, 1861, RG 109, NA. See also Myers to Sharp, June 18, July 21, Aug. 18, 1861, Compiled Service Records of Confederate General and Staff Officers and Nonregimental Enlisted Men (Compiled Service Records), M331, roll 223, *Ses–Sha,* RG 109, NA; Myers to Leroy P. Walker, Aug. 23, 1861, Quartermaster Department, Letters Sent to the Secretary of War, April 1861–Jan. 1864, Chap. 5, vol. 157, RG 109, NA; Wyne to James A. Seddon, Feb. 12, 1864, Letters Received, 1861–1865, M437, roll 144, Apr.–Dec. 1864 and Dec. 1863–Apr. 1864, RG 109, NA; *Richmond Examiner,* July 19, 1861; and Clark to Benjamin, Feb. 9, 1862, Letters Received, 1861–1865, M437, roll 28, Feb. 1862, RG 109, NA. *Richmond Dispatch,* July 20, 1861; Black, *Railroads,* 88–89.

7. Festus P. Summers, *The Baltimore And Ohio in the Civil War,* 94–100; Thomas Weber, *The Northern Railroads in the Civil War, 1861–1865,* 77; Mary Anna Jackson, *Life and Letters of General Thomas J. Jackson,* 162. Jackson regretfully confided to his wife that the destruction of "so many fine locomotives, cars, and railroad property was a sad work, but I had my orders, and my duty was to obey." Ibid., 167. See also Imboden, "Jackson at Harpers Ferry," 122–23; *Baltimore American and Commercial Advertiser,* June 25, 1861; *Baltimore Sun,* June 25, 1861; and *Washington Evening Star,* June 25, 1861. A foundry firm built the passenger locomotives at Taunton, Massachusetts, while a Baltimore manufacturing company built the "Camelbacks," the heavy freight train engines. *Baltimore Sun,* June 25, 26, 1861. A technical description of Camelbacks, or "Camels," and a reference to the Confederate action at Martinsburg is offered in Turner, *Victory Rode the Rails,* 40, 43, 75–76.

8. Fennimore P. Jones, *Three Years' Campaign of the "Ninth N.Y.S.M."* 28; *OR* 2:472, 949.

9. Summers, *Baltimore and Ohio,* 96–100; Angus J. Johnston, *Virginia Railroads,* 24; *Baltimore American and Commercial Advertiser,* June 25, 26, July 11, 17, 1861. Johnston's action at Martinsburg also aroused the anger and contempt of a Jefferson County farmer near Winchester. In a letter the pro-Union farmer declared that Johnston "has done little else than destroy property since he has been at the Ferry. All the cars and engines were taken off or destroyed from the Baltimore and Ohio Railroad." *Washington Evening Star,* Aug. 3, 1861.

10. Johnston, *Narrative,* 28. Unlike Johnston and other Confederate generals in 1861, Robert E. Lee placed a relatively higher value on railroad equipment at the beginning of the war. As the commander of the Virginia state forces in April 1861, Lee publicly supported a Virginia railroad president's plan that urged military protection of rolling stock. In May 1861, Lee ordered his subordinates around Alexandria, Virginia, to save rolling stock by building a branch line between two railroads to carry off the equipment in anticipation of a Federal cavalry raid against the threatened machinery. Yet Lee also called for the destruction of the rolling stock if a spur track could not be constructed, and, since one could not be, Confederate troops destroyed much of the equipment. Rebel cavalry spared, however, two subsequently redesignated engines: the General Johnston and the General Beauregard. *OR* 4:240–41, 724–25; George H. Terrett to Lee, May 16, 1861, Lee to Terrett, May 22, 1861, and Lee to Eppa Hunton, June 10, 1861, Records of Command Headquarters,

Letters Sent, Apr. 24–Nov. 4, 1861, and Registered Letters and Telegrams Received, May 13–29, 1861, M998, rolls 1 and 3, Records of the Virginia Forces, 1861, RG 109, NA; Black, *Railroads*, 56–57, 88; Turner, *Victory Rode the Rails*, 63–71, 107, 233.

11. *OR* 2:904, 910, 940.

12. *OR* 2:806, 894–95; Johnston, *Narrative*, 33–34; Turner, *Victory Rode the Rails*, 87–88; T. Harry Williams, *P. G. T. Beauregard, Napoleon in Gray*, 71–80; William C. Davis, *Battle at Bull Run: A History of the First Major Campaign of the Civil War*, 132, 135–43.

13. *OR* 2:485–86; *Washington Evening Post*, July 26, 1861; Johnston, *Narrative*, 36–37; Pierre G. T. Beauregard, "The First Battle of Bull Run," 200; Alfred Roman, *The Military Operations of General Beauregard in the War between the States, 1861 to 1865* 1:91; Lucius B. Northrop to Jefferson Davis, Apr. 29, 1879, quoted in Dunbar Rowland, ed., *Jefferson Davis, Constitutionalist: His Letters, Papers and Speeches* 8:386; Williams, *Napoleon in Gray*, 71–80; Summers, *Baltimore and Ohio*, 99–100. Some accounts of the Manassas Gap Railroad operation have suggested that Johnston, Beauregard, and War Department officials had previously planned the mobilized troop movement to Manassas Junction to effect a concentration of force at Bull Run. For example, see Black, *Railroads*, 61; Turner, *Victory Rode the Rails*, 88; and Joseph B. Mitchell, *Military Leaders in the Civil War*, 177. Other discussions of that operation have corrected this error, particularly Johnston, *Virginia Railroads*, 28–31, and Davis, *Bull Run*, 135–43. The latter accounts have emphasized the improvised nature of the Manassas Gap troop movement. Yet none of these accounts has noted that Beauregard, and not Johnston or Davis, sent rolling stock to Piedmont to transport Johnston's troops to Manassas Junction—an action that possibly prevented a Confederate defeat at Bull Run.

14. Jackson, *Life and Letters*, 177; John G. Barrett, ed., *Yankee Rebel: The Civil War Journal of Edmund DeWitt Patterson*, 7; *OR* 2:473; Johnston, *Narrative*, 37; Imboden, "Jackson at Harper's Ferry," 115; Washington Hands, "From Baltimore to First Bull Run," 63; H. T. Childs, "Turney's First Tennessee Regiment," 165; *Richmond Examiner*, July 27, 31, Aug. 17, 1861; *Charleston Courier*, July 31, 1861. Beauregard tried one Manassas Gap train conductor at Manassas Junction, found him guilty of the "vilest treachery," and ordered his execution. *Richmond Examiner*, July 31, 1861. After the outbreak of battle, similar delays and suspected acts of treason (compounded by errors made by Rebel troops using the hand-operated brakes of railroad cars) slowed the movement of troop trains to Manassas Junction from Richmond. For example, see V. E. Turner and H. C. Wall, "Twenty-third Regiment," 190–91.

15. *Richmond Examiner*, July 27, Dec. 11, 1861; *New Orleans Picayune*, quoted in *Richmond Examiner*, Aug. 9, 1861; *Richmond Dispatch*, Sept. 23, Oct. 9, 1861, Jan. 31, 1862; Black, *Railroads*, 88. The General Johnston, an 1859 vintage, Massachusetts-built locomotive, was sold by the Confederate agent Sharp to the Richmond, Fredericksburg & Potomac Railroad on September 24, 1861, for $8,000—a purchase price defrayed by the company's acceptance of an equivalent value of government transportation on its tracks. Valuation Receipt, Oct. 14, 1861, Citizens or Business Firms, Richmond, Fredericksburg & Potomac Railroad, M346, roll 861, RG 109, NA; *OR* 2:985; Govan and Livingood, *Johnston*, 42–58.

16. Angus J. Johnston, *Virginia Railroads*, 2–5; *Richmond Dispatch*, Jan. 18, Feb. 10, 17, 1862; *Richmond Enquirer*, Feb. 7, 1862; *Richmond Examiner*, Jan 23, 1862.

17. *OR*, ser. 4, 1:874, 1038; ser. 1, 51:2, 1071–72. Johnston, *Narrative*, 27, 67–68; Govan and Livingood, *Johnston*, 59–69; S. T. Stuart to W. B. Blair, Dec. 11, 1861,

Letters Received, 1861–1865, M437, roll 19, Dec. 1861, RG 109, NA. Meanwhile, the War Department assigned Beauregard to duty elsewhere in the Confederacy. Williams, *Napoleon in Gray,* 69–70, 96, 98.

18. Williams to Moore, Oct. 16, Nov. 4, 1861, chap. 6, vol. 367: 45–46, 95–96, Medical Department, Medical Director of Army of Potomac, Letters Sent, Sept. 1861–1862 (Medical Director, Letters Sent, 1861–1862), RG 109, NA. For a biographical sketch of Moore, whom the Confederate Congress confirmed as surgeon general of the Confederate States Army on November 29, 1861, see H. R. McIlwaine, "Surgical Department C.S.A.—Dr. Samuel Preston Moore," 406–7. The civilian complaints about inadequate transportation afforded sick and wounded troops between Manassas Junction and Charlottesville reached General Beauregard and Secretary of War Benjamin. The railroad officials pleaded innocence, though, explaining to one especially disturbed Charlottesville resident that they operated "under military rule, and can only do as ordered." S. W. Ficklin to Benjamin, Oct. 12, 1861, Letters Received, 1861–1865, M437, roll 12, Sept.–Oct. 1861, RG 109, NA. Benjamin apparently failed to ameliorate the situation between Manassas Junction and Charlottesville by ordering a reversal of Johnston's decision on the question of sick trains. Johnston proved more cooperative and sensitive, however, concerning other matters, such as his ordering that passes be issued for the transportation of disabled soldiers homeward over the East Tennessee & Virginia Railroad. See L. L. Ross to Johnston, Oct. 12, 1861, C. W. Elgin to Williams, Oct. 19, 1861, chap. 6, vol. 369:51, Medical Department, Letters Received by Surgeon Thomas H. Williams, Inspector of Various Hospitals in Virginia, 1862, RG 109, NA. See also Williams to Thomas G. Rhett, Jan. 6, 1862, and Williams to Hugh Rice, Jan. 6, 1862, chap. 6, vol. 367:239–40, 242, Medical Director, Letters Sent, 1861–1862, RG 109, NA.

19. *Charleston Courier,* Nov. 25, 27, 29, 1861, Jan. 22, 25, 1862; James Longstreet, *From Manassas to Appomattox,* 61; Smith to Rhett, Jan. 28, 1862, Military Departments, chap. 2, vol. 971:2, Letters Sent, Maj. Gen. E. Kirby Smith's Division, Army of the Potomac, Nov. 1861–Dec. 1862, RG 109, NA.

20. More specific references to Barbour's mismanagement of Confederate resources are offered in succeeding sections of the narrative. As late as December 1879, however, former Commissary General Northrop, in referring to Barbour (whom he did not specifically name but correctly identified), complained to Jefferson Davis that "Joe Johnston had a Q'master of his own selection I believe who was a defaulter of millions lost gambling I heard who bought at high prices 50000 or 60000 bushels of corn at high prices which was in exposed localities all of which was lost" to the enemy. Northrop to Davis, Dec. 15, 1879, quoted in Rowland, *Jefferson Davis* 8:433.

21. James W. Ripley to Henry K. Craig, Apr. 14, 1859, Special File 1812–1912, Reports of Inspections of Arsenals and Depots, 1832–1860, 1892, Records of the Office of the Chief of Ordnance, RG 156, NA; Craig to Barbour, Oct. 6, 1859, Letters to Ordnance Officers, vol. 19, Apr. 8, 1859–Apr. 16, 1860, RG 156, NA; Barbour to Craig, Nov. 23, 1859, Ordnance Department, OCO–Document File 1797–1894, File No. 1859B–1859C, RG 156, NA; Barbour to Craig, Mar. 21, 1861, Ordnance Department, OCO–Document File, File No. 1860Z–1861B, RG 156, NA. See also Barbour to Andrew Johnson, Aug. 3, 9, 1865, with supporting documents, Case Files of Applications from Former Confederates for Presidential Pardons ("Amnesty Papers") 1865–1867, M1003, roll 56, *Ab–Bl,* Records of the Adjutant General's Office, 1780s–1917, RG 94, NA; and Service Record of Alfred M. Barbour, Compiled Service

Records, M331, roll 15, *Bar–Bark*, RG 109, NA. Described by one Richmond paper in 1862 as a "quiet and elegant gentleman," Barbour enjoyed spacious accommodations before the war. Indeed, in February 1862 a Federal artillery unit occupied the stately "grounds and mansion" of his former residence at Harpers Ferry. *Richmond Dispatch*, Jan. 27, Feb. 3, 1862; John H. Rhodes, *The History of Battery B, First Regiment Rhode Island Light Artillery in the War to Preserve the Union, 1861–1865*, 61.

22. Jackson to Sharp, Dec. 22, 1861, and Barbour to Sharp, Feb. 5, 1862, Compiled Service Records, M331, roll 223, *Ses–Sha*, RG 109, NA; Sharp to Jackson, Dec. 11, 1861, Turner Ashby to Jackson, Dec. 12, 1861, and Jackson to Benjamin, Dec. 13, 1861, Letters Received, 1861–1865, M437, roll 18, Nov.–Dec. 1861, RG 109, NA; Angus J. Johnston, *Virginia Railroads*, 35–36.

23. Johnston to Benjamin, Dec. 30, 1861, Letters Received, 1861–1865, M437, roll 20, Dec. 1861–Jan. 1862, RG 109, NA. Alfred L. Rives to Johnston, Feb. 25, 1862, Letters and Telegrams Sent by the Engineer Bureau of the Confederate War Department, 1861–1864, M628, roll 1, Aug. 1861– Oct. 1862, RG 109, NA; James L. Nichols, *Confederate Engineers*, 18–19, 28; Angus J. Johnston, *Virginia Railroads*, 36, 264–65. "Beeline" remark quoted in Frank Moore, ed., *The Rebellion Record* 4:288. Barbour to Sharp, Mar. 1, 1862, Compiled Service Records, M331, roll 223, *Ses–Sha*, RG 109, NA; *OR* 5:1081, 1088.

24. J. F. Bell to Johnston, Feb. 3, 1862, Williams to Rhett, Feb. 3, 1862, and Barbour to Williams, Feb. 13, 1862, Medical Department, chap. 6, vol. 372, Letters Received by Surgeon Thomas H. Williams, Medical Director of the Army of the Potomac and Inspector of Hospitals in Virginia, 1862, RG 109, NA; Williams to Moore, Feb. 3, 1862, and Williams to Barbour, Feb. 7, 12, 1862, Medical Department, chap. 6, vol. 460, Letters Sent, Medical Director's Office, Army of the Potomac, Jan.–May 1862, RG 109, NA; Barbour to Powell, Feb. 10, 1862, Compiled Service Records, M331, roll 15, *Bar–Bark*, RG 109, NA. Powell also failed to provide transportation homeward for furloughed soldiers belonging to Major General Smith's division north of Manassas Junction. Accordingly, Smith complained to Barbour about Powell's "neglect, or refusal" to furnish transportation for Smith's troops on leave. Smith to Barbour, Feb. 9, 1862, Military Departments, Letters Sent, E. Kirby Smith's Division, 1861–1862, RG 109, NA.

25. *OR* 4:1081; Johnston, *Narrative*, 97–98; Northrop to Davis, Jan. 26, 1881, Jan. 14, 1885, quoted in Rowland, *Jefferson Davis* 8:582–83, 9:326–27.

26. Johnston, *Narrative*, 97; John S. Barbour to Benjamin, Nov. 23, 1861, Letters Received, 1861–1865, M437, roll 16, Nov. 1861, RG 109, NA; Moore, *Rebellion Record*, 4:284; Williams to Barbour, Feb. 24, 25, 26, 1862, and Williams to Bell, Feb. 24, 25, 1862, Medical Department, Letters Sent, Medical Director's Office, Jan.–May 1862, RG 109, NA.

27. *OR* 5:1093; ser. 4, 1:1039, 1083; Sharp to Edward C. Marshall, June 20, 1862, Citizens or Business Firms, Manassas Gap Railroad, M346, roll 652, RG 109, NA. See also Peter V. Daniel to Lee, June 17, 1864, Letters Received, 1861–1865, M437, roll 125, Dec. 1863–Oct. 1864, RG 109, NA; and Douglas Southall Freeman, *Lee's Lieutenants* 1:683; Angus J. Johnston, *Virginia Railroads*, 41.

28. Barbour to Sharp, Mar. 1, 1862, Compiled Service Records, M331, roll 223, *Ses–Sha*, RG 109, NA; Telegram, Williams to Johnston, Mar. 3, 1862, and Williams to Benjamin Blackford, Mar. 4, 7, 1862, Medical Department, Letters Sent, Medical Director's Office, Jan.–May 1862, RG 109, NA.

29. Special Orders No. 67, Mar. 3, 1862, Military Departments, chap. 2, vol. 89:120, Special Orders, Army of Northern Virginia, Oct. 1861–Dec. 1862, RG 109,

NA. See also former Lieutenant General Jubal A. Early to Davis, Sept. 22, 1877, quoted in Rowland, *Jefferson Davis* 8:3. In his postwar letter to Davis, Early also said of Trimble that other Confederate commanders made "some complaint that he took care to send all the baggage of his own brigade to the rear, while valuable public stores were lost" at Manassas Junction. Ibid. For more on Trimble's railroad background, see William M. Grace, "Isaac Ridgeway Trimble," 1–34; and Myers to Johnston, Mar. 7, 1862, Letters and Telegrams Sent, 1861–1865, M900, roll 2, Dec. 16, 1861–Mar. 29, 1862, RG 109, NA.

30. *OR*, ser. 4, 1:1038–39; Northrop (summarizing and quoting the contents of a letter from Noland to Northrop, n.d.) to Davis, Jan. 26, 1881, Jan. 14, Mar. 9, 1885, quoted in Rowland, *Jefferson Davis* 8:582–83, 9:326–27, 352; Voucher, Jan. 30, 1862, J. M. D. Goldsborough File, Citizens or Business Firms, M346, roll 359, *Gog–Gom*, RG 109, NA.

31. *OR* 5:1088; ser. 4, 1:605–8, 611; ser. 1, 47: 2, 1303, 1308. Noland to Northrop, Mar. 27, 1862, and Northrop to George W. Randolph, Apr. 1, 1862, Letters Received, 1861–1865, M437, roll 60, Apr.–June 1862, RG 109, NA; *Baltimore Sun*, Mar. 17, 1862. See also Lucius B. Northrop, "The Confederate Commissariat at Manassas," 261; Hudson Strode, *Jefferson Davis* 1:218–19; Angus J. Johnston, *Virginia Railroads*, 38–43; and Jubal A. Early, *War Memoirs: Autobiographical Sketch and Narrative of the War between the States*, 55. For harsher postwar assessments of Johnston's handling of railroad transportation during the evacuation of northern Virginia in 1862, see Early to Davis, Sept. 22, 1877, Northrop to Davis, Mar. 31, 1878, Jan. 29, Dec. 20, 1879, Jan. 26, 1881, Jan. 14, Feb. 2, 25, Mar. 9, 27, Aug. 22, Dec. 25, 1885, Davis to Northrop, Apr. 9, May 20, 1879, Jan. 14, Aug. 3, 1880, Feb. 1, 1881, and Davis to Marcus J. Wright, Oct. 14, 1880, quoted in Rowland, *Jefferson Davis* 8:3, 145–46, 341, 375, 391, 436–37, 438–39, 482, 502–3, 580–86, 587; and 9:326–27, 338–39, 346, 352, 355–56, 384–85, 400–402. For an incisive discussion of the Johnston and Davis feud, see Richard M. McMurry, " 'The Enemy at Richmond': Joseph E. Johnston and the Confederate Government," 5–31.

32. Myers to Johnston, Mar. 18, 22, 1862, Letters and Telegrams Sent, 1861–1865, M900, roll 2, Dec. 16, 1861–Mar. 29, 1862, RG 109, NA; *OR* 11:3, 401–2, 406–7, 408; Sharp to Marshall, June 20, 1862, Citizens or Business Firms, Manassas Gap Railroad, M346, roll 652, RG 109, NA; Daniel to Lee, June 17, 1864, Letters Received, 1861–1865, M437, roll 125, Dec. 1863–Oct. 1864, RG 109, NA.

33. *Washington Evening Star*, Mar. 12, 13, 1862; *Baltimore Sun*, Mar. 13, 14, 17, 1862; Gilbert Frederick, *The Story of a Regiment*, 39, 45–46. The damage done to the Manassas Gap Railroad's engine cost the Confederate government $1,640 to repair, a sum paid through Sharp to Manassas Gap superintendent Hugh Rice in February 1863. Voucher 22, Feb. 16, 1863, Citizens or Business Firms, M346, roll 854, *Rhu-Rice*, RG 109, NA; George A. Hussey, *History of the Ninth Regiment*, 115. See also *OR* 5:55, 514–16, 550–51; and Fennimore P. Jones, *Three Years' Campaign*, 74–76.

34. Special Orders No. 76, Mar. 12, 1862, Military Departments, Special Orders, Army of Northern Virginia, 1861–1862, RG 109, NA. Previously, in January 1862, Johnston named Lieutenant Edwin Barbour to the post of ordnance depot commandant at Culpeper Court House. In a reflection of his preference for saving ordnance rather than subsistence stores, Johnston instructed the officer, "In case of pressing necessity for ammunition for this army, he will divert the necessary Rail Road transportation from any other employment" to supply the Confederate army at Centreville. Special Orders No. 12, Jan. 9, 1862, Military Departments, Special Orders, Army of Northern Virginia, 1861–1862, RG 109, NA. *OR* 51:2, 504; 52: 2, 1073. See

also Cornelius Boyle to Randolph, May 19, 1862, Letters Received, 1861–1865, M437, roll 33, Apr.–June 1862, RG 109, NA; and Johnston, *Narrative*, 107–8.

35. Williams to Moore, Apr. 16, 1862, Medical Department, Letters Sent, Medical Director's Office, Jan.–May 1862, RG 109, NA.

36. *OR* 4:233, 236; 51:2, 1074. Native Virginians like Johnston, soldiers and civilians alike, expressed strong suspicion of Northerners in Confederate railroad service. For other revealing examples, see Henry D. Whitcomb to Governor John Letcher, Aug. 7, 1861, Letters Received, 1861–1865, M437, roll 6, July–Aug. 1861, RG 109, NA; Whitcomb to Seddon, Oct. 31, 1863, Letters Received, 1861–1865, M437, roll 117, Aug.–Dec. 1863 and Dec. 1862–Dec. 1863, RG 109, NA; and Anonymous to Davis, Aug. 15, 1861, Letters Received, 1861–1865, M437, roll 7, July–Aug. 1861, RG 109, NA. For a treatment of the head of the Confederate Railroad Bureau, New Hampshire–born Colonel William M. Wadley, see Black, *Railroads*, 107–23.

37. *OR* 11:3, 405. See also Myers to Randolph, Mar. 29, 1862, Letters Received, 1861–1865, M437, roll 59, Feb.–Apr. 1862, RG 109, NA. For other references to Johnston's use of the northern and central Virginia railroads, see Turner, *Victory Rode the Rails*, 128–35; and Thornton A. Washington to Johnston, Apr. 3, 1862, Military Departments, Letters Sent by Gen. R. E. Lee from Headquarters at Richmond, Mar.–Aug. 1862, Military Departments, RG 109, NA.

38. Myers to Johnston, July 29, 1861, Letters and Telegrams Sent, 1861–1865, M900, roll 1, Mar. 25–Sept. 4, 1861, RG 109, NA; Myers to Randolph, Sept. 5, 1862, Compiled Service Records, M331, roll 165, *Murr–My*, RG 109, NA. In the fall of 1861, the Quartermaster Department used a number of black state penitentiary convicts on corduroy road projects in northern Virginia and on the fortifications around Richmond. See Letcher to Benjamin, Dec. 4, 1861, and J. T. Pendleton to Letcher, Dec. 3, 1861, Letters Received, 1861–1865, M437, roll 17, Nov.–Dec. 1861, RG 109, NA. For more on the use of black workers on Virginia railroads, see James H. Brewer, *The Confederate Negro: Virginia's Craftsmen and Military Laborers, 1861–1865*, 79–94; and Johnston to Sharp, Apr. 1, 1862, Compiled Service Records, M331, roll 223, *Ses–Sha*, RG 109, NA.

39. *OR* 11:3, 423, 543–44; Johnston, *Narrative*, 110; Walter H. Taylor to Whitcomb, May 22, 1862, Military Departments, RG 109, NA; Lee to Johnston, May 5, 1862, Military Departments, RG 109, NA.

40. *OR* 11:3, 477, 506, 533, 555; Johnston, *Narrative*, 112–16; *OR* 11:3, 533, 555; Govan and Livingood, *Johnston*, 59–157; Longstreet, *From Manassas to Appomattox* 100.

2. Paralysis and Conflict in the West

1. John B. Jones, *A Rebel War Clerk's Diary at the Confederate States Capital* 1:190; Clement Eaton, *A History of the Southern Confederacy*, 191–95; *OR*, 19, pt. 2:622–23; 16, pt. 1:1087; Ulysses S. Grant, *Personal Memoirs of U. S. Grant* 1:422–23.

2. *OR* 15:820; Govan and Livingood, *Johnston*, 162.

3. Johnston to Myers, Aug. 12, 1862, Letters Received, Quartermaster General, 1861–1865, M469, roll 1, Apr. 1861–Mar. 1862, War Department Collection of Confederate Records, RG 109, NA; *OR*, 17, pt. 2:780; C. Vann Woodward, ed., *Mary Chesnut's Civil War*, 468. See also Rembert W. Patrick, *Jefferson Davis and His Cabinet*, 135–36. Unfortunately, Johnston thereafter adopted an increasingly distrustful atti-

tude toward the Richmond authorities, and this adversely affected his handling of the railroads in Tennessee, Alabama, and Mississippi. For a perceptive comment by a War Department official concerning Johnston's uncommunicativeness, see Edward Younger, ed., *Inside the Confederate Government: The Diary of Robert Garlick Hill Kean, Head of the Bureau of War*, 50.

4. Black, *Railroads*, 1–11; Turner, *Victory Rode the Rails*, 22, 30–32.

5. Johnston, *Narrative*, 148–49; John B. Jones, *Diary* 1:190.

6. Special Orders No. 12, Dec. 23, 1862, Orders and Circulars, Dept. No. 2, Army of the West, RG 109, NA.

7. Johnston, *Narrative*, 153–55; *OR*, 17, pt. 2:780; 23, pt. 2:745.

8. Barbour to Ewell, Dec. 14, 1862, Letters Received, Departmental Records, Department of Alabama, Mississippi, and East Louisiana, box 1, Dec. 1862, Jan. 1–July 4, 1863, RG 109, NA. For additional detail on the shortage of shoes and clothing in the Confederate Trans-Mississippi Department, see Robert L. Kerby, *Kirby Smith's Confederacy: The Trans-Mississippi South, 1863–1865*, 64–68.

9. *OR*, 20, pt. 1:669; Special Orders No. 4, Jan. 7, 1863, Orders and Circulars, RG 109, NA. See also Oliver P. Temple, *East Tennessee and the Civil War*, 366–411; Grant, *Memoirs* 1:432–33, 437–38.

10. James L. Nichols, *The Confederate Quartermaster in the Trans-Mississippi*, 91; *OR*, 17, pt. 2:764, 770; *Mobile Advertiser and Register*, Jan. 1, 1863; Black, *Railroads*, 131.

11. *Mobile Advertiser and Register*, Jan. 1, Feb. 4, 10, 19, 1863; T. H. Hamilton to Johnston, Feb. 19, 1863, Letters Received, Departmental Records, box 1, RG 109, NA; *OR*, 15, pt. 1:938, 971.

12. *OR*, 24, pt. 3:625; 52, pt. 2:508–9.

13. *OR*, 23, pt. 2:685; 28, pt. 4:806. See also Patrick, *Cabinet*, 132–49. Even before the issuance of Pemberton's order, the shortage of corn around Mobile threatened disaster. Early in November 1862, a Mobile citizen warned a War Department official that "the most immediate enemy in Mobile is starvation. Corn meal is $4.25 per bushel" and the food could "not be had at that." *OR*, 15, pt. 3:670.

14. *OR*, 17, pt. 2:834; 23, pt. 2:695; 32:646. *Daily Chattanooga Rebel*, Jan. 20, 1863.

15. *OR*, ser. 3, 3:178, 180, 288, 293; John S. Claybrook, Thomas Martin, and John W. Sloss to Johnston, Mar. 12, 1862, John S. Claybrook File, Confederate Papers Relating to Citizens or Business Firms, M346, roll 171, *Clarn–Clay*, RG 109, NA; Thomas L. Connelly, *Autumn of Glory: The Army of Tennessee, 1862–1865*, 114–15; Grant, *Memoirs* 2:46. In the fall of 1863, Brigadier General Grenville M. Dodge, the head of Grant's railroad reconstruction corps, rebuilt the entire Nashville & Decatur Railroad Line (including the reconstruction of 102 miles of track and 182 bridges) in forty days. Ibid. Dodge, however, employed a reserve force of eight thousand Union troops and thousands of black laborers to complete the reconstruction work. Stanley P. Hirshson, *Grenville M. Dodge: Soldier, Politician, Railroad Pioneer*, 81. In contrast to Dodge's achievement, by using fewer laborers Johnston and Bragg needed five months to repair the shorter Columbia and Decatur section of the railroad. See also Special Order No. 13, Jan. 30, 1863, Orders and Circulars, RG 109, NA.

16. *OR*, 23, pt. 2:663; Charles C. Ramsdell, "The Confederate Government and the Railroads," 794–810. For further explanation and analysis of Confederate railway policy, see Black, *Railroads*, 107–23, 130, 294–95; and Turner, *Victory Rode the Rails*, 233–46.

17. Goodwin to Bragg, including a map of a proposed railroad route, Apr. 20, 1862, John W. Goodwin File, Citizens or Business Firms, M346, roll 363, *Goodw–Gooz*, RG 109, NA; Thomas Jordan to Tate, with a copy of an "Act to provide for the connection of the Rail Road from Selma in Ala to Meridian in Missi," July 4, 1862, Selma & Meridian Railroad, Citizens or Business Firms, M346, roll 916, *Sel*, RG 109, NA.

18. John S. Bransford to Myers, Feb. 17, 1863, Nashville & Chattanooga Railroad, Citizens or Business Firms, M346, roll 732, *Nap–Nas*, RG 109, NA. Previously, Bransford had supervised government transportation at Murfreesboro. By late January 1863, Bragg had made him chief of transportation for the Army of Tennessee at Chattanooga, described as the "most important railroad point in the South." *Daily Chattanooga Rebel*, Jan. 3, 29, 1863; Edmund W. Cole to Myers, Feb. 17, 1863, Nashville & Chattanooga Railroad, Citizens or Business Firms, M346, roll 732, *Nap–Nas*, RG 109, NA; Special Orders No. 21, Jan. 27, 1863, No. 35, Feb. 10, 1863, No. 89, Apr. 5, 1863, Departmental Records, Department and Army of Tennessee, Bragg-Hardee, Nov. 1862–Dec. 1863, RG 109, NA. See also *Daily Chattanooga Rebel*, Mar. 7, 1863, and Sumner A. Cunningham, "Col. E. W. Cole and His Work," 276–77.

19. H.R. 12, Jan. 29, 1863, with endorsements, Nashville & Chattanooga Railroad, Citizens or Business Firms, M346, roll 732, *Nap–Nas*, RG 109, NA. See also *Journal of the Congress of the Confederate States of America, 1861–1865*, 6:56.

20. Rives to Johnston, Feb. 4, 1863, Gilmer to Johnston, Feb. 19, Mar. 9, 1863, and Gilmer to Northrop, Feb. 11, 1863, Letters and Telegrams Sent, Engineer Bureau, 1861–1864, M628, roll 2, Oct. 1862–May 1863, RG 109, NA. See also Rives to Johnston, Feb. 4, 1863, and Gilmer to Johnston, Feb. 19, 1863, Letters Received, Departmental Records, box 1, RG 109, NA; and *OR*, 32, pt. 2:647; 23, pt. 2:663, 732.

21. *Mobile Advertiser and Register*, Apr. 2, 1863; McMicken to Goodwin, Apr. 1, 1863, Letters Received, Departmental Records, RG 109, NA.

22. Voucher No. 12, June 21, 1863, George P. Gates, Citizens or Business Firms, 346, roll 340, *Gas–Gat*, RG 109, NA; Voucher No. 12, June 21, 1863, W. S. Higgins, Citizens or Business Firms, M346, roll 442, *Hico–Higg*, RG 109, NA. As a matter of perspective, it should be emphasized that Pemberton in Mississippi showed as much incompetence as Johnston and Bragg exemplified in Tennessee in repairing railroad facilities needed by the military. Johnston and Bragg, however, procrastinated and neglected, while Pemberton vacillated. Having previously ordered Mississippi & Tennessee officials to repair their bridges "as speedily as possible" between Grenada and Panola in northern Mississippi, Pemberton early in February 1863 abruptly ordered the reconstruction work suspended because he anticipated renewed Federal cavalry attacks against the trestles. The railroad officials, though, had already procured timber for the framing of the Howe Truss bridges needed to cross the Yockaney and Tallahatchie rivers, and they required government assistance to complete the work that they had undertaken at their own expense. F. M. White (president, Mississippi & Tennessee Railroad) to Pemberton, Feb. 2, 1863, Citizens or Business Firms, M346, roll 1,098, *White, E.–White, I.*, RG 109, NA. See also A. S. Livermore (General Superintendent, Mississippi & Tennessee Railroad) to Seddon, Mar. 7, 1863, Letters Received, Secretary of War, 1861–1865, M437, roll 100, Feb.–Sept. 1863, RG 109, NA.

23. *OR*, 32, pt. 2:647; 23, pt. 2:663, 732; *Mobile Evening News*, June 25, 1863; Gilmer to Lincoln P. Grant, May 18, 1863, Letters and Telegrams Sent, Engineer

Bureau, 1861–1864, M628, roll 2, RG 109, NA. See also Frederick W. Smith to William R. Hunt, with an endorsement by Gilmer, May 16, 1863, Letters Received, Secretary of War, 1861–1865, M437, roll 111, Apr.–July 1863, RG 109, NA.

24. William H. McCardle to Pemberton, Jan. 30, 1863, Letters Received, Departmental Records, box 1, RG 109, NA; *Mobile Advertiser and Register,* Apr. 2, 1863.

25. McCardle to Pemberton, Jan. 30, 1863, Letters Received, Departmental Records, box 1, RG 109, NA; *Daily Chattanooga Rebel,* Jan. 23, 1863; *Mobile Advertiser and Register,* Jan. 23, Feb. 17, 1863; Voucher 22, July 30, 1863, A. L. Maxwell & Co., Citizens or Business Firms, M346, roll 669, *Mav–Max,* RG 109, NA. See also Temple, *East Tennessee,* 366–411.

26. Johnston to Abert, Feb. 25, 1850, Dec. 1, 1851, Feb. 16, 29, May 8, 1852, Letters Received, I–J, 1838–1853, Topographical Engineers, M506, roll 36, Records of the Office of the Chief of Engineers, RG 77, NA; Abert to Johnston, Jan. 2, 1852, Letters Issued, vol. 16, Apr. 22, 1853–Dec. 5, 1853, Topographical Bureau, M66, RG 77, NA; Abert to Johnston, Mar. 29, 1852, Letters Issued, vol. 14, Aug. 1851–Aug. 1852, Topographical Bureau, RG 77, NA.

27. *OR,* 32, pt. 2:647; Myers to Barbour, Apr. 16, 1863, Letters and Telegrams Sent, Quartermaster General, 1861–1865, M900, roll 3, Feb. 10, 1863–Feb. 3, 1864, RG 109, NA. See also Myers to Seddon, Jan. 8, 26, 1863, Letters Sent to the Secretary of War, Apr. 1, 1861–Jan. 6, 1864, Letters and Telegrams Sent, Quartermaster General, 1861–1865, M900, roll 5, RG 109, NA; Myers to Wadley, Mar. 2, 1863, Myers to Pemberton, Mar. 2, 1863, Letters and Telegrams Sent, Quartermaster General, 1861–1865, M900, roll 3, Feb. 10–Feb. 3, 1864, RG 109, NA; and Seddon to Wadley, Feb. 23, 25, Mar. 23, 1863, Telegrams Sent, Secretary of War, 1861–1865, M524, No. 1747, RG 109, NA; *Mobile Advertiser and Register,* Dec. 14, 1862; Johnston, *Narrative,* 163.

28. Barbour to Johnston, Mar. 3, 1863, Letters Received, Departmental Records, box 1, RG 109, NA. *OR,* 23, pt. 2:685; 24, pt. 3:623, 670.

29. William T. Sherman to John Sherman, Jan. 25, 1863, quoted in Rachel Thorndike Sherman, ed., *The Sherman Letters,* 184.

30. *OR,* 24, pt. 3:650–52.

3. The Grenada Disaster

1. Johnston, *Narrative,* 171–74.

2. Pemberton to Johnston, Feb. 2, 1863, and Morris Emanuel to Johnston, Feb. 2, 1863, Letters Received, Departmental Records, box 1, RG 109, NA. Johnston also neglected to order the return to Chattanooga of a great quantity of Nashville & Chattanooga iron that Confederate quartermasters had "seized in transit at Memphis and sent to Mississippi by Government order" in 1862. The Nashville & Chattanooga superintendent Cole requested that Johnston authorize recovery of both the commandeered iron and other appropriated wheels and axles of partly destroyed railroad cars, the iron in particular being "*badly* needed on this road to repair the track" between Chattanooga, Tennessee, and Stevenson, Alabama. Cole to Ewell, Apr. 18, 1863, Letters Received, Departmental Records, box 1, RG 109, NA. Apparently, Johnston's belated concern over the reconstruction of the Central Southern and Tennessee & Alabama Central railroads and his increasing preoccupation with military affairs in Mississippi caused him to neglect the matter of diverted Nashville & Chattanooga property.

3. *OR*, 24, pt. 3:670, 875; Johnston, *Narrative*, 28–29, 252, 455. Johnston's preoccupation with arranging transportation for Confederate troops from Mobile to Jackson led him to compound an error of judgment made by Major Livingston Mims, chief quartermaster of the Department of Alabama, Mississippi, and East Louisiana, and by Major Barbour, his own chief quartermaster, in May 1863. He contributed to the loss of government cloth at Meridian and Mobile—cloth stolen by Confederate troops from unguarded railroad cars. Although Johnston and Barbour continued to deny Mobile & Ohio officials the use of military guards, Johnston defended Barbour against Quartermaster General Lawton's subsequent attacks on Barbour's alleged "looseness and inefficiency." Affidavits of William M. Boyce, Eugene V. Early, and C. E. Carr, Aug. 5, Sept. 9, 1863, Jan. 14, 1864, Letters Received, Quartermaster General, 1861–1865, M469, roll 8, Jan.–May 1864, RG 109, NA; Milton Brown to William H. Dameron, Nov. 4, 1863, Letters Received, Departmental Records, box 3, Sept. 30–Dec. 1863, RG 109, NA; Johnston to Fleming, Nov. 3, 1863, Military Departments, Telegrams Sent, Gen. J. E. Johnston's Command, June–Dec. 1863, chap. 2, vol. $236\frac{3}{4}$, RG 109, NA; Lawton to Johnston, Oct. 27, 1863, W. F. Alexander to Congressman W. H. Smith, Jan. 6, 1864, Letters and Telegrams Sent, Quartermaster General, 1861–1865, M900, roll 3, Feb. 10, 1863–Feb. 3, 1864, RG 109, NA. See also Myers to George W. Randolph, Oct. 21, 1862, Letters Sent, Secretary of War, Apr. 1, 1861–Jan. 6, 1864, Letters Sent, Quartermaster General, 1861–1865, M900, roll 5, RG 109, NA; and Barbour to Pierre G. T. Beauregard, Nov. 8, 1863, Compiled Service Records, M331, roll 15, *Bar–Bark*, RG 109, NA.

4. Grant, *Memoirs* 1:507–8; Johnston, *Narrative*, 171–74, 176–78; *Daily Chattanooga Rebel*, May 28, 1863; *Mobile Advertiser and Register*, May 22, 1863; Charles R. Woods to J. M. Paddock, May 25, 1863, U.S. Army Generals' Reports of Civil War Service, 1864–1887, Woods, Charles R., 2:306–7, Report No. 23, M1098, roll 1, vols. 1 and 2, Records of the Adjutant General's Office, 1780s–1917, RG 94, NA; John K. Bettersworth, ed., *Mississippi in the Confederacy as They Saw It*, 203–4; *Richmond Dispatch*, June 25, July 26, 1861, Jan. 31, 1862.

5. Mims to Johnston, July 27, 1871, quoted in Johnston, *Narrative*, 567–68; Special Orders 23, Jan. 28, 1864, Departmental Records, Army of Tennessee, Special Orders, Adjutant and Inspector General's Office, 1863–1865, RG 109, NA. Johnston's trip from Canton to Jackson late in May 1863 further impressed on him the extent of the railroad damage. Accompanied by Lieutenant Colonel Arthur J. Freemantle, a British military observer, Johnston expressed frustration while he marched the last five miles of the distance to Jackson because the Federals had destroyed that length of New Orleans, Jackson & Great Northern Railroad north of the capital. Arthur James Lyons Freemantle, *The Freemantle Diary*, 84, 87, 99. Even uninterrupted railroad transportation between Jackson and Canton exasperated Johnston. Late in June 1863 he complained to his wife, "One of the unpleasantnesses of my present course of life is spending 6 hours a day on the way between this place, & Canton. Nothing is more wearisome than slow Rail Road travelling especially in passing over the same ground twice a day." Johnston to Lydia Johnston, June 28, 1863, Joseph E. Johnston Papers, box 5, vol. 6, Dispatch Book of Joseph E. Johnston, Jan. 1, 1864–Feb. 15, 1865, including copies of letters from J. E. Johnston to Lydia McLane Johnston, May 30, 1861–Aug. 27, 1863, Manuscripts and Rare Books Department, Earl Gregg Swem Library, College of William and Mary, Williamsburg, Va.

6. Albert D. Kirwan, ed., *Johnny Green of the Orphan Brigade: The Journal of a Confederate Soldier*, 78–79; *Chicago Times*, July 17, 1863.

7. Ewell to Thomas M. Cochran, June 9, 1863, Johnston to Tate, June 26, 1863, Ewell to Mayor Magnum (Commanding officer at Meridian), June 26, 1863, and Ewell to D. G. Cooper, June 26, 1863, Military Departments, Telegrams Sent, J. E. Johnston's Command, RG 109, NA. There were some Confederate commanders in the West who understood the necessity of promptly repairing railroad trestles on strategically critical lines of transportation. In June 1863, for example, while Johnston failed to hasten the reconstruction of the Pearl River bridge, Major General Simon B. Buckner at Knoxville, Tennessee, acted immediately to restore rail communications on the East Tennessee & Virginia Railroad. For the second time in the war, Federal cavalry burned the bridges over Flat Creek and at Strawberry Plains northeast of Knoxville, severing connections with Lee's Army of Northern Virginia. In referring to the bridges, Buckner urgently requested Bragg to "grant permission to [Anthony L.] Maxwell Bridge Builder to rebuild them at once." Bragg authorized Maxwell to commence the work and Buckner thereafter closely supervised the reconstruction project until its completion in August. See Buckner to Bragg, June 22, 1863, Military Departments, Telegrams Sent, Department of East Tennessee and Department of Western Virginia and East Tennessee, Apr. 1863–Sept. 1864, RG 109, NA.

8. Lamar to Mims, July 4, 1863, Ewell to Chalmers, July 14, 1863, Military Departments, Letters Sent, chap. 2, vol. $18\frac{1}{2}$, Department of the West, Feb. 16–Dec. 16, 1863 (Letters Sent, Department of the West, 1863), RG 109, NA. Early in July, Johnston ordered the Southern Railroad's superintendent to furnish Mississippi Governor John J. Pettus with one railroad car for the removal of state property from Jackson. Special Orders No. 128, July 8, 1863, Military Departments, Special Orders, Department of the West, May–Aug. 1863, chap. 2, vol. 181 (Military Departments, Special Orders, Department of the West), RG 109, NA; *Chicago Times*, July 28, 1863; *OR*, 24, pt. 3:1003–5, 1009.

9. *OR*, 24, pt. 3:509, 559; N. R. Jennings and George Fearn, with a copy of a resolution, to Johnston, Feb. 2, 1863, Letters Received, Departmental Records, box 1, RG 109, NA.

10. *Montgomery Mail*, July 21, 1863, quoted in *New York Tribune*, July 29, 1863. The source of the *Mail*'s information is unknown, but late in June Lieutenant Colonel Frederick W. Sims, head of the War Department's Railroad Bureau, authorized Major John M. Hottle to remove the Mississippi rolling stock east of the Alabama River—a mission Hottle proved unable to accomplish before the fall of Jackson in July. See Sims to Hottle, June 24, 1863, Compiled Service Records, M331, roll 226, *Simp–Slau*, RG 109, NA. See also Danville Leadbetter to J. B. Vaughan, Oct. 3, 1863, Engineer Department, Letters Sent, Engineer Office, Department of the Gulf, chap. 3, vol. 12, June 1863–Apr. 1864 (Letters Sent, Engineer Office), RG 109, NA; *Richmond Whig*, July 23, 1863, quoted in *New York Times*, July 25, 1863; and Davis to Lee, July 28, 1863, quoted in Rowland, *Jefferson Davis* 5:579.

11. Woods to R. M. Sawyer, July 25, 1863, Generals' Reports, vol. 2, 319–20, M1098, roll 1, RG 109, NA; Oscar Osburn Winther, ed., *With Sherman to the Sea: The Civil War Letters, Diaries, & Reminiscences of Theodore F. Upson*, 64.

12. *OR*, 24, pt. 3:559, 938; 52, pt. 2:509–10; 24, pt. 3:1018, 1022.

13. Davis to Goodman, July 22, 1863, quoted in Rowland, *Jefferson Davis* 5:574; *OR*, 52, pt. 2:512–13; Seddon to Johnston, July 24, 1863, Letters Received,

Departmental Records, box 2, July 5–Sept. 29, 1863, RG 109, NA. See also John B. Jones, *Diary* 1:386.

14. Special Orders No. 107, July 26, 1863, Military Departments, General and Special Orders, Circulars, Brig. Gen. James R. Chalmers' Brigade, Mar. 1863–Aug. 1864, RG 109, NA; *OR*, 24, pt. 3:1029, 1036–37.

15. Lamar to Chalmers, Aug. 1, 1863, Military Departments, Letters Sent, Department of the West, 1863, RG 109, NA; Lamar to Chalmers, Aug. 1, 1863, Papers of Confederate Notables, James R. Chalmers, 1861–1865, RG 109, NA.

16. Chalmers to Ewell, Aug. 12, 1863, Letters Received, Departmental Records, box 2, RG 109, NA. Furthermore, as Mississippi & Tennessee Superintendent A. S. Livermore later explained to Lieutenant General Polk (who in December 1863 succeeded Johnston as commander of Confederate forces in Mississippi), earlier in 1863 Federal forces removed "a large proportion of the negroes" from northern Mississippi, while neither Pemberton nor Johnston had issued standing orders for impressment of black laborers and repair tools and materials in "cases of absolute necessity" to accomplish an expeditious reconstruction of militarily important railroad facilities. Livermore to Polk, Jan. 13, 1864, Citizens or Business Firms, M346, roll 594, *Littlef–Liv*, RG 109, NA. See also Livermore to William F. Avent, June 26, 1863, Papers of Confederate Notables, James R. Chalmers, RG 109, NA; *OR*, 24, pt. 1:235. For an excellent discussion of the War Department's impressment policy and use of black laborers for the Confederate war effort, including railroads, see Bell Irvin Wiley, *Southern Negroes*, 110–33.

17. *Atlanta Appeal*, Aug. 10, 1863, quoted in *Charleston Mercury*, Aug. 12, 1863; and *Atlanta Appeal*, Aug. 16, 1863, quoted in *Daily Richmond Examiner*, Aug. 25, 1863.

18. Johnston, in his postwar *Narrative*, thus referred to the four-mile gap created by the uncompleted railroad connection and the unbridged Tombigbee River near Demopolis in western Alabama, and the fifty-five-mile trackless gap between Blue Mountain, Alabama, and Rome, Georgia. See Johnston's *Narrative*, 252, 455; and *OR*, 24, pt. 3:493.

19. *OR*, 24, pt. 3:1046, 1049; 30, pt. 4:4, 496. Gilmer to Johnston, Aug. 6, 8, 14, Letters and Telegrams Sent, Engineer Bureau, 1861–1864, M628, roll 3, May–Oct. 1863, RG 109, NA; Gilmer to Grant, Aug. 13, 1863, and Gilmer to Johnston, Aug. 14, 1863, Letters Received, Departmental Records, box 2, RG 109, NA.

20. Special Orders No. 132, July 11, 1863, Military Departments, Special Orders, Department of the West, RG 109, NA.

21. Johnston, *Narrative*, 454. Possible railroad company objections in July 1863 notwithstanding, in the fall of 1863 the Confederate Congress passed a law requiring the formation of a company of engineer troops within each infantry division of every Confederate army. Johnston ordered the creation of such units withing the Army of Tennessee in Dec. 1863, but he did not thereafter use such troops to rebuild the still incomplete Pearl River bridge. Special Orders No. 274, Dec. 14, 1863, Army of Tennessee, 1863, chap. 2, vol. $19\frac{1}{2}$, 242–43, RG 109, NA.

22. *OR*, 24, pt. 3:1017, 1048; 30, pt. 4:493. Johnston, *Narrative*, 254.

23. *OR*, 24, pt. 3:586; 30, pt. 4:502, 510–14. See also William F. Scott, *The Story of a Cavalry Regiment: The Career of the Fourth Iowa Veteran Volunteers*, 118–39; Edward A. Davenport, ed., *History of the Ninth Regiment Illinois Cavalry Volunteers*, 65–66; and Edwin C. Bearss, "The Great Railroad Raid," 147–60, 222–39. For a convincing defense of Chalmers's role in the Grenada affair, see *Mobile Advertiser and Register*, Jan. 26, 1864.

24. *OR*, 30, pt. 4:521–22. Appalled by the wasteful destruction of railroad property at Grenada in August 1863, Lieutenant General Lee, commanding in Mississippi in June 1864, issued orders prohibiting subordinate officers to destroy rolling stock without his express authorization unless Federal forces had either captured or threatened to capture such equipment. In justifying his order, Lee declared that Confederate commanders in the Southwest had perpetrated "immense mischief" and had "greatly abused" the "discretionary power" to destroy railroad property in Tennessee and Mississippi in 1862 and 1863. *Mobile Advertiser and Register,* June 29, 1864.

25. *Meridian Clarion,* Aug. 26[?], 1863, quoted in *Richmond Sentinel,* Sept. 7, 1863. The *Mobile Advertiser and Register* later estimated the financial loss of the equipment in Mississippi and other railroad property in Tennessee to amount to.$20 million. *Mobile Advertiser and Register,* June 29, 1864. Another railroad official, George B. Fleece, the chief engineer and general superintendent of the Memphis, Clarksville & Louisville Railroad, echoed Williams's complaint and criticized Johnston's failure to rescue the rolling stock at Grenada before the fall of Jackson in July 1863. Fleece contended that Johnston should have "reduced the equipment of said Roads to the very minimum" before Sherman's occupation of Jackson in July, and that in August a "wise aid at his post might easily have saved all" the railroad property. Fleece to Hon. Dr. Thomas Menees, with an endorsement by Sims, Jan. 22, 1864, Memphis, Clarksville & Louisville Railroad, Citizens or Business Firms, M346, roll 677, *Mem–Memphis* and Ohio Railroad, RG 109, NA.

26. Johnston, *Narrative,* 227, 454.

27. Rives to Samuel H. Lockett, Aug. 26, 1863, Letters and Telegrams Sent, Engineer Bureau, 1861–1864, M628, roll 3, RG 109, NA. See also Rives to George W. Mader, Sept. 10, 1863, Letters and Telegrams Sent, Engineer Bureau, 1861–1864, M628, roll 3, RG 109, NA.

28. *Mobile Advertiser and Register,* Aug. 23, 1863, quoted in *New Orleans Picayune,* Sept. 2, 1863; *Atlanta Appeal,* Aug. 23, 1863, quoted in *Augusta Daily Constitutionalist,* Aug. 24, 1863; *Jackson Mississippian,* Aug. 26, 1863, quoted in *Augusta Constitutionalist,* Aug. 27, 1863; *Daily Chattanooga Rebel,* Sept. 15[?], 1864, quoted in *Mobile Advertiser and Register,* Sept. 21, 1864; *Meridian Clarion,* Aug. 26[?], 1863, quoted in *Richmond Sentinel,* Sept. 7, 1863.

29. *OR*, 24, pt. 2:536, 553–54, 579; 52, pt. 2:1308. See also *Richmond Examiner,* Sept. 3, 1863; Johnston, *Narrative,* 454–55; William C. Harris, *Presidential Reconstruction in Mississippi,* 22–25; and James Wilford Garner, *Reconstruction in Mississippi,* 142–44.

30. A postwar controversy surrounding the Grenada affair arose in consequence of the publication in 1874 of Johnston's *Narrative,* in which he declared that his decision not to replace the bridge had not contributed to the destruction of the Mississippi rolling stock. In rebuttal, William H. McCardle (a bitter wartime enemy of Johnston and a loyal friend of Jefferson Davis), who had served as assistant adjutant general to Pemberton, in 1878 sent to Davis a letter from the erstwhile Mississippi Central superintendent Frost concerning Johnston's failure to reconstruct the Pearl River bridge. Frost charged that the "military at Jackson would make no move to rebuild without *orders* from Richmond, and no order was ever sent," while a safe temporary bridge "could have been built by a detail from the army *in a week's time!*" McCardle then received a letter from Davis in which the former Confederate commander in chief condemned Johnston's failure to rebuild the bridge. Concurring with

Davis's views, McCardle assured him that the War Department had scarcely refused Johnston "permission to build the bridge over Pearl River. The supposition would have been absurd. I also knew that his bull-headedness was the only obstacle in the way." For further discussion, see Benjamin G. Humphreys to Johnston, Jan. 10, 1870, Mims to Johnston, Oct. 8, 1873, quoted in Johnston, *Narrative*, 431–33; Samuel Cooper to McCardle, Dec. 4, 1863, Letters and Telegrams Sent by the Confederate Adjutant and Inspector General, 1861–1865, M627, roll 4, Nov.–Dec. 1863, RG 109, NA; *OR*, 24, pt. 3:1062, 1065; 52, pt. 2:576, 579–80; McCardle to Davis, Sept. 20, 1864, McCardle to Cooper, Nov. 7, 1864, Compiled Service Records, M331, roll 168, *McA–McCa*, RG 109, NA; McCardle to Davis, July 2, 1878, Davis to McCardle, July 25, 1878, McCardle to Davis, Aug. 26, 1878, and Davis to Northrop, Apr. 9, 1879, Jan. 14, 1880, quoted in Rowland, *Jefferson Davis* 8:224–25, 241–42, 261, 375, 439; and Jeffrey N. Lash, "Joseph E. Johnston's Grenada Blunder: A Failure in Command," 114–128.

31. Special Orders No. 176, Sept. 3, 1863, Special Orders, Army of Tennessee, 1863, pp. 21–22, RG 109, NA; Leadbetter to Glenn, July 17, 1863, Letters Sent, Engineer Office, RG 109, NA.

32. Glenn to Ewell, Sept. 10, 1863, Letters Received, Departmental Records, box 2, RG 109, NA.

33. Special Orders No. 184, Sept. 11, 1863, Special Orders, Army of Tennessee, 1863, p. 61, RG 109, NA; Ewell to Kenney, Sept. 11, 1863, Military Departments, Telegrams Sent, J. E. Johnston's Command, RG 109, NA. See also D. H. Kenney File, Citizens or Business Firms, M346, roll 543, *Kennen–Kens*, RG 109, NA.

34. C. F. Vance and A. S. Livermore to Chalmers, Sept. 7, 1863, Citizens or Business Firms, M346, roll 1,098, *White, E.–White, I.*, RG 109, NA.

35. Seddon to Johnston, Oct. 9, 1863, Telegrams Sent, Secretary of War, 1861–1865, M524, No. 1747, RG 109, NA. See also Gilmer to Seddon, Oct. 10, 1863, Letters Received, Secretary of War, 1861–1865, M437, roll 94, Nov.–Dec. 1863 and Dec. 1862–Mar. 1863, RG 109, NA; Johnston to Seddon, Oct. 9, 12, 1863, Military Departments, Telegrams Sent, J. E. Johnston's Command, RG 109, NA.

36. Barbour to Ewell, July 20, 1863, Letters Received, Departmental Records, box 2, RG 109, NA; Moore to Ewell, with an endorsement by Barbour to Ewell, Oct. 17, 1863, Letters Received, Departmental Records, box 3, RG 109, NA; Telegram, South-Western Telegraph Company, Oct. 23, 1863, Letters Received, Departmental Records, box 3, RG 109, NA. See also Strode, *Jefferson Davis* 1:484–87.

37. Ewell to Loring, Nov. 8, 1863, Military Departments, Telegrams Sent, J. E. Johnston's Command, RG 109, NA; Ewell to Loring, Dec. 9, 1863, and Ewell to Lee, Dec. 9, 1863, Military Departments, Letters Sent, Department of the West, 1863, RG 109, NA; Loring to Ewell, Dec. 6, 1863, and Ewell to Lee, Dec. 9, 1863, Letters Received, Departmental Records, box 3, RG 109, NA; *Brandon Republican*, Dec. 3, 1863, quoted in *Mobile Advertiser and Register*, Dec. 9, 1863. Although Loring recommended the services of the head of his pioneer corps, he avoided urging Johnston to employ troops for railroad repair work at Jackson. In January 1864, after Johnston's departure from Mississippi, Loring advised Lieutenant General Polk's assistant adjutant general, Lieutenant Colonel Thomas M. Jack, that he hesitated to use army troops to assist Lieutenant Colonel Lockett in an effort to "construct a fortification for the protection of the Bridge, at Jackson." Loring explained to Jack that his troops would perform railroad work of "immediate military necessity" north of Jackson with "cheerfulness," but that Lockett should use black laborers at the

Mississippi capital to obviate the "bad effect that this sort of work has upon a command." Clearly, Loring shared Johnston's reluctance to use Confederate troops for railroad work. See Loring to Jack, Jan. 18, 1864, Departmental Records, Department of Alabama, Mississippi, and East Louisiana, Letters Received, 1864, Nos. 1–1200, box 4, No. 15, RG 109, NA.

38. Rives to Minor Meriwether, Dec. 5, 12, 1863, and Rives to Lockett, Dec. 16, 1863, Feb. 4, 1864, Letters and Telegrams Sent, Engineer Bureau, 1861–1864, M628, roll 4, RG 109, NA. Lockett purchased 107 axes and 48 axe handles at Meridian in Jan. 1864, tools "needed for chopping rail wood & bridge timbers." Special Requisition, Jan. 22, 1864, Unfiled Papers and Slips Belonging in Confederate Compiled Service Records, M347, roll 238, *Ll–Lof*, RG 109, NA. Colonel Tate, engaged in directing the reconstruction of the Mississippi Central Railroad in May 1864, advised Major General Lee that he, Tate, would have to suspend the repair work because Federal cavalry had seized a portion of the railroad around Canton. He assured Lee, however, that he would resume the work shortly, "except Pearl River bridge which must be postponed." Tate to Lee, May 14, 1864, Departmental Records, Telegrams Received, Dec. 2, 1863–June 30, 1864, Nos. 1–826, Department of Alabama, Mississippi, and East Louisiana, RG 109, NA. See also Joseph H. Parks, *General Leonidas Polk C.S.A.: The Fighting Bishop*, 359–61. Sadly for the Confederate war effort, William T. Sherman continued to order the destruction of the Pearl River bridge. During the Atlanta campaign in northwest Georgia late in June 1864, Sherman learned that the Confederates had finally begun rebuilding the bridge. He therefore directed Major General Henry W. Slocum, commanding officer of the district and post of Vicksburg, to destroy the trestle over the Pearl, observing, "that Railroad Bridge at Jackson is worth more to the Confederacy than all the population of Vicksburg & I trust to you that it is not rebuilt but on the contrary other points are also destroyed." Slocum reached Jackson in July 1864 and wrecked the partially raised Pearl River bridge, again crippling Confederate rail transportation operations in central Mississippi. See Sherman to Slocum, June 28, 1864, and Sherman to Lorenzo Thomas, July 9, 1864, Generals' Papers and Books, General William T. Sherman, vol. 2, Letters Sent, June 27–Aug. 14, 1864, RG 94, NA.

39. Polk to Wirt Adams, May 6, 1864, Military Departments, Letters Sent, chap. 2, vol. 8¾, Department of Alabama, Mississippi, and East Louisiana, RG 109, NA.

40. *OR*, 30, pt. 4:529–30, 541; Johnston, *Narrative*, 253–54.

41. Barbour to Ewell, July 20, 1863, Letters Received; Departmental Records, box 2, RG 109, NA.

42. Special Orders No. 103, June 13, 1863, Military Departments, Special Orders, Department of the West, RG 109, NA. Johnston recognized the notoriously bad condition of the Southern Railroad as early as February 1863 when Pemberton sought his and the War Department's assistance in procuring railroad construction materials for the repair of dilapidated tracks and trestles between Vicksburg and Meridian. Seddon to Wadley, Feb. 23, 25 1863, Telegrams Sent, Secretary of War, 1861–1865, M524, No. 1747, RG 109, NA; Myers to Wadley, Mar. 2, 1863, Letters Sent, Quartermaster General, 1861–1865, M900, roll 3, Feb. 10, 1863–Feb. 3, 1864, RG 109, NA. See also Freemantle, *Diary*, 99–100; and Kirwan, *Orphan Brigade*, 85.

43. *OR*, 30, pt. 4:464, 651; Johnston, *Narrative*, 228, 255; Johnston to Lee, Oct. 2, 1863, Letters Received, Departmental Records, box 3, RG 109, NA.

44. Daniel Ruggles to Ewell, June 29, 1863, Departmental Records, Letters Received, box 1, RG 109, NA; Fleming to Johnston, Sept. 24, 1863, Departmental

Records, Letters Received, box 2, RG 109, NA; *OR*, 30, pt. 4:464, 651; Ewell to Robert V. Richardson, Nov. 5, 1863, and Johnston to Cooper, Nov. 4, 1863, Military Departments, Telegrams Sent, J. E. Johnston's Command, RG 109, NA.

45. Johnston to Brown, Nov. 19, 1863, MD, TS, JEJ's C, RG 109, NA; Lamar to Richardson, Nov. 8, 1863, Military Departments, Letters Sent, Department of the West, 1863, RG 109, NA; Special Orders No. 207, Oct. 7, 1863, Special Orders, Army of Tennessee, 1863, pp. 113–14, RG 109, NA; Jeffrey N. Lash, "Major George Whitfield and Confederate Railway Policy, 1863–1865," 117–29.

46. Grady McWhiney, *Braxton Bragg and Confederate Defeat* 1:384, 387; *OR*, 47, pt. 2:1309.

47. Lawton to Tate, Nov. 30, 1863, Tate to Johnston, Dec. 7, 1863, Letters Received, Departmental Records, box 3, RG 109, NA.

48. Johnston to Davis, Nov. 4, 1863, Johnston to Bocock, Nov. 7, 1863, Johnston to Seddon, Nov. 24, 1863, Ewell to Maury, Dec. 18, 1863, and Ewell to Bocock, Dec. 18, 1863, Military Departments, Telegrams Sent, J. E. Johnston's Command, RG 109, NA; Leadbetter to Vaughan, Oct. 3, 1863, Victor von Sheliha to Cassius C. Clay, Dec. 29, 1863, Letters Sent, Engineer Office, RG 109, NA. See also Livermore to Polk, Jan. 24, 1864, Citizens or Business Firms, M346, roll 594, *Littlef–Liv,* RG 109, NA.

49. Meriwether to George W. Brent, Dec. 29, 1864, Meriwether to Taylor, Jan. 5, 1865, A. L. Maxwell & Co., Citizens or Business Firms, M346, roll 669, *Mav–Max,* RG 109, NA; Jeffrey N. Lash, "Anthony L. Maxwell, Jr.: A Yankee Bridge Contractor for the Confederacy, 1862–1865."

50. Polk to Seddon, May 4, 1864, Military Departments, Letters Sent, Department of Alabama, Mississippi, and East Louisiana, RG 109, NA.

51. *OR*, 32, pt. 2:510; Johnston, *Narrative*, 261–71.

4. Politics, Logistics, and Supply in Georgia

1. B. H. Liddell Hart, *Sherman: Soldier, Realist, American,* 233; Black, *Railroads,* 158–59, 195–96.

2. Thomas A. Walker to Seddon, Aug. 15, 1863, with an endorsement by Johnston, Aug. 18, 1863, Letters Received, Secretary of War, 1861–1865, M437, roll 117, Aug.–Dec. 1863, Dec. 1862–Dec. 1863, RG 109, NA. See also Rives to Seddon, Sept. 4, 1863, Letters Received, Secretary of War, 1861–1865, roll 117, RG 109, NA; Gilmer to Seddon, Oct. 10, 1863, Letters Received, Secretary of War, 1861–1865, roll 94, Oct.–Dec. 1863 and Dec. 1862–Mar. 1863, RG 109, NA; and Rives to Lockett, Oct. 16, 1863, and Rives to Meriwether, Dec. 5, 12, 1863, Letters and Telegrams Sent, Engineer Bureau, 1861–1864, M628, roll 4, Oct. 1863–May 1864, RG 109, NA.

3. Black, *Railroads,* 5, 9; *OR*, 32, pt. 2:565.

4. Black, *Railroads,* 7, 9, 10, 12, 38, 208–13; T. Conn Bryan, *Confederate Georgia,* 110–17; Marjorie Douglass, *Florida: The Long Frontier,* 186.

5. *Savannah Republican*, Dec. 28, 1863; *Mobile Advertiser and Register,* Jan. 8, 1864. See also S. W. Colors[?] to E. L. Gardenstiss[?], Jan. 15, 1864, Letters Received, Secretary of War, 1861–1865, M437, roll 122, Oct.–Dec. 1864 and Dec. 1863–Feb. 1864, RG 109, NA.

6. John H. Reese to A. R. Wright, Jan. 4, 1864, Letters Received, Secretary of War, 1861–1865, M437, roll 139, Dec. 1863–Sept. 1864, RG 109, NA.

7. *Atlanta Confederacy*, Jan. 7[?], 1864, quoted in *Richmond Sentinel*, Jan. 14, 1864.

8. *OR*, 32, pt. 2:510; Johnston, *Narrative*, 262–69.

9. *OR*, 31, pt. 3:698–99; 32, pt. 2:528; Black, *Railroads*, 194–96, 329; Allen D. Candler, *The Confederate Records of the State of Georgia* 3:450.

10. *Savannah Republican*, Feb. 5, 1864; Black, *Railroads*, 21–22, 127.

11. *OR*, 30, pt. 2:548–49; *Savannah Republican*, Jan. 28, 1864; Candler, *Confederate Records*, 451; Black, *Railroads*, 21–22, 127; Louise B. Hill, *Joseph E. Brown and the Confederacy*, 10, 16, 26–28, 42, 68, 79, 127, 129–30.

12. Lawton to Brown, Jan. 14, 1864, Letters and Telegrams Sent, Quartermaster General, 1861–1865, M900, roll 3, Feb. 10, 1863–Feb. 3, 1864, RG 109, NA. Davis also urged the Georgia delegation in the Confederate Congress to impress on Brown the necessity of an immediate improvement in Western & Atlantic operations. *Savannah Republican*, Jan. 28, 1864; *OR*, 52, pt. 2:602; 32, pt. 2:565; Candler, *Confederate Records*, 454–56.

13. Phillips to J. P. Jones, Jan. 18, 1864, with an endorsement by Jones to McMicken, Jan. 22, 1864, Military Departments, Army of Tennessee, Endorsements on Letters Received 1863–1864, Letters Sent, 1864, and Special Orders, 1864 (Military Departments, Army of Tennessee, 1864), chap. 2, vol. 15$\frac{1}{2}$: 387–88, RG 109, NA. Johnston did, however, accept Phillips's recommendations for apprehending citizens traveling aboard freight trains to the front from Atlanta in violation of military orders. Previously he had complained to Phillips about railroad conductors permitting civilians to take freight trains to Dalton, whereupon Phillips suggested that he and Major General Benjamin J. Hill, the Army of Tennessee's provost marshal general, take disciplinary measures against offending conductors and passengers. Johnston then ordered Hill to implement Phillips's punitive measures. See Jones to Phillips, Mar. 25, Apr. 9, 1864, endorsement of a letter from Phillips to Jones, Apr. 11, 1864, Military Departments, Army of Tennessee, 1864, chap. 2, vol. 15$\frac{1}{2}$: 134, 146, 359–60, RG 109, NA; Lawton to Johnston, Jan. 21, 1864, Letters and Telegrams Sent, Quartermaster General, 1861–1865, M900, roll 3, RG109, NA.

14. Lawton to Johnston, Jan. 13, 1864, Letters and Telegrams Sent, Quartermaster General, 1861–1865, M900, roll 3, RG 109, NA; [Illegible] to Cobb, Feb. 1, 1864, Letters Received, Secretary of War, 1861–1865, M437, roll 122, RG 109, NA; Proceedings of Court of Inquiry, Mar. 2, 1865, Letters Received, Confederate Adjutant and Inspector General, 1861–1865, M474, roll 153, Jan.–Apr. 1865 A(2–251), Jan.–Feb. 1865 B(1–354), RG 109, NA; inspection report concerning the conduct of Lieutenant Colonel M. B. McMicken (including censure of his "great want of system & capacity" and his "intemperate habits"), Sept. 27, 1864, Compiled Service Records of Confederate General and Staff Officers and Nonregimental Enlisted Men (Compiled Service Records), M331, roll 174, *McMe–McW*, RG 109, NA.

15. Phillips to Lawton, Apr. 12, 1864, Lawton to Johnston, May 2, 1864, Letters and Telegrams Sent, Quartermaster General, 1861–1865, M900, roll 4, Feb. 5, 1864–Jan. 28, 1865, RG 109, NA; Edward King to Davis, Nov. 21, 1861, Letters Received, Secretary of War, 1861–1865, M437, roll 16, Nov. 1861, RG 109, NA; Affidavits of William M. Boyce, Eugene V. Early, and C. F. Carr, Aug. 5, Sept. 9, 1863, Jan. 14, 1864, Letters Received by the Confederate Quartermaster General, 1861–1865, M469, roll 8, Jan.–May 1864, RG 109, NA; Milton Brown to William H. Dameron, Nov. 4, 1863, Letters Received, Departmental Records, Department of Alabama, Mississippi, and East Louisiana (Letters Received, Departmental Records), box 3, Sept. 30–Dec. 1863, RG 109, NA.

16. *OR*, 32, pt. 2:552, 557; Lawton to Johnston, Oct. 27, 1863, W. F. Alexander to Congressman W. N. H. Smith, Jan. 6, 1864, Letters and Telegrams Sent, Quartermaster General, 1861–1865, M900, roll 3, RG 109, NA; and Barbour to Beauregard, Nov. 8, 1863, Compiled Service Records, M331, roll 15, *Bar–Bark*, RG 109, NA.

17. *OR*, 32, pt. 2:708; Candler, *Confederate Records*, 463–64; Black, *Railroads*, 21, 32, 128–29. Brown offered this explanation to justify inaction. He sought to have a former Western & Atlantic employee, Joseph R. Tucker, detailed from the Confederate army for service on the railroad. Brown assured Secretary of War Seddon that he needed Tucker to maintain the "main channel" of transportation for supplying Johnston's army. Seddon refused Brown's request, however, because the Railroad Bureau chief, Lieutenant Colonel Sims (who obtained Quartermaster General Lawton's endorsement) had earlier reported to Seddon that Tucker scarcely qualified as a skilled mechanic and that Brown had all the men necessary to operate and maintain the State Railroad. Brown to Seddon, Mar. 22, 1864, with an endorsement by Sims to Seddon, Apr. 1, 1864, Letters Received, Secretary of War, 1861–1865, M437, roll 143, Feb.–Dec. 1864, Jan.–Dec. 1864, Dec. 1863–Apr. 1864, RG 109, NA.

18. *Atlanta Intelligencer,* Jan. 28[?], 1864, quoted in *Savannah Republican,* Feb. 1, 1864; *Savannah Republican,* Jan. 28, Feb. 1, 5, 1864. See also *Richmond Sentinel,* Jan. 11, 1864, concerning the State Railroad's failure to provide fresh water for sick soldiers being transported to hospitals in Atlanta.

19. Johnston, *Narrative,* 278; *OR*, 32, pt. 2:564–65, 592, 603, 698; *Charleston Courier,* Feb. 1, 1864; *Charleston Mercury,* Feb. 12, 1864; Lawton to McMicken, Mar. 31, 1864, Lawton to John M. Hottle, Mar. 30, 1864, Lawton to J. S. Calhoun, Apr. 1, 1864, Letters and Telegrams Sent, Quartermaster General, 1861–1865, M900, roll 4, RG 109, NA. See also *Charleston Mercury,* Apr. 5, 1864.

20. Frank L. Owsley, *King Cotton Diplomacy,* 250–91. For an excellent analysis of the Richmond Government's blockade-running policy and discussion of its promotion of the Wilmington cotton traffic, see Richard D. Goff, *Confederate Supply,* 175–77.

21. *OR*, 52, pt. 2:585–86.

22. *OR*, 52, pt. 2:593; 32, pt. 2:537, 592.

23. *OR*, 32, pt. 2:612, 614, 809; Chandler, *Confederate Records*, 457–58; Beauregard to Johnston, Feb. 9, 1864, and Beauregard to Gilmer, Feb. 9, 1864, Military Departments, Telegrams Sent, Department of South Carolina, Georgia, and Florida, July 1863–Feb. 1864, chap. 2, vol. 45:174, RG 109, NA; Black, *Railroads,* 138–42.

24. *OR*, 32, pt. 2:707; 30, pt. 4:514, 521–22. Johnston, *Narrative,* 252–53, 454–55; Black, *Railroads,* 238–41. The *Mobile Advertiser and Register* recognized the relationship between the supply problems of Johnston's and Robert E. Lee's armies and the destruction of rolling stock in Tennessee and Mississippi in 1862 and 1863. Declaring that Confederate commanders had needlessly sacrificed sixty locomotives and eight hundred cars in the Southwest, the paper complained, "It is hardly too much to say that the rolling stock destroyed in these two States, would, if in existence, suffice for all the requirements of the armies of the Confederacy." *Mobile Advertiser and Register,* June 29, 1864.

25. *OR*, 52, pt. 2:607–8, 616, 621, 623.

26. Wallace to Sims, Jan. 23, 1864, Campbell B. Wallace File, Confederate Papers Relating to Citizens or Business Firms, M346, roll 1,067, *Walla–Wallace,* RG 109, NA.

27. Ibid.

28. *OR*, 30, pt. 4:514, 521; 32, pt. 2:775; 52, pt. 2:607–8, 616, 621, 623; A. K. Seago to Brown, Jan. 9, 1864, and a copy of a contract, Nov. 23, 1863, between A. K. Seago Company and the State of Georgia, Letters Received, Secretary of War, 1861–1865, M437, roll 140, Sept.–Dec. 1864 and Dec. 1863–1865, RG 109, NA; Sims to Lawton, Dec. 10, 1864, Letters Received, Secretary of War, 1861–1865, M437, roll 142, Sept.–Dec. 1864, Dec. 1863–Feb. 1864, RG 109, NA; Hill, *Brown*, 10, 16, 26–28, 42, 68, 79, 127, 129–30; Candler, *Confederate Records*, 456, 458, 464–67, 480–84; Paul D. Escott, "Georgia," 69–82.

29. Federal naval officers stationed along the Atlantic coast recognized the shortage of beef cattle in the Southeast. Commander Maxwell Woodhull reported to South Atlantic Squadron commander, Rear Admiral Samuel F. DuPont, on Oct. 7, 1862, from Jacksonville, Fla. "I have it from reliable sources" that commissary "agents are all over the state buying up all the cattle obtainable, paying any price so they can get the animals." U.S. Navy Department, *The War of the Rebellion: The Official Records of the Union and Confederate Navies*, series 1, 13:369; Lucius B. Northrop, "Resources of the Confederacy in February, 1865," 99; Mary E. Massey, *Ersatz in the Confederacy*, 61. For excellent discussions of the Commissary Department's search for cattle after July 1863, see Goff, *Confederate Supply*, 151–53; Douglass, *Florida*, 186; and Robert A. Taylor, "Rebel Beef: Florida Cattle and the Confederate Army, 1862–1864," 15–31.

30. *OR* 52:565, 585.

31. *OR*, 32, pt. 2:510, 647; 52, pt. 2:565, 585. Johnston's proposal apparently continued his earlier practice of using cattle drives as a means of supplying the Army of Tennessee. Late in the winter of 1863, while at Chattanooga, Johnston ordered the implementation of cattle drives from Kentucky to Tennessee. See Johnston to Daniel S. Donelson, Mar. 5, 1863, Letters Received, Departmental Records, box 1, Dec. 1862, Jan.–July 4, 1863, RG 109, NA.

32. *OR*, 32, pt. 2:510.

33. *OR*, 32, pt. 2:522, 527; Kirwan, *Orphan Brigade*, 118–19; James H. M'Neilly, "Gen. Joseph E. Johnston," 555, and M'Neilly, "In Winter Quarters at Dalton, Ga.," 131–32. Despite the leanness of the beeves at Dalton, Johnston's troops fared better than Lee's veterans. On January 2, 1864, Northrop reduced Lee's troops to a quarter of a pound of beef per man. *OR* 33:1061, 1114–15; Goff, *Confederate Supply*, 197.

34. Ella Lonn, *Salt as a Factor in the Confederacy*, 17, 64–65.

35. *OR*, 32, pt. 2:565; Candler, *Confederate Records*, 454–56.

36. *OR*, 32, pt. 2:565, 645; Candler, *Confederate Records*, 454–58.

37. *OR*, 32, pt. 2:645; Candler, *Confederate Records*, 457–58; Kirwan, *Orphan Brigade*, 118. Despite Johnston's more efficient use of railroad transportation to ship cattle to Dalton, the "great and growing scarcity of meats" continued, prompting him on Jan. 24 to attempt to curtail indiscriminate discarding of meat by Army of Tennessee commissary agents and troops. Johnston instructed commissary officers to examine suspected lots of tainted meat more thoroughly before they condemned and abandoned the supplies. Special Orders No. 13, Jan. 24, 1864, Military Departments, Special Field Orders, Army of Tennessee, Jan. 1864, and Special Orders, chap. 2, vol. 350: 24; RG 109, NA.

38. Kirwan, *Orphan Brigade*, 118.

39. *OR*, 32, pt. 2:645; *Charleston Courier*, Jan. 28, Feb. 16, 1864; Thomas M. Jack to W. Millan, Feb. 3, 1864, Military Departments, Telegrams Sent, Department of Alabama, Mississippi, and East Louisiana, 1864, RG 109, NA.

5. The Atlanta Campaign

1. Andrew Ewing to Lawton, Apr. 21, 1864, Letters Received, Quartermaster General, 1861–1865, M469, roll 9, Jan.–May 1864, RG 109, NA; J. R. Viley to William Preston Johnston, Apr. 28, 1864, Letters Received, Secretary of War, 1861–1865, M437, roll 144, Apr.–Dec. 1864 and Dec. 1863–Apr. 1864, RG 109, NA. See also *Augusta Daily Constitutionalist*, May 4, 1864.

2. Wright to Mackall, Feb. 20, 22, 1864, Military Departments, Letters Sent, Commander of the Troops at Atlanta, July 1863–May 1864, chap. 2, vol. 186, RG 109, NA.

3. Wallace to Sims, Mar. 19, 1864, Campbell B. Wallace File, Confederate Papers Relating to Citizens or Business Firms, M346, roll 1,067, *Walla–Wallace*, RG 109, NA.

4. Rives to Grant, Apr. 26, 28, 1864, Rives to Presstman, Apr. 28, 1864, Letters and Telegrams Sent, Engineer Bureau, 1861–1864, M628, roll 6, RG 109, NA. See also Special Orders No. 274, Dec. 14, 1863, Special Orders, Army of Tennessee, 1863, chap. 2, vol. 19$\frac{1}{2}$, RG 109, NA.

5. Rives to Grant, Apr. 26, 28, Aug. 1, 1864, Rives to Presstman, Apr. 28, 1864, and Rives to Meriwether, Apr. 28, 1864, Letters and Telegrams Sent, Engineer Bureau, 1861–1864, M628, roll 6, RG 109, NA.

6. Jones to M. H. Coser, Apr. 5, 1864, Military Departments, Army of Tennessee, 1864, chap. 2, vol. 15$\frac{1}{2}$, p. 141, RG 109, NA.

7. Voucher No. 8, Jan. 18, 1864, Unfiled Papers and Slips Belonging in Confederate Compiled Service Records, M347, roll 230, *Le-Led*, RG 109, NA; Jones to commanding officer, 2d Regiment, near Georgia state line, Mar. 2, 1864, Military Departments, Army of Tennessee, 1864, chap. 2, vol. 15$\frac{1}{2}$, p. 113, RG 109, NA; Moore, *Rebellion Record* 10:686; Johnston, *Narrative*, 303.

8. Polk to Johnston, May 7, 1864, Military Departments, Letters Sent, chap. 2, vol. 8$\frac{3}{4}$, Department of Alabama, Mississippi, and East Louisiana, RG 109, NA; *OR*, 38, pt. 4:670, 680.

9. *OR*, 38, pt. 4:685, 691, 693, 694–95. See also William M. Polk, *Leonidas Polk, Bishop and General*, 347–50; and Parks, *Fighting Bishop*, 373–75.

10. Charles Wright, *A Corporal's Story: Experiences in the Ranks of Company C, 81st Ohio Vol. Infantry*, 95; Frank L. Byrne, ed., *The View from Headquarters: Civil War Letters of Harvey Reid*, 144; *Macon Telegraph*, May 15, 1864, quoted in *Charleston Courier*, May 17, 1864; John M. Davidson, "Additional Sketch Thirty-ninth Regiment (Second Artillery)," 2:741; *Augusta Daily Constitutionalist*, May 21, 1864; *Charleston Mercury*, May 19, 1864; Johnston, *Narrative*, 306–20; Polk, *Leonidas Polk*, 363; Oliver Otis Howard, *Autobiography of Oliver Otis Howard, Major General United States Army* 1:520.

11. Moore, *Rebellion Record* 11:47; William T. Sherman, *Memoirs of General William T. Sherman* 2:38–39. Regarding the Oostenoula River railroad bridge at Resaca, six hundred men of Sherman's railroad reconstruction corps rebuilt the trestle in six days. The completed structure, as photographed later in 1864, is shown in Ronald H. Bailey, et al., *The Battles for Atlanta*, 14; Jacob D. Cox, *Atlanta*, 61; *Charleston Courier*,

May 26, 1864. "Train flagged" remark quoted in W. H. Chamberlain, *History of the Eighty-first Regiment Ohio Infantry Volunteers*, 98.

12. Moore, *Rebellion Record* 11:47; Jacob D. Cox, *Military Reminiscences of the Civil War* 2:230. See also Cox, *Atlanta*, 33–143; Howard, *Autobiography*, 499–605; and *Mobile Advertiser and Register*, May 28, June 19, 1864.

13. Johnston, *Narrative*, 358–59; *Savannah Republican*, July 16, 1864; *Augusta Daily Constitutionalist*, May 25, 1865; *Charleston Courier*, May 23, 1864; *Charleston Mercury*, May 20, 23, 24, 25, 1864; Byrne, *Harvey Reid*, 153–54; H. I. Smith, *History of the Seventh Iowa Veteran Volunteer Infantry during the Civil War*, 136–37; J. W. Gaskill, *Footprints through Dixie*, 100.

14. *Mobile Advertiser and Register*, May 26, 1864; *Charleston Mercury*, May 27, 1864.

15. Conynghan, *Sherman's March*, 144; Sherman, *Memoirs* 2:46,57; *Charleston Courier*, June 11, 1864; Byrne, *Harvey Reid*, 158–59. *OR*, 34, pt. 3:1046, 1049; 30, pt. 4:513–21. Johnston, *Narrative*, 252–53, 454–55; H. W. Rood, *Story of the Service of Company E, and of the Twelfth Wisconsin Regiment, Veteran Volunteer Infantry in the War of the Rebellion*, 280, 295. Captured Confederate soldiers expressed admiration for Sherman's pioneer corps and particularly for his ability to maintain Union railroad communications despite the repeated destruction of Western & Atlantic tracks and trestles by raiding Rebel cavalry. One Confederate prisoner praised Sherman's ability to restore quickly broken lines of railway transportation, wryly observing, "old Bill Sherman carries a supply of ready made bridges" with his army. Gaskill, *Footprints*, 108. In truth, Sherman's carpenters and mechanics usually improvised replacement trestles by using spare timbers salvaged from partially destroyed Confederate fortifications and abandoned buildings. Indeed, Johnston, not Sherman, prepared duplicate bridges for the Atlanta campaign.

16. *OR*, 38, pt. 4:806, 991. As to the staff change, Barbour's troubles continued. Severely censured by Quartermaster General Lawton in 1863, Barbour was subjected to another attack by Lawton a year later. Moreover, in January 1864 the Richmond correspondent of the *Mobile Advertiser and Register* reported that Barbour qualified as an arch villain in the inefficient Confederate Quartermaster Department, a bureau "*filled*" with a troop of rascals." Others, in Mississippi, defended Barbour by praising his distinguished ancestry and antebellum political career in Virginia. See *Mobile Advertiser and Register*, Jan. 29, Feb. 3, 1864. For a War Department appraisal of Barbour's performance (and an accompanying favorable report on McMicken's conduct) in Georgia, see Eugene E. McLean to Samuel Cooper, Apr. 28, 1864, Letters Received, Office of the Quartermaster General, M634, roll 7, Entry 42, RG 109, NA. Whatever the merits of his service in Georgia, Barbour subsequently served under Johnston only briefly in North Carolina in the spring of 1865. "General Joe" remark quoted in *Charleston Mercury*, July 14, 1864. See also *Mobile Advertiser and Register*, June 24, 29, 1864. Balanced cargoes of corn and bacon notwithstanding, Confederate troops continued to lack fresh vegetables. Shipments of vegetables sent by citizens to Marietta by freight train, instead of by express train, prompted a war correspondent to remark, "Scarcely a freight train arrives here without a large number of boxes of vegetables, which have been on the road for weeks, and consequently, are perfectly rotten and worthless." Therefore, Johnston's men subsisted largely on "hard tack and bacon." *Savannah Republican*, July 2, 1864.

17. Johnston, *Narrative*, 345–46; *Charleston Courier*, June 20, 1864; W. H. Newlin et al., *A History of the Seventy-third Regiment of Illinois Infantry Volunteers*, 317; *OR*, 38, pt. 5:65; Cox, *Atlanta*, 61.

18. Chamberlain, *Ohio Infantry*, 119. "Yankees" remark in Newlin et al., *Illinois Infantry*, 316.

19. *Savannah Republican*, July 15, 1864. See also *Charleston Courier*, July 14, 1864; *Charleston Mercury*, July 14, 1864; and *Mobile Advertiser and Register*, July 14, 17, 1864.

20. Wright to Gorgas, June 2, 1864, Wright to Mackall, July 7, 1864, and Wright to H. Myers, July 8, 1864, Ordnance Department, chap. 4, vol. 16, Letters and Telegrams Sent, Atlanta Arsenal, Georgia, Feb.–July 1864, RG 109, NA.

21. *OR*, 38, pt. 5:879, 888.

22. *OR*, 38, pt. 2:908; 38, pt. 5:883. See also William H. Bragg, *Joe Brown's Army: The Georgia State Line*, 59–89. Brown subsequently declared that he had achieved a "perfect harmony" with Johnston during the Atlanta campaign. Brown to Seddon, Jan. 6, 1865, Letters Received, Secretary of War, 1861–1865, M437, roll 147, Oct. 1864–Mar. 1865, and 1862–1865, Dec. 1864–May 1865, RG 109, NA; *Mobile Advertiser and Register*, July 19, 20, 21, 1864; Black, *Railroads*, 250–52; Connelly, *Autumn of Glory* 2:281–426; Polk, *Leonidas Polk*, 347–75.

23. *OR*, 52, pt. 2:513; 47, pt. 2:1308. "Atlanta, and the railroads" remark in Jefferson Davis, *A Short History of the Confederate States of America*, 423. See also Davis to James Lyons, Aug. 13, 1876, quoted in Rowland, *Jefferson Davis* 7:517; Johnston, *Narrative*, 369, 371; and Govan and Livingood, *Johnston*, 323–38.

6. Chaos and Capitulation in North Carolina

1. Connelly, *Autumn of Glory*, 461–62, 477–514; Black, *Railroads*, 272–73; John B. Jones, *Diary* 2:425; Govan and Livingood, *Johnston*, 340–43.

2. *OR*, 47, pt. 2:1303, 1308. Referring to Johnston's Grenada blunder, Davis declared sixteen years later that "it is greatly to be regretted that the railroad-bridge across Pearl River was not so repaired that the large equipments of the [Mississippi] Central road might have been removed for use elsewhere and at other times. One of the serious embarrassments suffered in the last two years of the war was from the want of rolling stock with which to operate our railroads, as required for the transportation of troops and supplies." Jefferson Davis, *Rise and Fall* 2:425, 631; *Richmond Dispatch*, Feb. 27, 1865; *Raleigh Conservative*, Mar. 7, 17, 1865.

3. *OR*, 47, pt. 2:1247; Woodward, *Mary Chesnut's Civil War*, 725; Johnston, *Narrative*, 369, 371; Govan and Livingood, *Johnston*, 338.

4. *OR*, 47, pt. 2:1090, 1271; Johnston, *Narrative*, 371–72; Roman, *General Beauregard* 2:363.

5. *OR*, 47, pt. 2:1247, 1271; 49, pt. 1:757–58, 946; Black, *Railroads*, 275.

6. *OR*, 47, pt. 2:1271, 1320; 47, pt. 1:423; 45, pt. 2:640, 705–6; 44:995–96; 47, pt. 3:714, 727; 47, pt. 2:1108; Johnston, *Narrative*, 372; Sherman, *Memoirs* 2:274. "Corkscrew" remark in Nichols, *Great March*, 174; Black, *Railroads*, 268–71.

7. Black, *Railroads*, 31, 114, 148–52, 228; Nathaniel C. Hughes, *General William J. Hardee*, 266–72.

8. *OR*, 47, pt. 2:1239, 1290, 1297, 1311; Govan and Livingood, *Johnston*, 333, 338; Black, *Railroads*, 20; Hughes, *Hardee*, 266–72. Constant and heavy use for the transportation of troops and supplies largely accounted for the poor condition of South Carolina railroads and rolling stock. The Confederate Navy Department's conscription of railroad employees for use in torpedo boat construction at Charleston

compounded the problem. For example, in February 1864 Northeastern Railroad president Arthur J. Rannel questioned Railroad Bureau chief Sims about when the Richmond government would "see 'the error of its ways' in consuming [our] *skillful mechanical* labor, in the construction of gunboats?" He explained the damaging effects of the Navy Department's policy of impressing his mechanics and engineers and complained to Sims, "I am experiencing great difficulty and annoyance in getting the Mechanics, *absolutely* necessary for the *daily* repair of our Engines." Rannel to Sims, Feb. 4, 1864, Confederate Papers Relating to Citizens or Business Firms, M346, roll 747, *Nort–Norton, I.*, War Department Collection of Confederate Records, RG 109, NA.

9. *OR*, 47, pt. 2:1239. Powerful economic and political interests in the North Carolina legislature prevented the state's private railway companies from building their lines in conformity with the broad-gauged railroads of Virginia, Tennessee, and South Carolina. Legislators reasoned that a uniformity of gauges between the states would weaken the economy of the Tarheel State. They maintained that shipments of goods between Virginia, Tennessee, and South Carolina over the North Carolina railways would deprive the Tarheel State of the profits of that interstate traffic. The politicians also concluded that the construction of broad-gauged lines in North Carolina would divert the wealth of the state's mountain counties to the other three Southern states, thereby depriving the North Carolina Railroad of lucrative intrastate traffic. Black, *Railroads*, 43–44,148–53.

10. *OR*, 47, pt. 2:1311–12, 1425. For further discussion of the circumstances and controversy surrounding the gauge-change work between Greensboro and Danville, see Goff, *Confederate Supply*, 225–26; Frederick W. Sims, "Resources of the Confederacy in February, 1865," 121–22; and Frontis W. Johnston, *The Papers of Zebulon Baird Vance* 1:382. For a summary of Vance's wartime leadership in North Carolina, see John C. Barrett, "North Carolina," 149–61.

11. *OR*, 15:971; 52, pt. 2:602; 47, pt. 3:693, 724.

12. *OR*, 47, pt. 2:1298; Johnston, *Narrative*, 377–78.

13. *OR*, 47, pt. 1:1078; 47, pt. 2:1319, 1321, 1323, 1325, 1328, 1331, 1334, 1336.

14. *OR*, 47, pt. 2:1355–56, 1360, 1374, 1406–7. See also *Richmond Dispatch*, Mar. 20, 1865; and Gaskill, *Footprints*, 174.

15. *OR*, 47, pt. 2:1324, 1373, 1380, 1395. See also Special Orders No. 2, Mar. 12, 1865, Military Departments, chap. 2, vol. 349, Special Field Orders, Army of Tennessee, July 1864–Jan. 1865, and Special Orders, Gen. J. E. Johnston's Headquarters in North Carolina (Military Departments), RG 109, NA.

16. *OR*, 47, pt. 2:1361, 1371, 1374; *Raleigh Biblical Recorder*, n.d., quoted in *Richmond Dispatch*, Mar. 29, 1865.

17. *OR*, 47, pt. 2:1380, 1387–88; Special Orders No. 4, Mar. 14, 1865, Military Departments, RG 109, NA. See also *Richmond Dispatch*, Mar. 24, 1865.

18. *OR*, 47, pt. 2:1406–7; Johnston, *Narrative*, 394; *Raleigh Conservative*, Apr. 7, 1865.

19. Conynghan, *Sherman's March*, 362–63; Johnston, *Narrative*, 393; *OR*, 47, pt. 2:1323, 1455; 47, pt. 3:682, 683, 687.

20. *OR*, 47, pt. 2:1323, 1455; 47, pt. 3:687.

21. Ibid., 47, pt. 3:695–96, 789.

22. Ibid., 44:96; 45, pt. 2:786; 47, pt. 2:1323; 47, pt. 3:700, 703; Black, *Railroads*, 205–8.

23. *OR*, 47, pt. 3:683, 695–96, 700, 703, 718, 725, 760, 762, 765–66, 789; 54:996; 55, pt. 2:786; 57, pt. 1:712, 718, 722, 1058–59. See also Robert Herriot, "At Greensboro, N.C., in April, 1865," 101.

24. *OR*, 47, pt. 3:762, 765–66.

25. Robert Underwood Johnson and Clarence Clough Buel, "The Opposing Forces in the Campaign of the Carolinas," 698, 700.

26. *OR*, 42, pt. 2:1289; 47, pt. 3:102–3, 74; Edward Hagerman, "Field Transportation and Strategic Mobility in the Union Armies," 169–71. In fact, Sherman intended to establish two secondary bases in northeastern North Carolina on the Roanoke River and expected to draw supplies from Norfolk when the Federal army invaded southeastern Virginia.

27. *OR*, 47, pt. 1:30, 937; 47, pt. 3:774, 788–89. See also John G. Barrett, *The Civil War in North Carolina*, 357–59; Roman, *General Beauregard* 2:393; Johnston, *Narrative*, 400.

28. Lewis H. Webb, "Additional Sketch Thirteenth Battalion—Company A," 359; *OR*, 47, pt. 2:788; Barrett, *Civil War*, 355, 357. There was a staggering Confederate setback at Salisbury: Stoneman's cavalry destroyed 10,000 stands of arms, 1 million rounds of small arms ammunition, 3 magazines, 6 railroad depots, 75,000 military uniforms, 250,000 blankets, and 80,000 barrels of turpentine. They also burned 146,000 pounds of leather, bacon, salt, and saltpeter along with 60,000 bushels of wheat and corn, $15 million worth of Confederate currency, and $100,000 worth of medical supplies. *OR*, 49, pt. 1:334. See also Moore, *Rebellion Record* 11:358.

29. *OR*, 47, pt. 3:790; Johnston, *Narrative*, 397–401.

30. Concerning the well-stocked North Carolina depots, see an address by Vance to a meeting of the Southern Historical Society at White Sulphur Springs, W. Va., on Aug. 18, 1875, *Southern Historical Society Papers*, 513; Nichols, *Great March*, 309; *OR*, 47, pt. 3:802.

31. R. A. Lambert, "In the Battle of Bentonville, N.C.," 222; I. G. Bradwell, "Making Our Way Home from Appomattox," 102.

32. *OR*, 47, pt. 3:320, 850; N. A. Pinney, *History of the 104th Regiment Ohio Volunteer Infantry from 1862 to 1865*, 85–86; Johnston, *Narrative*, 417–19.

Bibliography

I. Government Records in the National Archives

A. Bound Documents

Record Group 94, Records of the Adjutant General's Office, 1780s–1917

Generals' Papers and Books, General William T. Sherman, Vol. 11: Letters Sent, June 27–August 14, 1864.

Record Group 109, War Department Collection of Confederate Records

Departmental Records. Army of Tennessee, Special Orders, Adjutant and Inspector General's Office, 1863–1865.

———. Department of Alabama, Mississippi, and East Louisiana, Letters Received, 1862–1864.

———. Department of Alabama, Mississippi, and East Louisiana, Telegrams Received, December 2, 1863–June 30, 1864.

———. Department No. 2, Army of the West, Orders and Circulars, 1862.

Engineer Department. Letters Sent, Engineer Office, Department of the Gulf, June 1863–April 1864.

———. Papers of Various Confederate Notables, Brigadier General James R. Chalmers, Letters and Telegrams Sent and Received, 1861–1865.

Medical Department. Army of Northern Virginia, Letters Sent, Medical Director's Office, Army of the Potomac, January–May 1862; Letters Received by Surgeon Thomas H. Williams, Inspector of Various Hospitals in Virginia, 1862.

Military Departments. Army of Northern Virginia, Letters Sent by Gen. R. E. Lee from Headquarters at Richmond, March–August 1862.

———. Army of Northern Virginia, Letters Sent, Edmund Kirby Smith's Division, 1861–1862.

———. Army of Northern Virginia, Special Orders, October 1861–December 1862.

―――. Army of Tennessee, Endorsements on Letters Received 1863–1864; Letters Sent, 1864; and Special Orders, 1864.

―――. Army of Tennessee, Special Field Orders, July 1864–January 1865, and Special Orders, Gen. J. E. Johnston's Headquarters in North Carolina.

―――. Army of Tennessee, Special Orders, 1863.

―――. Letters Sent, Commander of the Troops at Atlanta, July 1863–May 1864.

―――. Letters Sent, Department of Alabama, Mississippi, and East Louisiana, 1863–1864.

―――. Letters Sent, Department of the West, February 16–December 16, 1863.

―――. Special Orders, Department of the West, May–August 1863.

―――. Telegrams Sent, Department of Alabama, Mississippi, and East Louisiana, 1864.

―――. Telegrams Sent, Department of East Tennessee and Department of Western Virginia and East Tennessee, April 1863–September 1864.

―――. Telegrams Sent, Department of South Carolina, Georgia, and Florida, July 1863–February 1864.

―――. General and Special Orders, Circulars, Brig. Gen. James R. Chalmers' Brigade, March 1863–August 1864.

―――. Telegrams Sent, Gen. J. E. Johnston's Command, June–December 1863.

Ordnance Department. Letters and Telegrams Sent, Atlanta Arsenal, Georgia, February–July 1864.

Record Group 156, Records of the Office of the Chief of Ordnance

Letters to Ordnance Officers, April 8, 1859–April 16, 1860.

OCO—Document File 1797–1894, Nos. 1859B–1859C and 1860Z–1861B.

Reports of Inspections of Arsenals and Depots, 1832–1860, 1892.

Government Publications

U.S. Navy Department, *The War of the Rebellion: A Compilation of the Official Records of the Union and Confederate Navies*. 28 vols. and Index. Washington, D.C.: Government Printing Office, 1894–1927.

U.S. War Department, *The War of the Rebellion: A Compilation of the Official Records of the Union and Confederate Armies*. 128 vols. and Index. Washington, D.C.: Government Printing Office, 1880–1901.

B. Microfilm Publications

Record Group 77, Records of the Office of the Chief of Engineers

M506, Letters Issued, Vol. 14: August 1851–August 1852, and Vol. 16: April 22, 1853–December 5, 1853, Topographical Bureau, War Department.

M506, Letters Received, I–J, 1838–1853, Topographical Engineers, War Department.

Record Group 92, Records of the Office of the Quartermaster General

M475, Letters Sent by the Office of the Quartermaster General, Main Series, 1818–1870.

Record Group 94, Records of the Adjutant General's Office, 1780s–1917

M1003, Case Files of Applications from Former Confederates for Presidential Pardons ("Amnesty Papers") 1865–1867.
M1098, U.S. Army Generals' Reports of Civil War Service, 1864–1887.

Record Group 109, War Department Collection of Confederate Records

M331, Compiled Service Records of Confederate General and Staff Officers and Nonregimental Enlisted Men.
M346, Confederate Papers Relating to Citizens or Business Firms.
M347, Unfiled Papers and Slips Belonging in Confederate Compiled Service Records.
M437, Letters Received by the Confederate Secretary of War, 1861–1865.
M469, Letters Received by the Confederate Quartermaster General, 1861–1865.
M474, Letters Received by the Confederate Adjutant and Inspector General, 1861–1865.
M524, Telegrams Sent by the Confederate Secretary of War, 1861–1865.
M627, Letters and Telegrams Sent by the Confederate Adjutant and Inspector General, 1861–1865.
M628, Letters and Telegrams Sent by the Engineer Bureau of the Confederate War Department, 1861–1864.
M634, Letters Received, Office of the Quartermaster General.
M900, Letters and Telegrams Sent by the Confederate Quartermaster General, 1861–1865.
M998, Records of the Virginia Forces, 1861.

II. Manuscript Collection

Joseph E. Johnston Papers, Manuscripts and Rare Books Department, Earl Gregg Swem Library, College of William and Mary, Williamsburg, Virginia.

III. Books and Monographs

Bailey, Ronald H. et al. *The Battles for Atlanta (The Civil War): Sherman Moves East.* Alexandria, Va.: Time-Life Books, 1985.

Bain, William E., ed. *B & O in the Civil War, from the papers of Wm. Prescott Smith*. Denver: Sage Books, 1966.

Barrett, John G. *The Civil War in North Carolina*. Chapel Hill: University of North Carolina Press, 1963.

———, ed. *Yankee Rebel: The Civil War Journal of Edmund Dewitt Patterson*. Chapel Hill: University of North Carolina Press, 1966.

Bettersworth, John K., ed. *Mississippi in the Confederacy as They Saw It*. Baton Rouge: Louisiana State University Press, 1961.

Black, Robert C. *The Railroads of the Confederacy*. Chapel Hill: University of North Carolina Press, 1952.

Boatner, Mark Mayo. *The Civil War Dictionary*. New York: David McKay, 1959.

Bragg, William H. *Joe Brown's Army: The Georgia State Line, 1862–1865*. Macon, Ga.: Mercer University Press, 1987.

Brewer, James H. *The Confederate Negro: Virginia's Craftsmen and Military Laborers, 1861–1865*. Durham: Duke University Press, 1969.

Bryan, T. Conn. *Confederate Georgia*. Athens: University of Georgia Press, 1953.

Byrne, Frank L., ed. *The View from Headquarters: Civil War Letters of Harvey Reid*. Madison: State Historical Society of Wisconsin, 1965.

Candler, Allen D. *The Confederate Records of the State of Georgia, Compiled and Published under Authority of the Legislature*. 4 vols. Atlanta: Charles P. Byrd, 1909–10. Vol. 3: *Official Correspondence of Governor Joseph E. Brown, 1860–1865, Inclusive*.

Chamberlain, William H. *History of the Eighty-first Regiment Ohio Infantry Volunteers, during the War of the Rebellion*. Cincinnati: Gazette Steam Printing House, 1865.

Connelly, Thomas Lawrence. *Autumn of Glory: The Army of Tennessee, 1862–1865*. Baton Rouge: Louisiana State University Press, 1971.

Conynghan, David P. *Sherman's March through the South*. New York: Sheldon, 1865.

Cox, Jacob D. *Atlanta*. New York: Scribner's, 1882.

———. *Military Reminiscences of the Civil War*. 2 vols. New York: Scribner's, 1900.

Davenport, Edward A., ed. *History of the Ninth Regiment Illinois Cavalry Volunteers*. Chicago: Donohue and Henneberry, 1888.

Davis, Jefferson. *The Rise and Fall of the Confederate Government*. New York: D. Appleton, 1881. Reprint ed., with a Foreword by Bell I. Wiley. 2 vols. New York: Thomas Yoseloff, 1958.

———. *A Short History of the Confederate States of America*. New York: Belford Co., 1890.

Davis, William C. *Battle at Bull Run: A History of the First Major Campaign of the Civil War*. Garden City, N.Y.: Doubleday, 1977.

Douglass, Marjorie. *Florida: The Long Frontier*. New York: Harper, 1967.

Dowdey, Clifford, ed. *The Wartime Papers of R. E. Lee*. Boston and Toronto: Little, Brown, 1961.

Early, Jubal A. *War Memoirs: Autobiographical Sketch and Narrative of the War between the States*. N.p., 1912. Reprint ed. Edited and with an Introduction by Frank E. Vandiver. Bloomington: Indiana University Press, 1960.

Eaton, Clement. *A History of the Southern Confederacy*. New York: Macmillan, 1954.

Frederick, Gilbert. *The Story of a Regiment: Being a Record of the Military Services of the Fifty-seventh New York State Volunteer Infantry in the War of the Rebellion 1861–1865*. Chicago: C. H. Morgan, 1895.

Freeman, Douglas Southall. *Lee's Lieutenants*. Vol. 1: *From Manassas to Malvern Hill*. New York: Scribner's, 1942.

Freemantle, Arthur J. L. *The Freemantle Diary*. Edited and with an Introduction by Walter Lord. Boston: Little, Brown, 1954.

Garner, James W. *Reconstruction in Mississippi*. New York: Macmillan, 1901. Reprint ed. Gloucester, Mass.: Peter Smith, 1964.

Gaskill, J. W. *Footprints through Dixie: Everyday Life of the Man under a Musket on the Firing Line and in the Trenches 1862–1865 (from Diary of 1862–1865)*. Alliance, Ohio: privately published, 1919.

Goetzmann, William H. *Army Exploration in the American West, 1803–1863*. New Haven: Yale University Press, 1959.

Goff, Richard D. *Confederate Supply*. Durham: Duke University Press, 1969.

Govan, Gilbert E., and James W. Livingood. *A Different Valor: The Story of General Joseph E. Johnston, C.S.A.* Indianapolis: Bobbs-Merrill, 1956.

Grace, William M. "Isaac Ridgeway Trimble, the Indefatigable and Courageous." Master's thesis, Virginia Polytechnic Institute and State University, 1984.

Grant, Ulysses S. *Personal Memoirs of U. S. Grant*. 2 vols. New York: Charles L. Webster, 1886.

Hagerman, Edward. *The American Civil War and the Origins of Modern Warfare: Ideas, Organization, and Field Command*. Bloomington: Indiana University Press, 1988.

Harris, William C. *Presidential Reconstruction in Mississippi*. Baton Rouge: Louisiana State University Press, 1967.

Hart, B. H. Liddell. *Sherman: Soldier, Realist, American*. New York: Frederick A. Praeger, 1958.

Harwell, Richard, ed. *The Confederate Reader*. New York: Longmans, Green, 1957.

Henderson, G. F. R. *Stonewall Jackson and the American Civil War*. Introduction by Viscount Wolseley. 2 vols. London: Longmans, Green, 1900.

Hill, Louise B. *Joseph E. Brown and the Confederacy*. Chapel Hill: University of North Carolina Press, 1939. Reprint ed. Westport, Conn.: Greenwood Press, 1972.

Hirshson, Stanley P. *Grenville M. Dodge: Soldier, Politician, Railroad Pioneer*. Bloomington: Indiana University Press, 1967.

Howard, Oliver O. *Autobiography of Oliver Otis Howard, Major General United States Army*. 2 vols. New York: Baker and Taylor, 1908.

Hughes, Nathaniel C. *General William J. Hardee*. Baton Rouge: Louisiana State University Press, 1965.

Hughes, Robert M. *General Johnston*. New York: Appleton, 1897.

Hussey, George A. *History of the Ninth Regiment (Eighty-third N.Y. Volunteers), 1845–1888*. Edited by William Todd. New York: Press of J. S. Ogilvie, 1889.

Jackson, Mary Anna. *Life and Letters of General Thomas J. Jackson*. With an Introduction by Henry M. Field. New York: Harper and Brothers, 1892.

Johnston, Angus J. *Virginia Railroads in the Civil War*. Chapel Hill: University of North Carolina Press, 1961.

Johnston, Frontis W., ed. *The Papers of Zebulon Baird Vance*. 2 vols. Raleigh, N.C.: State Department of Archives and History, 1963. Vol. 1: *1843–1862*.

Johnston, Joseph E. *Narrative of Military Operations Directed during the Late War between the States*. New York: D. Appleton, 1874. Reprint ed. Bloomington: University of Indiana Press, 1959.

Jones, Fennimore P. *Three Years' Campaign of the "Ninth N.Y.S.M."* Privately published diary, 1865.

Jones, John B. *A Rebel War Clerk's Diary at the Confederate States Capital*. Philadelphia: Lippincott, 1866. Reprint ed., with an Introduction by Howard Swiggert. 2 vols. New York: Old Hickory Bookshop, 1935.

Journal of the Congress of the Confederate States of America, 1861–1865. Washington, D.C.: Government Printing Office, 1905.

Kerby, Robert L. *Kirby Smith's Confederacy: The Trans-Mississippi South, 1863–1865*. New York: Columbia University Press, 1972.

Kirwan, Albert D., ed. *Johnny Green of the Orphan Brigade: The Journal of a Confederate Soldier*. Lexington: University of Kentucky Press, 1956.

Longstreet, James. *From Manassas to Appomattox*. Philadelphia: Lippincott, 1896. Reprint ed. Edited and with an Introduction by James I. Robertson. Bloomington: Indiana University Press, 1960.

Lonn, Ella. *Salt as a Factor in the Confederacy*. New York: W. Neale, 1933. Reprint ed. Tuscaloosa: University of Alabama Press, 1965.

McWhiney, Grady. *Braxton Bragg and Confederate Defeat*, vol. 1: *Field Command*. New York: Columbia University Press, 1969.

Massey, Mary Elizabeth. *Ersatz in the Confederacy*. Columbia: University of South Carolina Press, 1952.

Mitchell, Joseph B. *Military Leaders in the Civil War*. New York: Putnam, 1972.

Moore, Frank, ed. *The Rebellion Record*. 12 vols. New York: Putnam, 1861–68.

Newlin, W. H. et al. *A History of the Seventy-third Regiment of Illinois Infantry Volunteers*. Washington, D.C.: Office of the Librarian of Congress, 1890.

Nichols, George W. *The Story of the Great March: The Diary of a Staff Officer*. New York: Harper and Brothers, 1866.

Nichols, James L. *Confederate Engineers*. Tuscaloosa, Ala.: Confederate Publishing Co., 1957.

——— . *The Confederate Quartermaster in the Trans-Mississippi*. Austin: University of Texas Press, 1964.

Owsley, Frank L. *King Cotton Diplomacy*. Chicago: University of Chicago Press, 1931.

Parks, Joseph H. *General Leonidas Polk C.S.A.: The Fighting Bishop*. Baton Rouge: Louisiana State University Press, 1962.

Patrick, Rembert, W. *Jefferson Davis and His Cabinet*. Baton Rouge: Louisiana State University Press, 1944.

Pinney, N. A. *History of the 104th Regiment Ohio Volunteer Infantry from 1862 to 1865*. Akron, Ohio: Werner and Lohman, 1886.

Polk, William M. *Leonidas Polk, Bishop and General*. 2 vols. New York: Longmans, Green, 1915.

Rhodes, John H. *The History of Battery B, First Regiment Rhode Island Light Artillery in the War to Preserve the Union 1861–1865*. Providence: Snow and Farnham, 1894.

Roman, Alfred. *The Military Operations of General Beauregard in the War between the States, 1861 to 1865*. 2 vols. New York: Harper and Brothers, 1884.

Rood, H. W. *Story of the Service of Company E, and of the Twelfth Wisconsin Regiment, Veteran Volunteer Infantry in the War of the Rebellion*. Milwaukee: Swain and Tate, 1893.

Rowland, Dunbar, ed. *Jefferson Davis, Constitutionalist: His Letters, Papers and Speeches*. 10 vols. and Index. New York: Little and Ives, 1923.

Scott, William F. *The Story of a Cavalry Regiment: The Career of the Fourth Iowa Veteran Volunteers, from Kansas to Georgia 1861–1865*. New York: Putnam, 1893.

Sherman, William T. *Memoirs of William T. Sherman*. New York: Charles L. Webster, 1891. Reprint ed., with a Foreward by B. H. Liddell Hart. 2 vols. Bloomington: Indiana University Press, 1957.

Silver, James W., ed. *A Life for the Confederacy: The Diary of Private Robert A. Moore*. Jackson, Tenn.: McCowat-Mercer Press, 1959.

Smith, H. I. *History of the Seventh Iowa Veteran Volunteer Infantry during the Civil War*. Mason City, Iowa: Hitchcock, 1903.

Strode, Hudson. *Jefferson Davis*. 2 vols. New York: Harcourt, Brace, 1959–64. Vol. 1: *Confederate President*.

Summers, Festus P. *The Baltimore and Ohio in the Civil War*. New York: Putnam, 1939.

Temple, Oliver P. *East Tennessee and the Civil War*. Cincinnati: Robert Clarke Co., 1899.

Thorndike, Rachel S., ed. *The Sherman Letters*. New York: Scribner's, 1894. Reprint ed. New York: Da Capo Press, 1969.

Turner, George E. *Victory Rode the Rails: The Strategic Place of the Railroad in the Civil War*. Indianapolis: Bobbs-Merrill, 1953.

Vandiver, Frank E. *Rebel Brass: The Confederate Command System*. Introduction by T. Harry Williams. Baton Rouge: Louisiana State University Press, 1956.

Warner, Ezra J. *Generals in Grey: Lives of the Confederate Commanders.* Baton Rouge: Louisiana State University Press, 1959.

Weber, Thomas. *The Northern Railroads in the Civil War, 1861–1865.* New York: King's Crown, 1952.

Wiley, Bell Irvin. *Southern Negroes, 1861–1865.* New Haven: Yale University Press, 1965.

Williams, T. Harry. *P. G. T. Beauregard, Napoleon in Gray.* Baton Rouge: Louisiana State University Press, 1954.

Winther, Oscar Osburn. *With Sherman to the Sea: The Civil War Letters, Diaries, & Reminiscences of Theodore F. Upson.* Bloomington: Indiana University Press, 1958.

Woodward, C. Vann, ed. *Mary Chesnut's Civil War.* New Haven: Yale University Press, 1981.

Wright, Charles. *A Corporal's Story: Experiences in the Ranks of Company C, 81st Ohio Vol. Infantry, during the War for the Maintenance of the Union, 1861–1864.* Introduction by William H. Chamberlain. Philadelphia: James Beale, 1887.

Younger, Edward A., ed. *Inside the Confederate Government: The Diary of Robert Garlick Hill Kean, Head of the Bureau of War.* New York: Oxford University Press, 1957.

IV. Articles

Barrett, John G. "North Carolina." In *The Confederate Governors,* edited by W. Buck Yearns. Athens: University of Georgia Press, 1985.

Bearss, Edwin C. "The Great Railroad Raid." *Annals of Iowa* 40 (Fall and Winter 1969–70): 147–60, 222–39.

Beauregard, Pierre G. T. "The First Battle of Bull Run." In *Battles and Leaders of the Civil War,* edited by Robert Underwood Johnson and Clarence Clough Buel. 4 vols. New York: Century Co., 1884. Reprint ed., with an Introduction by Roy F. Nichols. New York: Thomas Yoseloff, 1956. 1:196–227.

Bradwell, I. G. "Making Our Way Home from Appomattox." *Confederate Veteran* 29 (March 1921): 102–3.

Childs, H. T. "Turney's First Tennessee Regiment." *Confederate Veteran* 25 (April 1917): 164–66.

Cunningham, Sumner A., ed. "Col. E. W. Cole and His Work." *Confederate Veteran* 7 (June 1899): 276–77.

Davidson, John M. "Additional Sketch Thirty-ninth Regiment (Second Artillery)." In vol. 2 of *Histories of the Several Regiments and Battalions from North Carolina in the Great War 1861–1965, Written by Members of the Respective Commands,* edited by Walter Clark. 4 vols. Goldsboro, N.C.: Nash Brothers, 1901.

Escott, Paul D. "Georgia." *The Confederate Governors,* edited by W. Buck Yearns. Athens: University of Georgia Press, 1985.

Hagerman, Edgar. "Field Transportation and Strategic Mobility in the Union Armies." *Civil War History* 34 (June 1988): 143–71.

Hands, Washington. "From Baltimore to First Bull Run." *Confederate Veteran* 7 (February 1899): 62–63.

Herriot, Robert. "At Greensboro, N.C., in April, 1865," *Confederate Veteran* 30 (March 1922): 101–2.

Imboden, John D. "Jackson at Harper's Ferry in 1861." In *Battles and Leaders of the Civil War,* edited by Robert Underwood Johnson and Clarence Clough Buel. 4 vols. New York: Century, 1884. Reprint ed., with an Introduction by Roy F. Nichols. New York: Thomas Yoseloff, 1956. 1: 111–25.

Johnson, Robert Underwood, and Clarence Clough Buel. "The Opposing Forces in the Campaign of the Carolinas." In *Battles and Leaders of the Civil War,* edited by Robert Underwood Johnson and Clarence Clough Buel. 4 vols. New York: Century, 1884. Reprint ed., with an Introduction by Roy F. Nichols. New York: Thomas Yoseloff, 1956. 4: 696–700.

Lambert, R. A. "In the Battle of Bentonville, N.C." *Confederate Veteran* 37 (June 1929): 221–23.

Lash, Jeffrey N. "Anthony L. Maxwell, Jr.: A Yankee Bridge Contractor for the Confederacy, 1862–1865." *Journal of Confederate History* 6 (Fall 1990): 24–55.

——— . "Joseph E. Johnston's Grenada Blunder: A Failure in Command." *Civil War History* 23 (June 1977): 114–28.

——— . "Major George Whitfield and Confederate Railway Policy, 1863–1865." *Journal of Mississippi History* (Fall 1980): 117–39.

McIlwaine, H. R. "Surgical Department C.S.A.—Dr. Samuel Preston Moore." *Confederate Veteran* 33 (November 1925): 406–7.

McMurry, Richard M. " 'The Enemy at Richmond': Joseph E. Johnston and the Confederate Government." *Civil War History* 27 (March 1981): 5–31.

M'Neilly, James H. "Gen. Joseph E. Johnston." *Confederate Veteran* 25 (December 1917): 554–66.

——— . "In Winter Quarters at Dalton, Ga." *Confederate Veteran* 28 (April 1920): 130–32, 157.

Northrop, Lucius B. "The Confederate Commissariat at Manassas." In *Battles and Leaders of the Civil War,* edited by Robert Underwood Johnson and Clarence Clough Buel. 4 vols. New York: Century, 1884. Reprint ed., with an Introduction by Roy F. Nichols. New York: Thomas Yoseloff, 1956. 1: 261.

——— . "Resources of the Confederacy in February, 1865." *Southern Historical Society Papers* 2 (August 1876): 85–105.

Ramsdell, Charles C. "The Confederate Government and the Railroads." *American Historical Review* 32 (July 1917): 794–810.

Sims, Frederick W. "Resources of the Confederacy in February, 1865." *Southern Historical Society Papers* 2 (September 1876): 113–28.

Taylor, Robert A. "Rebel Beef: Florida Cattle and the Confederate Army, 1862–1864." *Florida Historical Quarterly* 67 (July 1988): 15–31.

Turner, V. E., and H. C. Wall. "Twenty-third Regiment." In vol. 2 of *Histories of the Several Regiments and Battalions from North Carolina in the Great War 1861–1865, Written by Members of the Respective Commands*, edited by Walter Clark. 4 vols. Goldsboro, N.C.: Nash Brothers, 1901.

Vance, Zebulon B. "From an Address by Zebulon B. Vance to a Meeting of the Southern Historical Society at White Sulphur Springs, West Virginia, on August 18, 1875." *Southern Historical Society Papers* 14 (January 1886): 506–21.

Webb, Lewis H. "Additional Sketch Thirteenth Battalion—Company A." In vol. 4 of *Histories of Several Regiments and Battalions from North Carolina in the Great War 1861–1865, Written by Members of the Respective Commands*, edited by Walter Clark. 4 vols. Goldsboro, N.C.: Nash Brothers, 1901.

Woodward, Earl F. "Internal Improvements in Texas in the Early 1850s." *Southwestern Historical Quarterly* 76 (October 1972): 161–82.

V. Newspapers

Augusta Daily Constitutionalist, 1863–64.
Baltimore American and Commercial Advertiser, 1861.
Baltimore Sun, 1861–62.
Charleston Courier, 1861–62, 1864.
Charleston Mercury, 1863–64.
Chicago Times, 1863.
Daily Chattanooga Rebel, 1863.
Mobile Advertiser and Register, 1863–64.
Mobile Evening News, 1863.
New Orleans Picayune, 1863.
New York Times, 1863.
New York Tribune, 1863.
Raleigh Conservative, 1865.
Richmond Dispatch, 1861–62, 1865.
Richmond Examiner, 1861–62.
Richmond Sentinel, 1863–65.
Savannah Republican, 1864.
Washington Evening Star, 1861–62.

Index

DESTROYER OF THE IRON HORSE

was composed in 10½/12 Caslon 540 roman & italic
and Caslon 224 bold & bold italic
on a Xyvision system with Linotron 202 output
by BookMasters, Inc.;
with display type and initial capitals set
by Dix Type, Inc.;
printed by sheet-fed offset on 50-pound Glatfelter B-16 stock,
Smyth sewn and bound over .088″ binders' boards
in Holliston Roxite cloth, with 80-pound Rainbow Antique endleaves,
and wrapped with dust jackets printed in two colors
on 80-pound enamel stock and film laminated
by BookCrafters, Inc.;
designed by Will Underwood;
and published by

THE KENT STATE UNIVERSITY PRESS
Kent, Ohio 44242